Demons and Development

Hegemony and Experience

Critical Studies in Anthropology and History

SERIES EDITORS   Hermann Rebel and William Roseberry

DEMONS *and Development*

The Struggle for Community in a Sri Lankan Village

JAMES BROW

The University of Arizona Press   Tucson

The University of Arizona Press
Copyright © 1996
The Arizona Board of Regents
All rights reserved

FIRST PRINTING

Library of Congress Cataloging-in-Publication Data

Brow, James.
Demons and development : the struggle for community in a Sri Lankan village /
James B. Brow.
p. cm. — (Hegemony and experience)
Includes bibliographical references and index.
ISBN 0-8165-1638-3 (acid-free paper). — ISBN 0-8165-1639-1 (pbk. : acid-free paper)
1. Ethnology—Sri Lanka—Anuradhapura (District) 2. Anuradhapura (Sri Lanka :
District)—Social conditions. 3. Anuradhapura (Sri Lanka : District)—Religious life and
customs. 4. Vedda (Sri Lankan people)—Social conditions. 5. Community.
6. Nationalism—Sri Lanka. I. Title. II. Series.
GN635.S72B76   1996
305.8′0095493—dc20   96-9982
CIP

British Library Cataloguing-in-Publication Data
A catalogue record for this book is available from the British Library.

for

Judy,

Ranjani,

and

Geoffrey

Contents

Illustrations

Acknowledgments

This book has been a long time in the making, and in the course of its composition I have benefited from the criticisms and suggestions of numerous colleagues, students, and friends. Those whose comments have been particularly valuable include Ana María Alonso, Arjun Appadurai, Amy Burce, Mary Crain, Val Daniel, Nick Dirks, Steve Feld, Doug Foley, Ted Gordon, Calla Jacobson, Man-Hyung Lee, Jose Limon, Liz Nissan, Daniel Nugent, Gananath Obeyesekere, Michael Roberts, Henry Selby, Nick Siegel, P. G. Somaratne, Jonathan Spencer, Jock Stirrat, Ted Swedenburg, Serena Tennekoon, Carol Trosset, and Mike Woost. If there are any others whom I have overlooked, and whose names should be added to this list, I beg their pardons. I am also grateful to Kyle Woodson, Buck Van Winkle, and Sam Wilson for help with the maps and figure, and to John Bodinger de Uriarte for help with the photographs.

Publication of this book was made possible in part by a grant from the College of Liberal Arts at the University of Texas at Austin. Field research in 1983, upon which the present account is principally based, was supported by the Joint Committee on South Asia of the American Council of Learned Societies and the Social Science Research Council, by the Wenner-Gren Foundation for Anthropological Research, and by the University of Texas at Austin. Earlier field research was funded by the Smithsonian Institution and by the National Science Foundation.

The present text includes some material that previously appeared in the following books and journals: *American Ethnologist* 15:2, May 1988, published by the American Ethnological Society, a section of the American Anthropological Association (Brow 1988); *Anthropological Quarterly* 63:1, January 1990, published by the Catholic University of America Press (Brow 1990a, 1990b); and *Sri Lanka: History and the Roots of Conflict*, edited by Jonathan Spencer and published in London by Routledge (Brow 1990c).

Acknowledgments

An earlier version of chapter 4 was published as chapter 9 of *Agrarian Change in Sri Lanka,* edited by myself and Joe Weeramunda and published in New Delhi by Sage Publications India Pvt. Ltd. (Brow and Weeramunda 1992). In each case thanks are due to the publishers and copyright holders for permission to reproduce that material here.

Abbreviations

AGA	assistant government agent
CID	Criminal Investigation Department
DRO	divisional revenue officer
GA	government agent
MP	member of parliament
RDS	rural development society
SLFP	Sri Lanka Freedom Party
UNP	United National Party

Cast of Characters

Notes

1. The ages are given as of 1983.
2. The names of Kukulewa villagers given here are mostly pseudonyms.
3. On formal occasions a villager commonly prefixes his personal name with that of his father, linking the two names with the possessive form *ge*. Thus Bandathe will refer to himself, or be referred to by others, as Herathamy ge Bandathe (i.e., Herathamy's Bandathe). Likewise his children will be known as Bandathe ge Wijepala, Bandathe ge Ukkumenike, etc. The father's name is often reduced to an initial; thus Herathamy ge Bandathe becomes H. Bandathe. These patronymics are omitted here. The descendants of Albert and Millie Fernando, members of the Karava caste and immigrants from the Western Province, provide a partial exception to this rule as some of them (e.g. Anthony, James) at times employ Fernando as a surname that is inherited in the male line.

Residents of Samadigama

Jinadasa: 41 years old; son of Anthony Fernando; organized the local branch of the UNP in the mid-1970s; treasurer of the UNP from 1975 to 1982, then president; treasurer of the RDS from 1977; employed in Anuradhapura by the Ceylon Petroleum Corporation; the dominant figure in Samadigama.

Wijeratne: 37 years old; son of Punchibanda and Rosalyn Fernando; Jinadasa's cross-cousin (father's sister's son) and his chief lieutenant; assistant secretary of the UNP from 1975 to 1979, then president from 1979 to 1982, and then secretary; president of the RDS from 1974 to 1977, then secretary; in 1983 became possessed by a god or demon that claimed to be the village's guardian deity; brother of Seelawathie.

Seelawathie: 35 years old; daughter of Punchibanda and Rosalyn Fernando, sister of Wijeratne and wife of Dharmaratne; in 1983 became possessed by a demon that subsequently appeared to demonstrate an ability to locate lost objects and to cure minor ailments.

Dharmaratne: 42 years old; husband of Seelawathie; became vice-president of the UNP in 1979.

Cast of Characters

Anthony: 63 years old; eldest son of Albert and Millie Fernando; father of Jinadasa, Malietana, Sugathapala, Sita, and others; a shopkeeper and trader most of his life, in 1983 he was running a small stall at the crossroads in Sippukulama, about three miles from Kukulewa on the Anuradhapura-Trincomalee road; had abandoned his wife to live with Ukkuhamy, a widow who was allocated a house in Samadigama.

Malietana: 31 years old; sister of Jinadasa; unmarried with three children; became a member of the UNP committee in 1982.

Sugathapala: 28 years old; brother of Jinadasa; became treasurer of the UNP in 1982.

Sita: 18 years old; sister of Jinadasa; trained as a community organizer by Sarvodaya; made herself the custodian of the community hall in Samadigama; became a member of the UNP committee in 1982.

Dissanayake: 25 years old; became assistant secretary of the UNP in 1982; the only party official by that time who was not closely related to Jinadasa.

Herathamy, 55 years old; Menikrala, 59 years old; Sellathe, 58 years old; Muthubanda, 58 years old: all mature men who had supported the UNP and had acquired houses in Samadigama, but all of whom had become dissatisfied with Jinadasa's leadership by 1983.

Residents of Kukulewa

Wannihamy: 60 years old; a successful shopkeeper since the 1960s and the most prosperous man in the village; a longtime supporter of the SLFP, he served as president of the Kukulewa branch of the party from 1976 to 1980, and as treasurer thereafter.

Naidurala: 55 years old; skilled in the treatment of children's ailments; president of the local branch of the UNP from 1975 to 1979, and president of the RDS from 1978 to 1979; was removed from both offices, principally because he was unwilling to see the benefits of the housing project go exclusively to UNP supporters.

Sumanapala: 33 years old; son of Undiyarala, the former *gamarāla;* secretary of the RDS from 1974 to 1977, and president from 1977 to 1978; vice-president of the SLFP from 1976 to 1980, and president thereafter; one of the principal organizers of *gambädi rājakāriya* in Kukulewa in 1983.

Wimaladasa: 28 years old; son of Dingiribanda, the *kapurāla* in Kukulewa; secretary of the SLFP from 1980; a successful entrepreneur in 1983, many villagers were dependent on the employment he could offer them.

Tikiribanda: 57 years old; son of Bandathe, the former *vel vidāne;* not an office holder in either political party; one of the organizers of *gambädi rājakāriya* in Kukulewa in 1983.

Cast of Characters

James: 54 years old; younger brother of Anthony; a UNP supporter who failed to get a house in Samadigama, although both his sons did; joined the group of UNP dissidents in 1983.

Ritual Specialists

Ukkubanda: 57 years old; the *kapurāla* in Samadigama.

Dingiribanda: 68 years old; the *kapurāla* in Kukulewa; closely associated with Wannihamy, the shopkeeper, and identified with the SLFP.

Ukkurala: 82 years old; mother's brother of Dingiribanda and Bandathe Vidane; reputedly skillful in dealing with demons, he came to serve the deity possessing Seelawathie in Samadigama.

Kalubanda: 55 years old and almost blind; an *udäkki kapuvā* and close observer of the ways of gods and demons, one who enjoyed reciting the myths about them; a householder in Samadigama, and father of Dissanayake.

Kandathe: 64 years old; a *vedarāla* and *udäkki kapuvā;* a mediator in disputes between Kukulewa and Samadigama, he had children who had received houses in Samadigama but he himself continued to live in Kukulewa.

Kapuruhamy: 69 years old; the *kapurāla* of the shrine where Kandappu's ornaments were kept, he had served as assistant to the former *anumätirāla*.

Premadasa: 31 years old; son of Dingiribanda, whom he was in the process of succeeding as the Kukulewa *kapurāla* in 1983; had at one time supported the UNP although several of his family, and especially his father and his brother Wimaladasa, were prominently identified with the SLFP.

Jothipala: 22 years old; youngest son of Kandappu *anumätirāla;* took care of his father's god's ornaments.

Deceased

Bandathe: died 1976; *vel vidāne* from about 1930 until 1962 and the most powerful man in Kukulewa for most of that time; supporter of the UNP; father of Tikiribanda.

Kandappu: died 1978; a famous *anumätirāla*.

Undiyarala: died 1981; former *gamarāla;* father of Sumanapala.

Cast of Characters

Outsiders

Ranasinghe Premadasa: prime minister in the UNP government that came to power in 1977; the driving force behind the Village Awakening Program.

E.L.B. Hurulle: minister of cultural affairs in the UNP government and MP for Horuwopotana.

Yasapala Herath: MP for Anuradhapura East, the constituency that included Kukulewa.

A. T. Ariyaratne: founder and leader of Sarvodaya Shramadana, an independent grassroots organization that greatly influenced the Village Awakening Program.

P. K. Dissanayake: the government agent for Anuradhapura District at the time that Samadigama was built.

Demons and Development

Chapter 1   *Ceremony*
                in Samadigama

AUGUST 3, 1983. Preparations for the ceremony began early in the morning and continued at a leisurely pace throughout the day. A group of young men erected a frame of thin wooden poles next to the large solitary tree that stood beside the road leading into the village. At the base of the tree was a set of stones marked with the signs of Pulleyar, the elephant-headed god who is lord of the jungle. The men covered the wooden frame with branches of a coconut tree, and then carried into it a bed that they placed at the back of the makeshift shrine, against the wall opposite the narrow entrance. The bed was next decorated to serve as the altar at which the major gods would receive their offerings. Above the altar was hung the sacred cloth that depicts the god Pulleyar, the great god Kataragama with his two consorts, Thevali and Valliamma, and Bahirava, lord of the earth and guardian of buried treasure.

I was told that the ceremony was intended to bring divine protection to the village and to ensure its prosperity. It was held once a year and was the only ceremony in Samadigama in which everyone was expected to participate. Those who were organizing it had already visited each household in the village to ask for a measure of rice, half a coconut, and a little money. Not all the food was destined for consumption by the gods. They would receive their special offerings first, but a portion of the milk-rice and oil-cakes that were prepared for the gods was reserved for the people themselves, who would conclude the ceremony with a rare communal meal of rice and curry.

The people had held this ceremony in Samadigama in each of the three years since the village was built. Samadigama had been developed as a model village under the Village Awakening Program initiated by the new government that had been elected in 1977. Indeed the prime minister himself had come to Samadigama to preside at the ceremonial opening in 1980, and had planted in the center of the village a sapling taken from the

3

sacred bo-tree in Anuradhapura, one of the most venerable places of Buddhist worship in Sri Lanka. Before 1980 the people of Samadigama had held the ceremony in Kukulewa, the village from which all the families that occupied the sixty new houses built by the government had come. Kukulewa was immediately adjacent to Samadigama, and many people still thought of the new houses as part of the old village, as an extension of Kukulewa rather than a distinct community. However, the anger and resentment over the way the new houses had been allocated had cut so deep that they had been obliged to perform the ceremony separately in the two places. Social relations between those who had remained in Kukulewa and those who had moved to Samadigama had improved somewhat by 1983, but much bitterness still remained.

Anticipation and excitement had been rising in Samadigama as the day of the ceremony approached, for there had been signs of unusual supernatural activity. A number of people had been afflicted by demons during the previous few months. This in itself was not uncommon, but there was a case that commanded particular attention. One day when Seelawathie was out in the jungle collecting firewood, she was frightened by a sudden apparition. After she returned home she fell ill and was treated for demonic possession. In the course of her treatment she went into trance, and the demon who possessed her spoke through her voice and said that he had been sent to ruin Samadigama by certain people in Kukulewa. This accusation was challenged, but it brought the issue of social relations between the two villages back into sharp focus. Subsequently Seelawathie continued to go into trance, and seemed to show some skill in curing ailments and finding lost objects, so that some people became convinced that she was possessed, not by a demon compelled by sorcery, but by a benevolently disposed god. Then her brother, Wijeratne, also began to go into trance, and intimated that he would do so at the ceremony itself. And there were other portents as well to suggest that Samadigama was about to be divinely favored. Ukkubanda, the priest in charge of the communal ceremony in Samadigama, was one of those who felt the excitement.

Ukkubanda: There are signs that a god is coming to Samadigama to make it his permanent home. Last week Wijeratne had a dream in which he saw three people dressed in white coming into the village. He met them near the bo-tree and asked them who they were. They looked like the members of a family—

4

father, mother, and child. The child said that the two adults were the member of parliament and his wife. And with that word they disappeared. We take it as a sign that a god is coming to make this village his home.

On the evening before the main ceremony about thirty villagers gathered at the shrine as two drummers began to play their instruments and chant invocations of the gods, drawing attention to the ceremony to be performed on their behalf and inviting their attendance the next day. Ukkubanda supervised their performance. Several respected elders who had been specially invited sat inside the shrine, chewing betel and quietly conversing among themselves. Others remained outside and mingled with their friends.

After a while Wijeratne, who had been sitting inside the shrine with the elders, got up and stepped outside. A few moments later he began to tremble, then suddenly threw his arms up in the air and cried out as he entered the initial stage of trance, when the god first mounts his human vehicle. For several minutes he thrashed wildly about, while those close to him struggled to hold him upright. Eventually he quieted down, still quivering with the presence of whatever god or demon was possessing him, but steadier on his feet as he moved into full trance. Then he began to dance to the rhythm of the drums. After a while he approached the priest and asked permission to enter the shrine to make an offering to the major gods. Ukkubanda gave his permission, and someone handed Wijeratne a few betel leaves. He carried these into the shrine and made his offering. When he came out again he continued to dance for several minutes. Then he stopped and began to speak in the language of the gods, which is not readily understood by all. The priest and the drummers listened closely, and everyone else also clustered around, intent on what was being said.

Wijeratne's god: I am a very powerful god. I have been in thirty-two villages, including Kukulewa, and everywhere I have watched over the interests of Kuveni's children. Now I have come to this village to give you my message. When the kings built this new village and planted the bo-tree here, the village became sacred. The tree is a branch of the Sri Maha Bodhi tree in Anuradhapura, where the Black God lives. Because of the bo-tree, the village is divinely blessed.

In the beginning people used to treat the bo-tree with proper respect. But later women began to go there to make offerings even when they were unclean. Menstruating women would walk across the sacred area around the bo-tree. This made the gods angry. And then the villagers, who had been united when they first came to Samadigama, began to fall out among themselves. They became jealous of one another and started to fight over petty things.

All this happened because the gods were displeased. Therefore you must keep that sacred place very clean. Before you make offerings to the gods you should make offerings at the bo-tree. That will attract the attention of the gods, who will then give their blessings to the village. I will come again tomorrow to give you instructions before you make the offerings.

After he had delivered his message the god left Wijeratne, who was led away to recover himself. The drumming and chanting were concluded a few minutes later. Afterward the performers, organizers, and invited guests ate together and discussed arrangements for the ceremony on the following day.

The next morning there was a bustle of activity in front of the shrine as people made ready for the ceremony in the afternoon. Children were dispatched to fetch firewood and haul water, and both men and women busied themselves cleaning and cooking rice and vegetables for the feast. The two groups worked separately; the men prepared the food to be offered to the gods while the women cooked the larger quantities that would be distributed among the people. Every now and then a drummer played his instrument and sang, chanting praise to the gods and reciting their myths.

In the middle of the morning, as the preparations continued, there was a flurry of excitement as Seelawathie, veiled and dressed entirely in white, emerged from her house and walked down toward the shrine, followed by a procession of about thirty villagers. As she approached the shrine the drummers began to play, and she quickly went into trance. She brushed aside her veil, let down her hair so that it covered her face, and began to dance. She was soon followed into trance by her brother, Wijeratne, who again began to speak in the language of the gods, which his sister helped interpret to the audience.

Seelawathie's god: The god who speaks through the brother of my vehicle-woman wants to see the two villages united again. He says the people should forget their jealousies and quarrels, and should bring together Samadigama and Kukulewa into a single community. He wants to see just one performance of the ceremony next year, in which members of both villages participate together.

At this point one man in the audience called out a remark that threw the challenge back at the gods.

Ranbanda: It will be very difficult to bring the people of the two villages together. That's up to the gods. It's up to the gods to make the people into one harmonious group.

But the god ignored this interruption and went on to announce that he would come again later, just before the afternoon ceremony, to give a further message. Then the gods left. Wijeratne and Seelawathie were laid down on mats and given water to drink to help them regain their own senses. Wijeratne recovered first and was soon on his feet again. Seelawathie took a little longer, and then led her procession back to her house.

Excitement spread through the village. Many people believed that Samadigama was about to be blessed. Seelawathie's and Wijeratne's possession seemed to herald the arrival of a powerful god who would take up residence in the village. Some speculated that it might be the return of the same god who had watched over Kukulewa at an earlier time. That god had used a man named Kandappu as his vehicle, and before that Kandappu's father, who had brought the god's sacred ornaments to the village, had been the medium through whom the god conveyed his messages and afforded his protection. But many people believed that the god had left the village when Kandappu died in 1978, either because of sorcery or because there was no one left who was sufficiently virtuous to be his vehicle. Now people began to recall images of a distant past when, through the mediumship of Kandappu's father, the benevolent gaze of the god had rested on the village and made it prosperous and contented. Word of the god's visit and his promise to return for the ceremony spread rapidly, and more and more people began to converge on the shrine. They came in large numbers not only from Samadigama but also from Kukulewa, and a few even arrived from more distant villages. By the time Ukkubanda began the ceremony in midafternoon, several hundred people were gathered at the shrine.

Accompanied by the playing and chanting of the drummers, Ukkubanda approached the gods, beginning inside the shrine with Pulleyar,

Kataragama, and the other major gods, and then stepping outside to make offerings to the lesser gods and demons. An offering at the bo-tree was not neglected. Wijeratne and Seelawathie, who again arrived in procession, quickly went into trance. Two men who had come from Kukulewa, sons of Kandappu the former medium, also showed signs of becoming possessed. They began to tremble, as if they felt a god alight on them, but they did not move into full trance and were led to the side to recover themselves.

Wijeratne again asked the priest's permission to make an offering to Pulleyar and Kataragama, then proceeded into the shrine to do so. Seelawathie had also brought an offering for Kataragama, but she went straight into the shrine to present it without asking Ukkubanda's permission. This made the priest furious, and he angrily demanded to know what kind of god it was who would enter his shrine without permission. Later he would say that he himself was possessed at the time, and that he would not have spoken like that to a god if he had been in his own senses. Then Wijeratne's god began to speak.

Wijeratne's god: I am a watcher for the god who used to live in Kukulewa. The god who spoke through the old vehicle-man is still in the village. He sent me to give you the message that he wants to come again. He has a tender regard for Kuveni's children. But you, the children of Kuveni, are now jealous of one another. Your minds are not clean and you hate one another. You even hate your own kinsmen. You, Kuveni's children, are all one kin group, but you have fallen out among yourselves. All who are kin should be united. The god wants you to come back together.

This is a village built by kings. A sacred bo-tree was planted here on the day the village was opened. With the blessing of the Black God who lives in the sacred bo-tree this village would have prospered. But women have been going to worship at the bo-tree when they were unclean. That made the place itself unclean and the village lost the blessing of the Black God. The bo-tree here is a branch of the sacred bo-tree in Anuradhapura. One is planted in every Awakening Village. Consequently every Awakening Village has the blessing of the gods.

But you must learn how to retain the favor of the gods. Build a fence around the bo-tree, and be very clean when you go there to worship. That in itself may bring the blessing of the gods. Get back together with the kin from whom you have been separated. Forget about your petty jealousies and disputes. That is my message to you. Make offerings to me on the seven auspicious days that fall after the next quarter of the moon. On each of these days I will come to give you my message. On the seventh day the powerful god who used to live in Kukulewa will come again to take care of you. So all of you unite. I came here earlier on seven different occasions and tried to speak to you through seven different people. But their minds were not good. They were greedy and jealous, so I left them. The man through whom I give my message now is better than those others. But even he is not the best.

While Wijeratne's god was speaking, Seelawathie remained in trance, swaying slightly from side to side and with her long hair concealing her face. The crowd remained quiet, but pressed in on all sides. Small children were lifted onto their fathers' shoulders to get a better view, and almost everyone gave rapt attention to the words and actions of the gods. After their message had been given the two gods danced for a few minutes longer, and then departed. Wijeratne and Seelawathie lay down to rest and recover their own senses.

At last it was time for the communal meal. But as preparations were made to serve the food, most of the visitors from Kukulewa began to drift away. When some were spotted heading down the road they were called back and invited to eat. They seemed to hesitate, and the invitation was repeated. But eventually they moved on again, back toward Kukulewa. One of them called out, and the cry was then repeated, "We came to see the god, not to eat."

Chapter 2　　　　　*Orientations*

I HAD BEEN living in Samadigama for six months when the events described in the previous chapter took place. I had come to the village at the beginning of 1983, intending to study how life had changed for its inhabitants in the fifteen years since my wife and I had first visited. Judy and I had lived in Kukulewa between 1968 and 1970, doing the ethnographic research on which I based my doctoral dissertation. In that work I concentrated mainly on kinship and economic life, analyzing the way agriculture was organized, tracing the inheritance of land, and delineating the patterns of marriage that connected the people of Kukulewa with one another and with their relatives in the thirty-two other villages in Anuradhapura District that were also inhabited by the "children of Kuveni." In choosing this emphasis I was building on the work of Edmund Leach, S. J. Tambiah, Gananath Obeyesekere, and Nur Yalman, all of whom had published important ethnographic studies of Sinhala kinship and land tenure in the previous few years.[1] But I was also mindful that as an ethnographic novice, with no previous experience of Sri Lanka and only a rudimentary command of the Sinhala language, it might be sensible to concentrate first on material aspects of social life that I could observe directly and sometimes even measure. After that, I could use whatever knowledge I had acquired to guide me into a more thorough exploration of how the people themselves construed the world that they inhabited. Accordingly, with Judy's skillful and energetic assistance, I spent countless hours collecting genealogies, investigating household budgets, and tramping through the paddy fields and swidden plots to record the agricultural work that was being done.

As my notebooks filled up, it became clear that life in Kukulewa was undergoing a fundamental transformation. From any long-term perspective the change was not abrupt or even dramatic, but its implications were enormous. In the first few weeks of research it had seemed that the pattern of life in Kukulewa was not unlike that which Leach (1961) had recorded in Pul Eliya, a village seventeen miles away where he had conducted field research in 1954. Pul Eliya was certainly less impoverished than Kukulewa, and its inhabitants belonged to a different caste, but on several occasions I suffered the disconcerting sensation that what I was observing was nothing other than a dramatic enactment of Leach's text. As our own research proceeded, however, I became increasingly conscious of the differences, which were attributable less to distinctions of wealth or status than to changes that had taken place in the region since the time of Leach's study. First of all, and perhaps most fundamentally, the virtual eradication of malaria in the 1940s had triggered a rapid growth of population that threatened the viability of established modes of livelihood. At the same time the villages, which had previously enjoyed a substantial measure of autonomy, were being steadily incorporated within regional, national, and even international circuits of power and exchange. Various social practices that had served to mark the inhabitants of the same village as members of a distinct community were under threat, while some had already been abandoned. For example, employment of a fellow villager for a cash wage, which Leach (1961:251) had reported as being incompatible with the norms of kinship in Pul Eliya, had become quite common in Kukulewa by 1968, although villagers were still unsure of its ethical propriety.

I wrote about these matters in the book that I developed from my dissertation (Brow 1978a), as well as in several other papers that I published over the next few years (Brow 1976, 1978b, 1980, 1981a). My interests at the time led me to center my work on the articulation of modes of production in Kukulewa. Although I focused much of my analysis on structural features of agrarian change, I also emphasized that transformations of the social relations of production were simultaneously processes of class formation in which changes in consciousness were decisive.[2] Nevertheless the accounts that I wrote still maintained what was then a conventional academic distance from the lives of the people being described, and they conveyed little sense of how the villagers themselves had experienced the changes.

When I returned to Kukulewa in 1983 it was this more subjective dimension of experience that I was most concerned to understand, along with documenting and analyzing the further changes in material conditions that had taken place since 1970. I was not at all sure how successful I would be in gaining access to the consciousness of Kukulewa villagers, but I did anticipate that it would be rewarding to investigate their expressions of "community," defined simply as "a sense of belonging together" (cf. Weber 1978:40). Our research in 1968–1970 had made it clear that the Kukulewa people's understanding of who they were was deeply rooted in their sense of belonging together as members of the same village. It was equally clear, as I have already indicated, that a number of customs that had formerly sustained the sense of community in Kukulewa were being altered or discarded. It seemed possible, then, that I might be able to grasp the villagers' experience of social change by exploring the cultural practices through which they expressed their sense of belonging together.

Until recently each village in Anuradhapura District was normally inhabited by members only of a single caste, whose interactions with one another were structured by codes of reciprocity and mutuality articulated in the idiom of kinship. Identification of the village as an appropriate site of community was thus a matter of kinship and caste. The caste identity of the Kukulewa villagers was succinctly expressed in the assertion (repeatedly made by Wijeratne's god at the ceremony described earlier) that they were "children of Kuveni." Kuveni was the indigenous demon princess whose ill-fated dalliance with Prince Vijaya, the legendary founder of the Sinhala nation, is recorded in the *Mahavamsa,* the Great Chronicle of the Sinhala people. By tracing their descent from this union, the people of Kukulewa identified themselves as Veddas, the reputed aboriginals of Sri Lanka.

It was this identity as a Vedda village that had drawn me to Kukulewa in the first place. Gananath Obeyesekere, my mentor when I was a graduate student at the University of Washington, had pointed out to me that the Veddas had received very little attention from professional anthropologists since the Seligmanns had published their classic study in 1911 (Seligmann and Seligmann 1911). He also advised me that there was a group of Veddas in Anuradhapura District who were barely even mentioned in the existing ethnographic record. It was, then, partly to fill this gap that I had originally chosen to work in Kukulewa, and although my early research focused on the changing modes of production in the village, I had also been concerned from the very beginning with questions of identity.

The people of Kukulewa were more obviously distinguished from other inhabitants of the district by their greater poverty than by any differences of race or culture. Like the overwhelming majority of their neighbors they spoke Sinhala, professed Buddhism, and lived mainly from cultivation. Nevertheless, their designation as Veddas did set them apart from the Sinhala caste groups of Goyigama (Cultivators), Smiths, Potters, Washermen, and Drummers who inhabited the surrounding villages. Yet they were not totally different from their neighbors, since their myth of origin identified them not just as the children of Kuveni but also as descendants of Vijaya, the first Sinhala king. When we were in Kukulewa in 1968, most villagers were inclined to stress that the Veddas were distinct from the Sinhala, but they were already beginning to feel the pressures of an expansive Sinhala Buddhist nationalism. There were also suggestions that, after all, the Veddas were really no more than a particular kind of Sinhala. As I prepared to return to Kukulewa in 1983, I wondered whether the continuing incorporation of the village within national markets and national politics might have encouraged further movement in that direction or, alternatively, whether resistance to incorporation might have prompted renewed assertions of Vedda separateness.

Field Work

It was with thoughts such as these that I arrived in Kukulewa in January 1983, accompanied by P. G. Somaratne, my research assistant, and my eleven-year-old son Geoffrey. Our plan was that Judy and Ranjani, our daughter, would join us a couple of months later. We managed to rent one of the new houses in Samadigama, and while Geoffrey struggled to accommodate himself to the sudden changes of diet, language, and material comfort, Somaratne and I began to investigate the changes that had taken place in the village since my earlier research.

As before, we began by inquiring into the more material aspects of social life. We took a census of the village, updated genealogies, asked people about their sources of income and patterns of consumption, and recorded the work being done in the paddy fields and swiddens. These inquiries generated an extensive body of information that detailed the village's continuing population growth and its ever deeper involvement in market relations. In itself, however, this information gave little indication as to how the villagers were experiencing these changes. In this respect, our initial understanding came less from our formal investigations than from what emerged out of our casual conversations.

One topic that kept coming up in conversation was that of the Village Awakening Program, also officially described as the Model Village Project. I had decided from the outset to include a detailed study of the project in my research. We soon began a systematic investigation, examining official records and consulting civil servants in Anuradhapura, but mainly relying on the memories of the villagers. It immediately became clear that although the events being described had taken place only three or four years earlier, they were already being remembered differently by villagers. This was hardly surprising, but I had not anticipated how revealingly the conflicting versions would differ in their treatment of the ethical issues that were central to the question of community. The political struggles generated by the project thus became the terrain on which I explored the problem that most intrigued me.

Somaratne's contribution to the collection of the villagers' narratives was invaluable and indispensable, as indeed it was to the research as a whole. I had met him at the University of Colombo, where he had recently completed his B.A. in sociology, working mainly under the supervision of Newton Gunasinghe, a brilliant scholar whose untimely death in 1988 was a grievous loss to Sri Lankan anthropology. Somaratne's background was semirural, and he had retained a gentle, unpretentious demeanor that quickly enabled him to establish intimate relations with the people of Kukulewa. By contrast, except when villagers had been drinking, in which condition their conversation was occasionally engaging but rarely lucid, I myself was usually treated with a certain reserve, and even deference. My personality may have encouraged this, but I also interpreted it both as a residue of the colonial past and as a result of the seemingly unshakable belief that my known acquaintance with government officials might possibly be turned to personal advantage.

My main contribution to the research, apart from obtaining the funding that made it possible, stemmed from my theoretical and methodological skills and my previous knowledge of the village. Somaratne, by contrast, although he possessed a native fluency in Sinhala culture, had little experience of ethnographic research and no previous knowledge of village life in Anuradhapura District. But as we moved beyond the standardized questions of demographic, genealogical, and economic inquiry, he proved much the more successful of us at drawing out the villagers and persuading them to speak openly about their particular concerns. In the course of time I encouraged him to work more independently, and although I continued to direct the research, as well as conduct a substantial portion of it, I came to rely on his discussions with the villagers for our most illuminating information. When we were alone in our house, we would discuss his interviews and observations at great length, probing their significance, examining their inconsistencies, and exploring their implications. I would then take the lead in indicating the directions further inquiries should take, but the primary work was largely his and if, as I hope it does, the story that is told here accurately conveys a sense of how the people of Kukulewa understood and responded to the changes they were experiencing, much of the credit belongs to Somaratne.

Somaratne also provided much of the continuity that is crucial to ethnographic research, for my own presence in the village turned out to be less constant than I had intended. Living conditions in Kukulewa, which were never less than harsh, had been aggravated by a prolonged drought that by April had lowered the water in the wells to a dangerous level. Consequently, when Judy and Ranjani arrived, we decided to rent a house in Anuradhapura town, twenty miles from Kukulewa, rather than risk the children's health by living in the village. This made for greater domestic comfort, but it also reduced the time I spent in the village. In addition I had to make a number of trips to Colombo, first to pay the convoluted series of bureaucratic dues that would eventually secure official approval of our research, and subsequently in connection with a conference on agrarian change that I was organizing for the following year.[3] Then, only a few weeks after Judy's arrival, we learned that her mother was dying of cancer in California, and we began to make plans for her and the children to return to the United States.

Finally, in the last week of July, after Judy and the children had left, and about ten days before the ceremony described in the previous chapter, the ethnic crisis in Sri Lanka suddenly erupted in a massive outbreak of violence in which hundreds of Tamils were brutally murdered.[4] These gruesome events had little immediate effect in Kukulewa, which was far from the scenes of greatest atrocity. Indeed I found some relief from the shock and horror by burying myself in the affairs of the village, whose own conflicts were just then coming to a head, although mercifully a less violent one. But my immersion in Kukulewa's parochial affairs also seemed like a self-indulgent evasion of the surrounding devastation. I persuaded myself, however, that the best way I could contribute to an understanding of the larger tragedy would be to continue my ethnographic research in the village. It might seem that demonic possession in Kukulewa had little connection with what Tambiah (1986) has aptly called the "ethnic fratricide" into which Sri Lanka was collapsing. In fact, the crisis of community in Kukulewa was precipitated by similar currents of ethnic chauvinism to those that were about to plunge the whole country into civil war. As will become clear, the Village Awakening Program in Samadigama was as much an exercise in Sinhala nationalism as in economic development, and the factional conflict that had divided Samadigama from Kukulewa was generated in large part by official efforts to incorporate the village within an expansionist Sinhala nation.

So I continued my field research in Kukulewa until October, while Somaratne remained in the village until the end of the year. During these last months, as I tried to come to terms with the traumatic events of July, I also left the village to seek the company of friends and colleagues. In this difficult period Jock Stirrat, Liz Nissan, Gananath and Ranjini Obeyesekere, Mike Woost, Jonathan Spencer, Colin Kirk, and Mark Whitaker all provided welcome companionship as well as stimulating thoughts on the ethnic crisis.

By the middle of June, Somaratne and I had already compiled a comprehensive record of the demographic and economic changes that had occurred since 1970. We had also collected numerous accounts of the Village Awakening Program, in the course of which we learned a good deal about local political struggles and the impact of the state's intrusion into village affairs. Discrepancies among these accounts not only indicated the strategic importance of the past as a site of struggle, but also exposed the contradictory principles to which villagers appealed in their assessments of recent events. But I still felt that we had as yet acquired only a modest understanding of their subjective dispositions and, in particular, of how the intense factional conflict was affecting their sense that membership in the same village and caste should be the primary focus of community. Our investigations into the Village Awakening Program had, however, reinforced the conviction that we would probably learn more by listening to them talk, in their own terms, about their own particular experiences and the specific issues that concerned them, than by throwing out abstract questions about social change or inviting them to make broad comparisons between the past and the present.

It was at this point that Seelawathie suffered her affliction, and from then on I allowed the chain of local events to dictate the course of research. The activities of gods and demons immediately became the liveliest topic of discussion in the village, and we had no difficulty in getting people to offer their interpretations of what was going on. We also attended the various ceremonies that were held, and recorded what was said and done. To a significant degree we thus withdrew to the wings of the local stage. No longer were the topics of our interviews one-sidedly determined by our own research agenda. At most we simply prompted the villagers to talk about matters that were already uppermost in their minds, and then tried to follow them where they led us.

I chose this strategy once I realized that the villagers were leading us exactly where I wanted to go. Their talk was of gods and demons, of sorcery and supernatural power, but the issues they were addressing in this prolific idiom encompassed those that I most wanted to explore. What constitutes a community? How should those who are bound together in the same community behave toward one another? What determines the boundaries of community, and under what circumstances can those boundaries legitimately be changed? Is Kukulewa a single village, or have Kukulewa and Samadigama become separate communities?

Constructions of Community

I began my account with a brief description of Seelawathie's possession and the subsequent ceremony in Samadigama because it was on these occasions that the issues of community were most dramatically expressed. The charge that Seelawathie's affliction was the result of sorcery practiced by her kin in Kukulewa, the appeals by Wijeratne's god for unity among the children of Kuveni, and the refusal of Kukulewa villagers to share in the collective meal—all these events were highly charged moments in a contentious struggle to define the terms and boundaries of the local community. At the same time the upheavals within Kukulewa were implicated in a much wider-ranging struggle for hegemony, in which the dominant ideological current was the strident Sinhala nationalism that was then being relentlessly disseminated from the centers of power in Sri Lanka. In this and the following section, I outline the conceptual framework and theoretical perspective that guide my attempt to understand these complex processes.

"Community" is defined here simply and broadly, following Max Weber (1978:40), as "a sense of belonging together," with the recognition that this typically combines both affective and cognitive components, both a feeling of solidarity and an understanding of shared identity. In refashioning the already established contrast between *gemeinschaft* and *gesellschaft*, Weber retained a fundamental distinction between communal relationships, in which "the orientation of social action . . . is based on a subjective feeling of the parties . . . that they belong together" (1978:40), and associative relationships, in which "the orientation of social action . . . rests on a rationally motivated adjustment of interests or a similarly motivated agreement" (1978:40–41), but he insisted that this was an ideal-typical contrast between analytically distinguishable tendencies that might in practice occur together, and he recognized that "the great majority of social relationships have this (communal) characteristic in some degree, while being at the same time determined by associative factors" (1978:41).

This formulation not only draws attention to "the constant interweaving of economic utility and social affinity" (Bendix 1962:476) but also recognizes that communalization, defined as any pattern of interaction that promotes a sense of belonging together, is ubiquitous in social life. Following Durkheim's lead, anthropologists have frequently examined the revitalization of community on ritual occasions similar to the ceremony in Samadigama described in chapter 1. They have given much less attention to the ways in which a sense of belonging together is constantly renewed in the mundane activities of daily life, as when a Kukulewa villager provides his labor to a kinsman on privileged terms that differ from those on which he would be employed by an outsider. In what follows, I try to situate these very different kinds of communalizing practices in relation to one another, in order to reveal connections between public assertions of community on ritual occasions and the ways in which a sense of belonging together is affirmed, negotiated, and sometimes denied in the ordinary course of everyday life.

Recent accounts of communalization have been greatly influenced by Benedict Anderson's (1983) study of the origins and spread of nationalism. Anderson's (1983:15) much cited definition of the nation as "an imagined political community" affirms that, at least in the particular case of the nation, the sense of belonging together depends upon an active process of imagining. It also seems tacitly to admit the possibility that an ideal of belonging together can be imagined without generating a concomitant feeling of solidarity. The reverse, however, is not possible. When Anderson claims that "all communities larger than primordial villages of face-to-face contact (and perhaps even these) are imagined" (1983:15; parentheses in the original), his tentative qualification is unwarranted. Communalization *always* contains an imaginative aspect.

Anderson (1983:16) claims that the nation is imagined as a community because it "is always conceived as a deep, horizontal comradeship." "Deep comradeship" certainly exemplifies what is to be understood by "a sense of belonging together," but any implication that communal relations are always exclusively horizontal should be resisted. As one moves along a scale of communal intensity—a scale that reaches its extreme at the point designated by Turner (1969) as "communitas," where all separations are dissolved—horizontal relations of equality may become more pronounced and vertical ties muted, but the latter are not incompatible with the experience of community, however uncongenial this may be to the purportedly egalitarian temper of our times. Communal relations may, in other words, possess both egalitarian and hierarchical dimensions.

Anderson's (1983:15) further observation that the nation is imagined as "inherently limited" applies also to other kinds of community. Just as "no nation imagines itself as coterminous with mankind" (1983:16), so every community is defined in opposition to others. Communalization is, then, a simultaneous and sometimes contentious process of inclusion and of exclusion, in the course of which differences among those who are incorporated are often erased or obscured, while differences between insiders and outsiders may be loudly proclaimed. The resulting pattern of polarization between communities and homogenization within them (cf. Tambiah 1986:120) is often reinforced by appeals to a past that represent a cultural distinction as an original and essential difference.

All communal relations are socially constructed. Even if sociobiologists were to find support for the claim that certain kinds of communal relations are genetically based, it would still be evident that the specific form of those relations is always culturally and historically determined. This applies to "primordial" relations as much as to any others. Geertz (1973: 259) recognizes this when he defines a primordial attachment as "one that stems from the 'givens'—or, more precisely, as culture is inevitably involved in such matters, the assumed 'givens'—of social existence."

Nevertheless, provided it is not simply used as an excuse to terminate sociological analysis prematurely, the identification of certain kinds of communal relations as primordial is important and revealing. It draws attention to the fact that some communal relations are felt to be more deeply binding than others, to the point where they "seem to flow more from a sense of natural . . . affinity than from social interaction" and come to possess "an ineffable, and at times overpowering, coerciveness in and of themselves" (Geertz 1973:259–60; cf. Anderson 1983:131–32). As the word implies, the inevitability of primordial relations is associated with the belief that they have existed from the very beginning. The term "primordialization" may then be used to describe the process—one that is often fundamental to struggles for hegemony—whereby certain communal relations are promoted and come to be experienced as if they possessed a natural and original fatality.

The primordial apprehension of community corresponds to the experience that Bourdieu (1977:164–71) calls "doxa," where the culturally constructed world is "seen as a self-evident and natural order" (1977:166) that is "taken for granted" (1977:167). Doxa prevails in the absence of contending opinions, where "what is essential goes without saying because it comes without saying" (1977:167). A doxic order is one that has successfully accomplished "the naturalization of its own arbitrariness" (1977: 164). One aspect of this is the primordialization of communal relations, which are experienced as ineluctable precisely because, as Anderson (1983:131) puts it, "in everything 'natural' there is always something unchosen." A field of doxa, however, always coexists with a field of opinion, also described by Bourdieu as a universe of discourse (1977:168), within which everything can be explicitly questioned. Where competing opinions confront one another the experience of primordiality can only be preserved by its incarceration in the doxic prison of innocence. Elsewhere, in the universe of discourse, prevailing understandings are always vulnerable to challenge.

Almost everywhere the sense of belonging together is nourished by being cultivated in the fertile soil of the past. Even newly established collectivities quickly compose histories for themselves that enhance their members' sense of shared identity, while solidarity is fortified by a people's knowledge that its communal relations enjoy a historical provenance. Communalization is further strengthened by the conviction that what ties a group of people together is not just a shared past but a common origin. Anthropologists hardly need to be reminded that claims of descent from a common ancestor are among the most effective and commonplace means by which human groups forge bonds of community. But what gives kinship its special potency as a basis of community is that it can draw upon the past not just to posit a common origin, but also to claim substantial identity in the present. Kinship thus provides a standard idiom of community for collectivities ranging from the family, the lineage, and the clan to the nation and the "race," and is extended also to include religious "brotherhoods," feminist "sisterhoods," "fraternal" orders of all kinds, and even the whole "family" of nations.

Despite the rhetoric of kinship, which typically asserts the primordiality of biological ties ("blood is thicker than water," etc.), the power of the past to shape communal relations in the present is a matter of culture rather than nature. What is at stake is not genetic affinity but the moral authority of tradition, the maintenance of which requires continuous cultural work. Various means are available to bolster the authority of tradition, of which one of the most widely adopted is its sacralization, as Weber (1978:215; emphasis added) noted when he described the ideal-type of traditional authority as "resting on an established belief in the *sanctity* of immemorial tradition."

Construction of an authoritative tradition that identifies all who accept it as members of the same political community is particularly prominent in the creation of nations and subnations. Tradition typically composes a version of the past that not only binds the members of the nation to one another, by proclaiming their shared descent and/or common experience, but also associates the nation as a whole with a particular territory that—maintaining the domestic imagery of the family—is its homeland. Such renditions of the past establish the enduring character of the national community despite all the ruptures and vicissitudes of history. The essential continuity of the nation is often also represented in the figure of the peasant, doubtless because his way of life seems endlessly to reproduce that of ancestral generations, while his (less often, her) intimate familiarity with the land epitomizes the nation's inviolable attachment to its territory.

Where norms of traditionalism prevail, behavior is legitimated by appeals to precedent. But memory is less stable than the events it recollects, and knowledge of what happened in the past is always subject to selective retention, innocent amnesia, and tendentious reinterpretation. Traditions are also invented (Hobsbawm and Ranger 1983). In other words, appeals to the authority of the past do not preclude innovation. Discussing traditional domination, Weber (1956:10; quoted in Bendix 1962:331) writes that "as a matter of principle it is out of the question to create new laws which deviate from the historical norms. However, new rights are created in fact, but only by way of 'recognizing' them as having been valid from 'time immemorial'." Innovation can thus evade the strictures even of a rigid traditionalism by appearing in the guise of preservation, recovery, or purification.

Throughout the contemporary world rapid and profound changes in the objective conditions of existence are constantly threatening the doxic foundations of established communities. At the same time, however, vigorous new projects of primordialization are scarcely less evident. Perhaps the most pervasive and forcefully propagated forms of contemporary primordialization are nationalism and ethnicism, the several components of which (kinship, language, religion, locality, etc.) interact both with one another and with communalization on other bases, especially class, in extremely complex and varied ways. This has certainly been the case in Sri Lanka, and more specifically in Kukulewa, which provides the present case in point.

I have already indicated that the experience of community in Kukulewa was formerly grounded in membership in a village, all of whose inhabitants were kin. This sense of belonging together was undoubtedly once taken for granted. However, in recent times massive changes in both the cultural and the material conditions of life have increasingly challenged its primordiality and have placed in jeopardy the propagation of socially constructed understandings of the world that previously were unquestioned. In particular, patterns of economic and political action that had sustained a sense of belonging together as members of the same village were undermined by the reorientation of agriculture from subsistence to the market and by the steady intrusion of state officials and party politics into village affairs. During the same period Kukulewa was opened up to the massive dissemination of Sinhala Buddhist nationalism. Proclaiming the common destiny of the Sinhala people, the teachings of the Buddha, and the island of Sri Lanka, nationalist discourse was vigorously propagated by the state and came to saturate the whole range of government activities, including projects of rural development such as the Village Awakening Program.

It will be shown in greater detail that these movements and activities were decisively shaped by appeals to the authority of the past, of the kind briefly described earlier. In the 1970s and 1980s the character of the Sinhala national community was principally imagined in terms not only of its territorial association with the island of Sri Lanka, but also of its historical association with the Buddha's teachings. The village community of Kukulewa likewise enjoyed both a sacred geography and a legitimating genealogy. In spatial terms it was generally believed that the village's boundaries had been authoritatively marked out by its tutelary deity. Along the temporal axis both the national and the local community defined themselves with reference to their founding ancestors, one of whom, it may be recalled, was even held in common. The Sinhala people looked to Vijaya as their first king and founder of their nation, while the Vedda people of Kukulewa traced their descent from Vijaya's liaison with Kuveni.

In this and other respects, processes of local and national communalization meshed comfortably together. The people of Kukulewa were frequently addressed by authorities as members of the Sinhala nation, and while this certainly called into question their identification of themselves as Veddas, it did not preclude continued attachment to the closely circumscribed bonds of caste and kinship that structured the village community. In many of its most prominent representations the Sinhala nation was itself imagined as a nation of villages, and the village community was even located at its moral core. Nevertheless the propagation of nationalist ideology through such official activities as the Village Awakening Program was profoundly contradictory and disruptive. This was largely due to the fact that Sinhala nationalism was most stridently carried into villages like Kukulewa by representatives of the major political parties, whose competition with one another had intensified local conflicts to the point of fracturing the very sense of village unity that was so loudly celebrated in nationalist rhetoric.

Cultural Hegemony

The dissemination of nationalist rhetoric in Kukulewa was not, however, simply part of a battle between political parties over which of them was the more authentic advocate of Sinhala Buddhism. It was also central to the process by which the ruling groups in Sri Lanka sought to win consent by binding people within the imagined community of the Sinhala nation. My account of communalization in the village is, therefore, simultaneously a study of cultural hegemony. It examines the media through which nationalist discourse was propagated in the village, and it explores the extent to which nationalist representations of social reality were accepted into the villagers' conventional understandings of the world. But along with assessing the success of superiors in educating consent by persuading villagers to take their assigned places in the national society, it also examines the ways in which the people of Kukulewa actively deployed their own indigenous cultural resources in response to such hegemonic strategies. It looks at evidence of resistance as well as acceptance, of refusal as well as accommodation and acquiescence, and at the tactical shifts between these different positions that villagers made as they struggled both to ensure their livelihood and to make sense of the changes they were experiencing.

In attempting to delineate these complex processes, I have adopted the theoretical perspective originally opened up by Antonio Gramsci and subsequently elaborated and refined by later scholars.[5] Gramsci's writings have proved immensely stimulating to scholars who integrate the analysis of structural constraints with that of human agency, who recognize that the persistence of cultural forms may be attributed as much to the exercise of power as to a spontaneous consensus about values, and who acknowledge the openness of historical processes. Central to Gramsci's arguments is his recognition that hegemony (like community) is a continuous process rather than a fixed state of affairs. Thus the *attainment* of hegemony, in the sense of a "state of 'total social authority' which, at certain specific conjunctures, a specific class alliance wins, by a combination of 'coercion' and 'consent', over the whole social formation" (Hall 1980a:331) is very rare. But the *struggle* for hegemony, understood as the process whereby the interests of other groups are coordinated with those of a dominant or potentially dominant group, through the creation of "not only a unison of economic and political aims, but also intellectual and moral unity" (Gramsci 1971:181) is continuous. Every hegemonic, or potentially hegemonic, movement attempts to contain competing understandings of the world within its own horizons. From this latter perspective communalization, which encompasses any attempt to create "intellectual and moral unity," (Gramsci 1971:57) can be seen to be an indispensable component of all hegemonic strategies.

Hegemony cannot adequately be understood simply by reference to the thesis of a more or less coherent and articulate "dominant ideology" (Abercrombie et al. 1980) that people either consciously accept or consciously reject. It can only be grasped as a process, one that is typically uneven, heterogeneous, and incomplete, and that operates at other levels of consciousness besides that of "mere opinion or mere manipulation" (Williams 1980:38). Its internal structures are normally fractured by contradictions, and although it may absorb some oppositional currents, it simultaneously generates others. Analysis must therefore examine the interplay between hegemonic and counter-hegemonic tendencies, attending closely to the complex movements through which, as Williams (1977:112) puts it, hegemony is continually "renewed, recreated, defended, and modified . . . (but) also continually resisted, limited, altered, challenged by pressures not all its own."

These movements traverse all levels of consciousness. For Williams (1977:109–10) one of the conceptual advantages of "hegemony" over "ideology" lies precisely in

> its refusal to equate consciousness with the articulate formal system which can be and ordinarily is abstracted as 'ideology.' It of course does not exclude the articulate and formal meanings, values and beliefs which a dominant class develops and propagates. But it does not equate these with consciousness, or rather it does not reduce consciousness to them. Instead it sees the relations of dominance and subordination, in their forms as practical consciousness, as in effect a saturation of the whole process of living . . . to such a depth that the pressures and limits of what can ultimately be seen as a specific economic, political and cultural system seem to most of us the pressures and limits of simple experience and common sense.

This formulation recalls Gramsci's (1971:331) assertion that "the relation between common sense and the upper level of philosophy is assured by 'politics'." For Gramsci (1971:323–31) "common sense" refers to the

general understandings of the world—themselves often disjointed, frag-
mentary, and even contradictory—that inform the practical, everyday
consciousness of ordinary people in a particular society at a particular
time. As Hall (1986a:20) argues, following Gramsci, common sense is "the
terrain of conceptions and categories on which the practical consciousness of the masses of the people is actually formed . . . (and) on which
more coherent ideologies and philosophies must contend for mastery."

Treatments of hegemony as encompassing both "the articulate upper
level of 'ideology'" (Williams 1977:110) and the normally taken-for-
granted understandings of common sense also connect with Bourdieu's
discussion of the relationship between a field of doxa, in which "the established cosmological and political order . . . goes without saying and therefore goes unquestioned" (1977:166), and a field of opinion defined by the
confrontation of orthodox and heterodox arguments that "recognize the
possibility of different and antagonistic beliefs" (1977:164). In turn this
distinction broadly corresponds to that which Giddens (1979:5) makes
between practical consciousness, informed by "tacit stocks of knowledge
which actors draw upon in the constitution of social activity," and discursive consciousness, "involving knowledge which actors are able to express
on the level of discourse." In each case the distinction is an analytical one
that opens up a necessary conceptual space within which to explore the
dialectical interplay between social conditioning and human agency.[6]

Discussions of this relationship have often taken as their point of depar-
ture Marx's celebrated assertion at the beginning of *The Eighteenth Bru-
maire of Louis Bonaparte:* "Men make their own history, but they do not
make it just as they please; they do not make it under circumstances
chosen by themselves, but under circumstances directly found, given and
transmitted from the past. The tradition of all the previous generations
weighs like a nightmare on the brain of the living" (Tucker 1978:595).

The variety of "circumstances" that determine people's ability to "make
their own history" is, of course, immense. Slightly modifying Marx's meta-
phor in his letter to Joseph Bloch of September 21–22, 1890, Engels referred to "the traditions that haunt human minds" but also identified
economic and political factors as among the more decisive of the "very
definite conditions and assumptions" under which "we make our history
ourselves" (Tucker 1978:761). Across this wide range of circumstances de-
lineation of the specific factors that condition agency has often been at-

tempted by means of some form of structural analysis, whether of modes of production, mythologies, or kinship systems, to mention only those whose deployment in anthropology has been particularly sophisticated. These kinds of structural analysis nevertheless remain external to agency. They may successfully identify the forces that restrict and limit practice, but they are unable to grasp the dynamic processes that constitute and generate it.[7] Attempting to make a virtue of necessity, history is then all too easily dismissed as "a process without a subject" (Althusser 1972:183), one in which men and women appear as the "supports" of structure (Althusser and Balibar 1970:112, 252), rather than as E. P. Thompson's (1978:88) "ever-baffled and ever-resurgent agents of an unmastered history."

Bourdieu's (1977:72) assertion that, although structural analysis (or, more generally, "methodological objectivism") is "a necessary moment in all research . . . (it) demands its own supersession," points from assessment of external conditions that constrain practice to elucidation of the determinate ways in which it is produced. The complexities of this process are well captured by Williams's (1977:87) fruitful reworking of the concept of "determination" to include both the (negative) setting of limits and the (positive) exertion of pressures. Within this formulation the social determination of action can be recognized as being simultaneously both a limiting and a constitutive process, one "with very powerful pressures which . . . are internalized and become 'individual wills' " (Williams 1977:87).[8]

Much is left unspecified here about the precise ways in which, through the process of internalization, pressures become transformed into individual wills. Nevertheless it is evident that the social formation of individual identities, no less than the constitution of collective identities that communalization entails, is a critical issue in any hegemonic struggle. Production of the subject positions in terms of which people fashion their sense of self establishes the framework within which everyday practices of domination and resistance are enacted. As Laclau and Mouffe (1982:100) succinctly put it, the concept of hegemony refers not to "an external relation between preconstituted social agents, but (to) the very process of the discursive constitution of those agents."

The level of consciousness at which Engels's "assumptions and conditions," once internalized, come to settle is historically and situationally variable. That, indeed, is what struggles for hegemony are largely about. Where the tradition of previous generations weighs most heavily, there doxa prevails. People's understandings are ensconced deep in their practical consciousness, inducing unquestioning adherence to established custom. Where, by contrast, the possibility is discursively entertained that things might be other than what they are, there agency affirms its potential. With this in mind Bourdieu argues that the boundary between the field of opinion and the field of doxa is a crucial site of hegemonic struggle: "the dominated classes have an interest in pushing back the limits of doxa and exposing the arbitrariness of the taken for granted; the dominant classes have an interest in defending the integrity of doxa or, short of this, of establishing in its place the necessarily imperfect substitute, orthodoxy" (1977:169). Put somewhat differently, to discuss what was previously unquestioned and therefore undiscussed involves an expansion of political consciousness, a movement against the prevailing hegemony. By contrast primordialization, as an instance of what Bourdieu (1977:184) claims is the tendency of "every established order . . . to produce . . . the naturalization of its own arbitrariness," entails a reduction of political consciousness and a strengthening of that established order.

As will be demonstrated throughout the account that follows, memories of the past are among the most crucial sites of hegemonic struggle. According to the Popular Memory Group (1982:211), popular memory is structured by two sets of relations—on the one hand, "the relation between dominant memory and oppositional forms" and, on the other, the relation between "public discourses" and "the more privatised sense of the past that is generated within a lived culture." Images and sentiments of community that are produced, contested, diffused, and modified on this terrain feature prominently in projects to promote or resist the intellectual and moral unity that defines an effective hegemony.[9]

These processes are neither uniform nor unassailable. The contradictions and distortions within any hegemonic discourse, as well as the discrepancies between it and the popular understandings of common sense, leave it ever vulnerable to penetration, criticism, and refusal. The struggle for hegemony is always an open-ended process of contestation as well as incorporation, of negotiation and resistance as much as of accommodation and consent.[10]

In examining this process the political connection that Gramsci discerned "between common sense and the upper level of philosophy" should be understood in the broadest possible terms. State officials and political parties are certainly among the major agencies that determine this relationship, but cultural, educational, and religious institutions, as well as the family and all kinds of voluntary organizations, are also fundamentally involved (Hall 1986a:21). As Williams (1977:110) stresses in the passage quoted earlier, the concept of hegemony looks at "relations of domination and subordination . . . as in effect a saturation of the whole process of living—not only of political and economic activity, nor only of manifest social activity, but of the whole substance of lived identities and relationships." In short, like communalization, hegemonic struggle is ubiquitous in social life.

It is precisely the ubiquity, as well as the open-endedness, of both communal and hegemonic processes that I try to capture in the narrative that follows. Much has been written on these themes in general terms, but detailed accounts of how they work themselves out in the quotidian routines of everyday life, which can only be based on deep and prolonged ethnographic research of the kind that anthropologists relish, remain relatively scarce. It is partly to remedy this deficiency, as well as to suggest some of the unexplored possibilities, that my account focuses on the shifting dispositions of the villagers' common sense. In the struggle for hegemony in Kukulewa common sense was both the central site of contestation and what was principally at stake. At the same time their common sense was the major cultural resource that villagers brought to bear in their efforts to forge moral standards and a sense of community appropriate to the novel circumstances in which they found themselves.

Plan of the Book

As far as possible I have composed my account in a form that allows the villagers to tell their own stories in their own words. My descriptions of events that I observed in 1983, such as Seelawathie's possession and Wijeratne's performance at the ceremony in Samadigama, not only include a good deal of what was said on those occasions but are also accompanied by other villagers' commentaries on those same events. Likewise my narrative of what happened in Kukulewa between the time the Village Awakening Program was initiated and my own return to the village in early 1983 is mainly carried by the recollections of villagers who participated in the events they describe. When their statements conflict with one another, as they frequently do, I make no attempt to impose either a purportedly authoritative version of what "really" happened or a misleadingly consensual version of how villagers interpreted what was going on. Rather, the disparities of memory and assessment are allowed to illustrate the factional disputes that racked the village and to reveal the shifting and often contradictory movements of common sense as it confronted Kukulewa's crisis of community. By providing a detailed ethnographic narrative of the discursive practices through which the consciousness of the villagers was expressed, I hope to capture the complexity of the hegemonic process, illuminating connections between its more or less simultaneous moments of consent, resistance, accommodation, and renewal.

If the villagers' discursive practices are to be comprehensible to my readers, however, it is necessary to describe not only what was said and done in the village, but also what was normally left unsaid. Most of the time in Kukulewa, as elsewhere, people interact with familiar others who already share with them a vast repertoire of common understandings. In the ordinary course of social life these understandings, which constitute the basis of the villagers' common sense and inform their practical consciousness, are taken for granted and remain unquestioned. They are also only rarely stated explicitly or scrutinized critically.

This defines one of the most challenging tasks of ethnographic research, which is precisely to reveal the normally unspoken premises that underlie social interaction. The ethnographer, moreover, must not only elicit this tacit knowledge but must also transmit it to his readers, who will otherwise be unable to grasp the local significance of what is described. Accordingly, my narrative is sometimes punctuated by passages that attempt to describe the implicit understandings that informed people's words and actions. For example, before reporting the villagers' responses to Seelawathie's possession, I have included a brief description of some generally held beliefs about supernatural powers. This account, which summarizes the knowledge I have derived from numerous conversations, interviews, and observations, as well as from the work of other scholars, describes what is not usually stated explicitly when villagers interact with one another, precisely because it is assumed to be understood.

To demonstrate how the struggle for community in Kukulewa was taking place within a larger hegemonic process of which it was, in a sense, no more than a specific instance, I also describe various aspects of Sri Lankan history and culture that impinged upon events in Kukulewa in the late 1970s and early 1980s. Just as my account of the doxic knowledge underlying local discursive practices provides the necessary context for understanding what villagers said and did as they strove to create a sense of belonging together in the village, this other material performs a similar function for the understanding of the larger hegemonic process in which the local struggle was embroiled. These interventions, which include a condensed account of the history of the region and of the place of the Veddas within it (chapter 3), an analysis of the economic changes that have taken place in Kukulewa in the last forty years (chapter 4), and a description of some general features of Sinhala nationalism (chapter 5), are mostly confined to the first half of the book. Thereafter it becomes increasingly feasible for the narrative to be carried forward in the words of the villagers themselves. Moreover, even in the early chapters, I make every effort to balance my own abstract account with relevant statements by the villagers themselves. For example, in chapter 4 my analysis of the economic changes that have taken place in Kukulewa is juxtaposed with direct quotations that demonstrate the analytical skill and moral fervor with which villagers addressed the economic issues that impinged most immediately on their lives.

Nevertheless it remains the case that, while it is necessary for me to contextualize the villagers' words and deeds to render them intelligible, the very process of contextualization inevitably constrains their discourse within the compass of my own project. This dilemma, which suspends the ethnographer between the impossibility of liberating his subjects from his own textual authority and his no less impossible claim to possession of the objective truth, has been widely discussed in recent years (see especially Clifford 1983; Clifford and Marcus 1986; Marcus and Fischer 1986). In the work at hand I have composed much of the narrative out of the spoken words of Kukulewa villagers, but I have also arranged their voices to fit my own narrative and interpretive project.

I make no claim, therefore, that my account is either comprehensive or objective, let alone that it is *the* authoritative and definitive account of what happened in Kukulewa. Like all accounts it is partial, in the twin senses of being both incomplete and one-sided, and that partiality is inescapably mine. Nevertheless, while I cannot avoid imposing myself as a screen between the people of Kukulewa and the reader, I am consoled by the thought that without my intervention few people would ever hear the voices of Kukulewa at all. This is not because the villagers are incapable of speaking for themselves. Far from it; they are as eloquent as anyone else. But inequalities in the distribution of power, wealth, and the technologies of communication virtually guarantee that, without the intervention of someone like myself, they would be heard only within a very narrow horizon.

What follows, then, is a story of how issues of community were addressed by the inhabitants of Kukulewa as they were caught up in the hegemonic project of Sinhala nationalism. The narrative is ultimately my rendition of what happened, but it aims also to provide a vehicle through which the villagers' own voices can be heard, as they drew on their common sense to wrestle with the disruptive threats and opportunities of what is still euphemistically referred to as "development" or "modernization."

Chapter 3   *Of Savages and Kings*

THE EVENTS recounted here took place in Kukulewa and are unique to it, but the general pattern of life from which they emerged is shared by other villages not only in Anuradhapura District, or Nuvarakalaviya, as it was formerly called, but also in other parts of the lowland Dry Zone that extends over two-thirds of Sri Lanka's land surface. This general pattern is grounded in two distinct forms of agriculture, both of which were established more than two thousand years ago. Since then the Dry Zone has suffered extreme vicissitudes of political fortune, but basic features of the pattern have endured. Only in the present generation has their continued reproduction been threatened by the combined effects of fundamental changes in ecology, technology, demography, economics, culture, and politics. In this chapter, which sketches the historical background against which more recent events have occurred, I concentrate on the more persistent patterns of action to the virtual exclusion of particular historical events.

The gently rolling landscape of Anuradhapura District is interrupted by numerous rocky outcrops, most of modest prominence but a few of which rise several hundred feet above the surrounding plains. Otherwise the undulating terrain is mainly shaped by the shallow valleys of the many small streams that run through the district. For most of the year the beds of these streams are dry, but with the coming of the monsoon rains they fill rapidly and often overflow their banks. The annual rainfall averages about fifty-five inches, but is highly variable. In some years there may be as many as eighty inches, in others less than thirty. Two-thirds of the rain normally falls between October and January, the period of the northeast monsoon, and this provides the water for the main cultivation season, called *maha*. Most of the remainder comes in April and May, and is sometimes sufficient for a second season of cultivation, known as *yala*. After the showers die out in May it remains dry for several months. The shallow soil

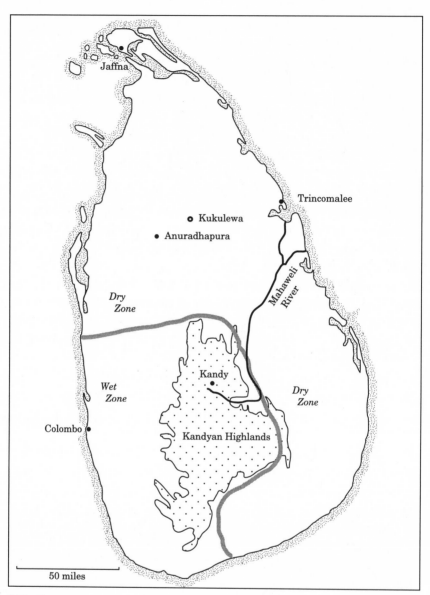

Sri Lanka

eventually cracks, the scrub jungle shrivels under a remorseless sun, and
a steadily strengthening wind blows dust everywhere. Then, when the
northeast monsoon arrives again, the landscape is suddenly transformed.
The vegetation becomes green and expansive, the stream beds fill with

water, and for a while the land is lush. But by January the rains slacken off and the withering heat sets in once more.

In order to secure their subsistence under these conditions the people who live in Anuradhapura District long ago devised two distinct modes of agriculture, one of which is dependent on direct rainfall and the other on irrigation. *Hēna,* anglicized as *chena,* is the local form of what is more generally known as shifting cultivation, swidden, or slash-and-burn. Under this regime a stretch of jungle is cut down a month or two before the rains are expected, and then burned. Ashes from the fire supply valuable nutrients to the soil, and if the rains are sufficient, the land will yield good returns for two years before its fertility drops sharply off. It is then abandoned and left to regenerate itself, ideally for as long as twenty years. Meanwhile the cultivator shifts his attention to other sites, which he works in succession and in similar manner.

The other form of agriculture, which is devoted exclusively to rice cultivation, requires the construction of a reservoir, or tank, in which the monsoon rains are collected and stored. An earth dam is built across one of the seasonal streams and water is impounded behind it. Permanent fields and irrigation ditches are laid out below the dam, or bund, and connected to the tank by means of sluices and channels. This permits the carefully controlled flow of water that rice cultivation requires. But successful paddy cultivation also demands a greater quantity of water than most village tanks can regularly provide. For this reason cultivators usually wait until they can see that the tank is going to fill before they begin to work their paddy fields. Under the prevailing conditions of unreliable rainfall this means that in many years they do not attempt irrigated rice cultivation at all. Chena cultivation is also jeopardized by a shortage of water, as well as by a sudden excess of rain and the unpredictable arrival of the monsoon, but it is less susceptible to such natural vagaries and has therefore long been recognized, by villagers if not always by colonial administrators, state officials, and experts in development, as the less uncertain means of livelihood.[1]

These two forms of agriculture have imposed a uniform pattern of settlement in the district. Each village normally contains a tank, the paddy fields it irrigates, a collection of wattle-and-daub houses clustered close to the tank bund, and a square mile or so of surrounding scrub jungle that separates it from its nearest neighbors. The jungle is exploited principally for chena cultivation, but is also a source of fuel, grazing land, wild plants, and game. The spacing of the villages reflects the need for jungle land, while the size of each settlement is conditioned by the available water supply. Particular tanks and villages have at times been abandoned, and new ones developed, but ecological constraints have, up until the very recent past, ensured the maintenance of the same basic pattern through all the turmoil of historical change.

Vicissitudes of History

This rural economy of chena and paddy cultivation provided the material foundations on which was raised the brilliant edifice of ancient Sinhala civilization.[2] From the third century B.C. Anuradhapura began to emerge as the capital of an expansive kingdom that came to dominate the Dry Zone and even to claim sovereignty over the whole island. Much is now unknown about the social organization of the ancient Anuradhapura kingdom, but the scale and splendor of its palaces, temples, and shrines, many of which remain in unexcavated ruin, attest not only to the aesthetic vision of its people but also to their rulers' ability to command a mass of concentrated labor. The royal government constructed a vast system of major irrigation works, a network of large tanks and canals that in some cases carried water many miles over precisely calculated gradients. These works demonstrate extraordinary engineering skill, but for the most part they were not connected to the cruder village tanks, which to that degree retained their local independence. On the other hand, the rulers could only have sustained the city of Anuradhapura with the labor service and tributary payments of the rural cultivators.

Extraction of a surplus from the villagers was secured not simply by the threat of coercion but also, and perhaps more decisively, by ideological means. Almost from its beginning Sinhala kingship was closely associated with Buddhism, which was introduced to the island in the third century B.C. Thereafter the king came to be represented as the protector of religion as well as of the people, one of whose principal responsibilities was the maintenance of Buddhist institutions. Buddhism in turn served both to unify the kingdom and to augment the authority of the king. One effect of this mutual enhancement was a powerful legitimation of the social hierarchy. Scrupulous performance of ascribed functions, from the righteous rule of the king to the faithful service of the peasant, was held to be both the sanctioned path to a more elevated status in one's next life and the means to ensure harmony not only in society but also in the larger cosmos. At this distance of time one cannot readily determine the extent to which peasant villagers actively embraced this rationalization of their subordination, but everything suggests that eventually its premises became deeply embedded in their culture. Similar principles were used to legitimate the later kingdom of Kandy, and even in the 1980s, more than 150 years after the British overthrew the last Sinhala king, the residue of this ancient ideology was still almost as palpable in Anuradhapura District as were the material remains of the civilization it sustained. In popular parlance it was still known as the *rājaraṭa*—the land of the kings.

Anuradhapura remained the center of Sinhala civilization for more than a thousand years, during which the power and abilities of its rulers varied greatly. At times its kings led conquering armies into South India; at other times they were themselves defeated and Anuradhapura fell into foreign hands. But despite the diversity of individual destinies, and scarcely noted by the monks who compiled the Mahavamsa, or Great Chronicle, the primary historical record of the period, one can also infer the long duration of an agrarian regime whose basic features were not much different in the eleventh century A.D., when the capital was moved to Polonnaruwa, forty miles to the southeast, than they had been a thousand years earlier.

Polonnaruwa served as the capital for two hundred years, and then the center of political gravity shifted again, this time to the southwest and out of the Dry Zone altogether. Ecological degradation, climatic change, and disease (especially the spread of malaria), as well as political turmoil, have all been advanced as factors contributing to this shift. However, while their relative causal weight remains controversial, their result is starkly clear. The city of Anuradhapura was left in ruins, and much of the Dry Zone, including Nuvarakalaviya, became isolated and impoverished. Population was drastically reduced, tanks fell into disrepair, and many villages and temples were deserted. Peasant cultivators continued their age-old struggle to make a living in the face of a harsh climate, a miserly soil, and endemic disease, but they no longer produced a substantial surplus. Local chieftains, known as Vanniyas, enjoyed virtually autonomous power in the region, and made little more than formal acknowledgment of any superior authority. Nuvarakalaviya thus came to form part of a broad arc of country, remote from the centers of power and supporting only a sparse population, that divided the mainly Sinhala-speaking regions of Sri Lanka from the predominantly Tamil-speaking areas to the north and east.

Nuvarakalaviya eventually came to be included as a province of the kingdom established in the central highlands toward the end of the fifteenth century, which was eventually successful in reuniting the interior of the island from its new capital in Kandy. But the kings of Kandy lacked the power to assert decisive authority at such a distance, and in any case they were increasingly preoccupied with the new European powers, led by the Portuguese, which from the beginning of the sixteenth century began to take control of Sri Lanka's coastline. Nevertheless, Nuvarakalaviya remained a part of the kingdom of Kandy for the next three hundred years, and during that time its social life was ordered by the same principles, many of them inherited from the Anuradhapura kingdom, that were now most elaborately articulated in the Kandyan heartland.

An overwhelmingly agrarian society, the kingdom of Kandy was fundamentally organized by its complex system of land tenure, integrated through the interlocking and mutually reinforcing institutions of kingship, religion, and caste. The king's sovereignty was expressed in his paramount landlordship of the whole kingdom. His subjects held land in return for the payment of grain and the performance of services, the intricate variety of which was associated with caste status, the more menial services being reserved for, and thus also defining, those of lower status. These forms of tribute and service were the dominant mode of surplus appropriation in the kingdom and provided the material means for the exercise of state authority. All rights to revenue and service were held to derive ultimately from the king, but in many cases they were effectively transferred, either to monastic institutions as acts of merit-making piety or to nobles and officials in compensation for their performance of administrative or military service.

The king himself was represented as a Bodhisattva, a future Buddha, and as an approximation of *cakravartin,* the ideal monarch and universal ruler. As the sacred mediator between human society and the cosmos of which it was a part, it was the king's task to maintain the harmony of both. This he accomplished by the virtuous performance of his duties. By acting to protect Buddhism and govern righteously he was believed to ensure the welfare and prosperity of the country. This came about both directly, by the magical efficacy of righteous rule itself, and indirectly, by the pleasure that virtuous conduct evoked among the gods, who then favored the king and his subjects with good fortune. Thus attainment of peace and prosperity was simultaneously a responsibility of kingship and a sign that the king was virtuous. When law and order were maintained, when the rains fell at the right time and in the right amounts so that the crops were bountiful, then the righteousness of the king's rule was confirmed. Conversely, there was always the risk that when social disorder broke out or natural disaster struck, it might be attributed to a lack of virtue in the king.

Thus the sanctity of Sinhala kingship did not permit the exercise of unrestrained power. The king might aspire to universal rule, but in order to preserve his legitimacy he had to attend to the welfare of his people, heed the advice of religious experts, and maintain traditional custom. The strongest constraint on royal power, however, probably stemmed from the segmentary structure of the Sinhala state.[3] The king presided over a polity composed of partially autonomous entities, each of which retained significant control over its own internal affairs. Moreover, kingship was not so much an absolutely unique imperial power as it was the most consummate manifestation of an exemplary principle that was less elaborately emulated at all levels of society. Regional lords, such as the Vanniya chiefs whose command of Nuvarakalaviya was virtually autonomous in Kandyan times, were in their own way petty kings who strove to reproduce on a smaller scale the greater kingdom that encompassed them. Even prominent villagers might share the same hierarchical aspirations, however much reduced. Anyone who controlled wealth, and especially land, could command a retinue, and everywhere the man to whom honor was given was one to whom others were beholden and service was owed, in return for which he offered his benevolent protection. In this sense kingship was ubiquitous, even in a province such as Nuvarakalaviya where the king's effective power was severely limited.[4] Compared with districts closer to the capital, neither material inequalities nor status differences were highly elaborated in Nuvarakalaviya, yet the imagery of kingship still flourished. Sustained both by the memory of Anuradhapura's ancient glories and by pervasive emulation of the royal model, it remained the most lucid expression of the hierarchical ideology through which the social order was articulated.

It is evident, however, that whatever the appeal of hierarchy, the tributary mode of production that it legitimated was no longer able to generate a sizable surplus in Nuvarakalaviya. Chena cultivation was resistant to the extraction of surplus, while wet-rice agriculture was irregular and unreliable. Large landowners were few, and most of those who did appropriate some surplus from the labor of others were themselves active cultivators. Nevertheless, insofar as hierarchical principles sustained even a modest flow of tributary services, they forestalled any tendency for the village economy to escape into isolation.

As in other parts of the kingdom the prevailing ideology obliged villagers in Nuvarakalaviya to perform services in return for their land rights. The principle was maintained that all rights ultimately originated with the king, and many kinds of services were thus known as *rājakāriya* (duty to the king), but in practice it was common for them to be owed to an intermediate superior, such as a Vanniya lord or a Buddhist monastery. Very often, especially in the case of lower ranking castes, the service was also performed for the benefit of neighboring villages. Unlike some other parts of the country, in Nuvarakalaviya the services attached to the lands in any village were normally all of the same kind, and correspondingly the inhabitants of any particular village were usually all members of the same caste group, known locally as a *variga*.

Maintenance of the system of caste services in Nuvarakalaviya was of crucial importance to the Vanniya lords, who themselves occupied the highest grade within the superior Goyigama (Cultivator) caste. Each local caste community, composed of a number of villages belonging to the same variga, enjoyed a measure of autonomy and possessed its own court, which held jurisdiction over its internal affairs, but appointment to these courts was in the hands of the local lord, whose approval was also necessary to ratify its decisions. In addition to the tribute and services that the Vanniyas claimed from their subordinates, the exercise of this privilege was one of the principal means by which they maintained their authority in the province.

Since all castes held land rights in return for the performance of their services, members of the Goyigama caste, which was the most numerous as well as the highest ranking caste in the district, enjoyed no monopoly of agriculture. Blacksmiths and Potters, who supplied neighboring villages as well as local lords with the products of their craft, and Washermen and Drummers, whose professional skills were indispensable to the proper

performance of various rituals, also inhabited their own villages and cultivated their own fields. For many of them their caste profession was not a
full-time occupation, or even their principal means of livelihood. Some
villages, however, were less well endowed with tanks and irrigated fields
than others, and in general these poorer sites were occupied by the lower
ranking castes. In some cases the members of these communities worked
as sharecropping tenants in the fields of neighboring villages with superior resources. Where such arrangements were regularly established,
sharecropping tenancy *(ande)* was commonly represented as a traditional
service owed by the lower caste group to its hierarchical superior.

All the evidence suggests that over the course of many generations the
principle of hierarchy embedded in the caste system became so deeply
sedimented in the culture that, while it always had to be renewed, for the
most part it was taken for granted as a matter of simple experience and
common sense. The fact that expressions of hierarchy were ubiquitous,
however, did not mean either that they were uniformly interpreted or that
superiors and inferiors necessarily agreed upon their mutual rights and
obligations. The exact ranking of the castes, the precise extent of a landlord's responsibilities to his tenant, the honor that attached to a particular
service—all these were matters that could be questioned. The righteous
ruler was enjoined to be generous to his subjects, but just how generous
did he have to be in order to be righteous? Landlord and tenant might
agree on the division of the crop between them, but to what extent could
the tenant justifiably call upon his landlord's assistance to cope with some
emergency, and what were the limits to the landlord's claims upon his
tenant's services outside agriculture? The answers to such questions were
never permanently fixed, but were continuously tested, negotiated, and
modified in the ongoing process of social life. Nevertheless, insofar as such
struggles focused on the mutual obligations of superiors and inferiors but
did not challenge their inegalitarian premises, they posed no threat to the
principle of hierarchy itself. Rather they served ultimately only to reproduce it.

In its continued isolation and poverty Nuvarakalaviya was of no more
than marginal interest to the foreign powers that pressed upon the kingdom of Kandy. When Robert Knox (1911), a British sailor who was a cap-
tive of the king of Kandy for eighteen years in the seventeenth century,
recounted his eventual escape through the district, he described it as a

wilderness. Neither the government in Kandy, nor the independent Tamil principality in the north, nor the intrusive Europeans paid close attention to what went on there. The Portuguese, and the Dutch who replaced them as the dominant European power in the mid-seventeenth century, both concentrated their commercial and military interests on the coastal areas, especially in the southwest, close to the sources of the lucrative trade in spices. And even the British, who overthrew the Kandyan kingdom at the beginning of the nineteenth century and proclaimed their authority over the whole island, did little at first to intervene in the affairs of Nuvarakalaviya.

Nevertheless, for Sri Lanka as a whole, the nineteenth century was a period of massive upheaval, as the British conquest was soon followed by the large-scale establishment of capitalist agriculture.[5] By the 1840s the central highlands were opened up to plantations of coffee, and later of tea and rubber, while coconut production was greatly expanded at lower elevations and Colombo was developed as the colony's capital, port, and commercial center. For much of the nineteenth century, however, Nuvarakalaviya was only marginally affected by these changes, and in many respects, even into the twentieth century the conditions of life in its villages remained much as they had been under the Kandyan kings. But eventually the effects of colonial rule were felt even in the most isolated areas. Especially after 1873, when Anuradhapura was established as the administrative center of the newly created North Central Province, within which Nuvarakalaviya was included, the state came to play a more intrusive role in village affairs, through land surveys and censuses, attempts to refurbish irrigation works, settlement of title to land, demands for tax, establishment of law courts and a police force, provision of education and welfare, and the construction of roads and railways. Even so, the local operations of the colonial bureaucracy that administered these policies retained a distinctly patrimonial style, and the exercise of authority preserved much of its traditionally hierarchical character. Under the British government agent in Anuradhapura the day-to-day administration of village affairs was left largely in the hands of a Sinhala official known as the *raṭe mahatmaya,* who, up until the office was abolished almost at the end of the colonial period, was always appointed from among the members of the Vanniya aristocracy. Thus although the raṭe mahatmaya was an official in the colonial bureaucracy he always also had an interest, by virtue of his presidential position in the system of caste courts, which were not themselves officially recognized by the British, in maintaining the hierarchical order of caste relations.[6]

As the colonial era drew to its close there were increasing signs that presaged a fundamental transformation of social life in Nuvarakalaviya, now officially known as Anuradhapura District. Independence was not attained until 1948, but the grant of universal suffrage in 1931 and the assumption of ministerial authority by indigenous politicians had already brought about a decisive realignment of official priorities, especially in agrarian policy. The new direction was most vigorously proclaimed by D. S. Senanayake, who served as minister of agriculture and lands before he became the first prime minister of Ceylon, as Sri Lanka was then still called. Prompted by the growing concern both to increase food production and to relieve the pressure of landlessness in the overcrowded Wet Zone, and doubtless also sensitive to the political advantages of a nationalist appeal to the past, Senanayake initiated a series of projects to restore the irrigation systems of the Dry Zone to their former splendor and prosperity.[7]

These projects, the scope of which was vastly expanded after 1948, were a major factor in the subsequent transformation of social relations in Anuradhapura District. Over the next thirty years agriculture was decisively reoriented from subsistence to the market, and state officials penetrated deeply into village life as they sought to implement successive policies of rural development.[8] Party politics also intensified, as villagers organized to gain access to the benefits of development. Facilitated by improved communications, these economic and political changes were accompanied by a massive surge in the propagation of Sinhala nationalism, which soon became a pervasive feature of almost all official discourse.[9]

Combined with the natural increase in population that followed the virtual eradication of malaria in the 1940s, these developments also contributed to a demographic explosion in the region. Large numbers of people from other parts of the island moved into what had formerly served as a kind of buffer zone between the Sinhalas and the Tamils, either in connection with one or other of the state projects or as individual migrants and settlers. These movements involved both Sinhala and Tamil people, but official projects generally favored Sinhala settlers, to which Tamils responded with vigorous assertions of their right to inhabit what they claimed were their "traditional homelands." As the struggle intensified both sides pointed to traces of ancient occupation, such as place names, ruined temples, and rock inscriptions that indicated an earlier religious or linguistic affiliation, as compelling evidence to support their right of possession. Under these conditions, marginal groups like the Veddas, who had formerly found refuge in the underpopulated buffer zone, came under increasing pressure to identify themselves with one side or the other of the major ethnic divide.

Aboriginal Claims

The Veddas are a famous people in Sri Lanka, but they are not at all well known. Most educated Sri Lankans firmly believe them to be the descendants of an aboriginal population of hunters and gatherers, now reduced to very small numbers but still retaining essential elements of their ancient culture. Their actual history, however, remains obscure. Among the texts cited by K.N.O. Dharmadasa in his recent review of "Veddas in the History of Sri Lanka" (1990a), the earliest one that refers to the Veddas as such *(väddo)* dates only from the thirteenth century. Scholars have rarely hesitated to interpret earlier textual mention either of hunters or of autochthons as referring to the ancestors of the people later known as Veddas, but this is speculation. After the thirteenth century there is increasing evidence that the Veddas formed a more or less distinct status group or ethnic community, but it is also clear that, while they may have been distinguished from the Sinhala, they were by no means segregated from them. Historical records identify them not only as isolated forest-dwellers but also as local chiefs and soldiers in the service of Sinhala kings. Academic research, however, has little to say about the Veddas' relations with the Sinhalas. For more than a hundred years Vedda scholarship has attended almost exclusively to the discovery and description of their supposedly pristine culture, uncontaminated by Sinhala influence. And in this endeavor they have commonly been described not only as possessing a distinct culture but also as constituting a distinct race.[10]

In this respect they were subject to the standard procedures of classification and regulation prescribed by nineteenth century colonial ideology. As Nissan and Stirrat (1987:10) summarize the situation, "different groups in Sri Lanka were, it was argued, different races and different races had different customs. Language, religion, custom and clothes were taken in various combinations as markers of racial variation." Thus the jungle-dwelling Veddas were identified as a pagan group of nomadic hunters and gatherers who were racially quite distinct from their Sinhala Buddhist and Tamil Hindu neighbors, who were settled agriculturalists. Some mixture of different races was admitted (and was often believed to result in "degeneracy" [Seligmann and Seligmann 1911:48]), but for the most part a strict correlation between race and culture was believed to hold. This conflation of biological and cultural characteristics, or rather the failure to distinguish them, is evident even in the best anthropological research of the colonial period. The Seligmanns' classic study of the Veddas, for example, which was published in 1911, begins with the revealing assertion (by C. G. Seligmann) that "with all my efforts I was able to meet only four families, and hear of two more, who I believe had never practiced cultivation. *Pure-blooded* Veddas are not quite so rare as the statement implies" (Seligmann and Seligmann 1911:vii; emphasis added).

Identification of the Veddas as a distinct race became part of the unquestioned common sense of urban, and especially educated, Sri Lankans, but in the rural areas there appears to have been a significantly different understanding of how Veddas and Sinhalas were related. Ethnographic reports from various parts of Sri Lanka contain scattered evidence that, when Sinhala villagers use the term "Vedda" *(vädda,* pl. *väddo),* they are primarily referring not to a group of people whom they consider racially distinct from themselves but to the absence of certain cultural characteristics. In this popular usage "Vedda" means something like "culturally deficient" or "uncivilized." In other words, Sinhala villagers describe as Veddas those among them who lack the cultural attributes that collectively define a civilized and distinctly Sinhala identity. Thus those who are ignorant of Buddhist teaching, or who live by foraging in the jungle or even from swidden cultivation rather than wet-rice agriculture, are always liable to be designated as Veddas. Spencer (1990a:144), for example, reporting how elderly men in a village in Sabaragamuva Province recalled the conditions under which they had formerly lived, quotes one old man as saying: "People in this village were like Veddas. They would group together, go to the jungle, kill the animals and eat. That was their work." And later (1990a:158), "we knew nothing of the *dharma* then."

In this instance the villager was saying only that his former way of life was *like* that of a Vedda. Often, however, what is posited is not just a similarity but an identity. Thus, in describing some communities of swidden cultivators in Uva Province, Yalman (1967:23) writes that "Sinhalese who live in established paddy-cultivating villages consider these people to be wild, backward and dangerous. They will often refer to them simply as Veddas. . . ."

Perera (1992:115) records a similar disposition in his account of an old village in Anuradhapura District that was absorbed into a government-sponsored development project. Referring to the inhabitants of the old village, who considered themselves to be respectable Sinhala of Goyigama caste, one of the new settlers remarked that "they do not have any social manners; they did not know how to laugh until very recently. They were aborigines (väddo)."

The people of Kukulewa were themselves by no means unanimous on the subject of their identity. In 1968, when I first visited the village, all of them acknowledged that they were Vedda, but some also claimed to be Sinhala as well. Some said that Veddas were quite distinct from the Sinhalas, while others said that the Veddas were simply one particular kind of Sinhala. In some cases the same individual would take one position on one occasion and the other on another. Similar ambiguities emerged when I began to inquire about the local caste hierarchy. At that time, even though a number of caste practices had already been abandoned, the salience of caste identities was scarcely questioned, but there was no agreement as to what the Veddas' caste profession had formerly been. Some people claimed that they had performed a religious service, acting as mediums with the spirit world. Others said that their duty was to provide jungle produce, especially game and honey. Others again argued that the Veddas stood completely outside the caste hierarchy and performed no services at all.

Each of these opinions was supported by appeals to the past, especially the latter two, both of which drew on the prevalent view that the Veddas were not just one among many Sinhala castes but a quite distinct kind of people, originally descended from the aboriginal population that had inhabited Sri Lanka before the arrival of the Sinhalas and that subsequently lived at, or even beyond, the margins of Sinhala civilization. The Veddas were not, however, totally separated from the Sinhalas by this myth, which also described the origins of the Sinhala people. The myth told of the arrival in Sri Lanka, on the day of the Buddha's enlightenment and with his blessing, of Prince Vijaya and his followers, from whom the Sinhalas reckoned their descent. Before sending back to India for a royal bride, Vijaya cohabited with the aboriginal Kuveni, who bore him two children from whose own subsequent union the Veddas were believed to be descended. Thus descent from Kuveni supported the Veddas' claim to be the original inhabitants of the island, while the connection to Vijaya established their kinship, if not with all the Sinhalas, then certainly with Sinhalas of royal status. Sinhala villagers, then, might (and did) interpret the presents of game and honey that the Veddas reputedly made to the Vanniya lords as an obligatory tribute to their hierarchical superiors, but the Veddas' own recollection was that these offerings were gifts among equals, which were reciprocated by presents of rice and cloth.

When discussing the distinctiveness of the Kukulewa people, however, their Sinhala neighbors usually put less emphasis on their purported ancestry than on the same features that were stressed by villagers elsewhere. What was thought to set the Veddas apart most clearly was their cultural deficiency and backwardness. Thus the categorical disjunction between Vedda and Sinhala coexisted in popular consciousness with awareness of a range of cultural variation that placed the Veddas and the Sinhalas on a single continuum. From this perspective the culture of Kukulewa could indeed appear as an impoverished version of the Sinhala culture of surrounding villages. Like their Sinhala neighbors, for example, the people of Kukulewa grew rice under irrigation, but their paddy fields were comparatively few and they depended for their subsistence more on swidden cultivation (or, in recent times, on wage labor outside the village). Again, the people of Kukulewa described themselves as Buddhists, but there was no temple in the village and only rarely did the people participate in Buddhist rites. To some extent, then, the lack of accord as to whether the people of Kukulewa were Vedda or Sinhala, or possibly both, might have reflected uncertainty as to just where they were positioned along the path to civilization.

In recent decades, however, not only in Anuradhapura District but also in other parts of the former buffer zone, Veddas have come under increasing pressure to identify themselves as Sinhala. Writing about Monaragala District, in the southeast of Sri Lanka, Vitebsky (1992:164) refers to "the subtle and complex process whereby the ambiguously placed villagers on the southern edge of the old Wedi Rata ('Vedda country') were coming to repudiate the Vedda strands in their ethnic identity in favor of defining themselves as Sinhalese of Goyigama caste from the Kandyan highlands." In this case, Vitebsky implies that as the villagers became more sophisticated they wanted to avoid any suggestion that they were uncivilized. Elsewhere the pressures were more direct. Dharmadasa's (1990b) account of recent Vedda history describes a number of projects that managed, to a greater or lesser extent, to assimilate or integrate the Veddas more closely into the mainstream of Sinhala society. These ranged from their resettlement under the Accelerated Mahaweli Development Project to the Buddhist missionary endeavors of Bhikku Silalankara among the Veddas at Dimbulagala. On the other hand, development funds were also sought to create a reservation on which Veddas could continue to pursue their purportedly traditional way of life (Gamage 1984; see also Hettige et al. 1993).

With the escalation of ethnic conflict, and the transformation of the former buffer zone into a line of direct confrontation between the Sinhalas and the Tamils, the Veddas in Anuradhapura District learned to put a greater stress on their Sinhala affinities. In the 1960s the Anuradhapura Veddas (a term I use in order to distinguish them from Veddas in other parts of the country, with whom they had no direct connection) occupied thirty-two villages and fourteen satellite hamlets, whose inhabitants composed a single variga. Genealogical research indicates that until a generation or two ago the Anuradhapura Vedda variga, although overwhelmingly endogamous, maintained a small number of marriage relationships with Tamil-speaking villages to the north (Brow 1978a:172–74, 203). By the 1980s the number of these marriages appears to have been much reduced. A corresponding movement can be detected in Kukulewa itself, where by 1983 the younger and better educated villagers asserted their Sinhala identity more strongly than did their elders and were uninterested in, or even embarrassed by, their Vedda origins.

There is no reason to suppose that such movements of ethnic consciousness are unprecedented. In an earlier work (Brow 1978a:26–39), in which I first pointed out that the categorical distinction between Sinhala and Vedda encompasses a continuous range of cultural variation, I also contrasted the conceptual stability of the categorical opposition with empirical indications of the ethnic transformation of actual groups and individuals. People who were once Vedda have become Sinhala, and people who were once Sinhala have become Vedda. In the 1980s the categorical distinction remained intact, and in Sinhala eyes the Veddas still represented the wildness and lack of civilization against which their own cultural accomplishments were to be measured. But ethnic transformations also continued, and the identity of the Anuradhapura Veddas remained, as ever, always open to reinterpretation.

       The Village Community
Confronts the Market

AS DESCRIBED IN the previous chap-
ter, the social order that prevailed in Anuradhapura District in Kandyan
and colonial times was structured by the hierarchical principles embodied
in the caste system. At the same time, those who lived in the same village
were normally all members of the same caste or subcaste (variga) and were
thus kinsmen of one another. In contrast, then, to the hierarchical structure of the larger society, social relations within each village were mainly
governed by norms of kinship that stressed the villagers' fundamental
equality of status and endorsed the practice of reciprocity and mutual aid
among them. The kinship order did also sanction striking inequalities of
age and gender, but it always contained them within its basic assertion of
the moral and substantial unity of all those whom it embraced. Under
these conditions, kinship, caste, and locality combined to make the village the primary focus of community.

The notion of "community" has often been very loosely and ambiguously defined, nowhere more so perhaps than in reference to the idea of
"the village community," so I should reiterate that I am following Max
Weber (1978:40) here in defining it simply as "a sense of belonging together." This subjective state typically includes both affective and cognitive components, both a feeling of solidarity and an understanding of
shared identity. For the sake of convenience I also use "community" to
describe a setting where the sense of belonging together exists, either as an
ideal or as an experience (as in "the village community"), as well as the
people who are supposed to share that sense ("the village community"
again). But I should emphasize that this usage does not assume any of the
other characteristics that have frequently been attributed to "the village
community," the most common of which have been autonomy, self-sufficiency, democracy, and egalitarianism. All these features were present in
the villages of Anuradhapura District to a significant degree, and they

undoubtedly helped sustain the sense of belonging together, but they do not define it. Nor do I mean to imply, by describing the village as a community, either that social life within it was ever perfectly harmonious or that villagers always subordinated pursuit of their individual interests to the discipline of communal norms.

With this definition in mind, it can be said that throughout the period of colonial rule the social organization of community in Kukulewa remained both segmentary and hierarchical, and was principally articulated in the idioms of kinship and caste. Those who belonged together in the same family *(pavula)* were for the most part also members of the same village *(gama),* which in turn formed part of the larger community of the caste (variga). Which of these segmentary divisions was the most salient varied with the particular context of social action, but all rested on the same principles. Apart from the internal hierarchies of age and gender, each defined an egalitarian community of kinsmen and caste fellows. At the same time the Vedda variga was only one caste in a system of castes that also constituted a community, although in this case the structure of community was hierarchical.[1]

Distinctions of caste and the commonality of kinship served to promote a collective identity that was focused most sharply on the village itself. Other villages of the Vedda variga were some distance away, while the neighboring villages with which the people of Kukulewa had regular dealings were all communities of different variga. In most practical situations the expressions *"gamē minissu"* (village people), *"apē näyō"* (our kinsmen), and *"apē minissu"* (our people) were used more or less interchangeably to invoke a collective identity that distinguished the people of Kukulewa from their neighbors. Yet those neighbors did also participate in the same caste system and were themselves distinguished from more complete outsiders, such as Tamils, Muslims, and Low Country Sinhalas, whose place in the traditional hierarchy of the region was less clearly defined, although some Low Country Sinhalas could be included in the even more extensive, if also more diffuse, community of Sinhala Buddhism.

The boundaries of the village community and the distinctive identity of those included within it were continuously reproduced by a vast array of conventional practices, both ceremonial and mundane, that encompassed virtually every facet of ordinary life. A sense of belonging together was constantly created and recreated in the daily routines of agricultural cooperation, in the taken-for-granted reciprocities of neighborliness, and in the common use of kinship terms in mutual address. It was also affirmed in conventional practices, such as endogamy within the variga, that similarly differentiated between the way villagers behaved among themselves and the way they behaved toward others. And it was also generated and regenerated on occasions of collective ceremony that explicitly identified the village as a privileged site of community.

Continually reproduced in these ways over the many generations during which there was little change in the basic conditions of rural life, everything suggests that the idea of the village community became deeply sedimented in the local culture. In each generation individuals were subjectively constituted by their assumption of the identities ascribed to them by membership in the kin-based community of the village and the variga. The primacy of these identities was taken for granted, and the communal attachment that bound a Kukulewa villager to his fellows was experienced as primordial, in the sense discussed in chapter 2.

The people of Kukulewa were distinguished from their neighbors not only by their identity as Veddas but also by their greater poverty. All the evidence indicates that, in the past as in the present, the Veddas were among the most impoverished communities in Anuradhapura District. Their tanks were generally smaller and less reliable than those of other groups, and in order to secure their subsistence they were often obliged to work as sharecropping tenants in the fields of their more prosperous neighbors. This dependency contradicted their claim to royal status, which derived from their descent from Prince Vijaya, but they nevertheless continued to invoke that status, even in accounting for their poverty. They said that originally they were the only inhabitants of the region, but when Sinhala people began to move in they were obliged, as the descendants of kings, to do what they could to provide them with the means of livelihood, so they gave them the best tank sites. Eventually so many people settled in the region that they themselves were left in possession of only the very poorest land.

Agriculture and Community

Although the people of Kukulewa were poorer than most of their neighbors, they followed basically the same mode of subsistence that prevailed throughout Anuradhapura District. They may have once depended more on foraging in the jungle, but even the earliest colonial records show that they were already cultivating paddy, and like other villagers in the region, they were doubtless also industrious chena farmers. Both forms of agriculture were governed by norms of kinship, but they were organized very differently. In general, chena land was considered to be the communal property of the whole village but was cultivated by households acting independently, while paddy land was held individually but required several households to cooperate in its cultivation.[2]

Chenas were cultivated in the jungle surrounding the village, on land to which anyone who was recognized as a member of the Vedda variga enjoyed access. Individual possession lasted only as long as a particular plot was kept in cultivation. After the initial clearing of the jungle, which was a male task, men and women worked alongside one another, producing a variety of crops of which the most important was millet. Members of different households sometimes joined together to clear the jungle, and subsequently to protect their growing crops, but for the most part chenas were worked by households operating separately; apart from reciprocal gifts between close kin, the crop was destined for consumption within the household that produced it.

Irrigated land, by contrast, was held in individual shares that were normally transferred by inheritance, although increasing monetization of the economy under colonial rule seems to have made sales and mortgages more frequent. Those who mortgaged their land usually continued to work it on andē (sharecropping tenancy), turning over half of what they produced as interest on the loan they had received. Paddy cultivation was mostly done by men, with women normally joining in only to reap the crop. The need for households to cooperate in paddy cultivation stemmed from several sources. First, villagers all drew their water through the same irrigation channels and therefore had to coordinate their activities. Second, shareholders in the village field had the collective responsibility both to maintain the irrigation works and to protect the growing crop. And third, paddy cultivation involved a comparatively complex technology, including the use of draft animals as well as human energy, and it demanded at times the concerted application of more labor than was typically available within a single household. This demand was met by institutionalized forms of reciprocal labor exchange between kinsmen belonging to different households.

Economic differentiation was not pronounced within the village. Individual possession of paddy land allowed its concentration in the hands of a few, but such concentrations were typically linked to the life cycle and did not develop into a permanent division between the landed and the landless. This resulted, on the one hand, from the low population density that permitted villagers to pioneer new settlements, with their own small tanks, in uninhabited parts of the district and, on the other, from the normal operation of the system of kinship and marriage. Endogamy within the village was approved, but the small size of the village impelled most of its young men and women to marry members of other Vedda villages, and they were then free to choose whether to live in the husband's or the wife's village. All children enjoyed equal rights of inheritance, but it was difficult to live in one village and work paddy land in another. Under these circumstances couples tended to reside in the village where their inheritance prospects were greater and to let their rights lapse where they were less, with the overall result that the more land a villager possessed the more likely his potential heirs were to press their claims. These practices did not prevent short-term concentrations of wealth in land, but they did provide an effective levelling mechanism in the long run.

Those who came to hold more paddy land than they could themselves work gave some of it out to their fellow villagers to work on andē. This created relations of dependency, but andē within the village was represented as an act of reciprocity and mutual assistance between status equals who were members of the same community. Similar representations were also made when land was worked on andē on behalf of proprietors who were unable to cultivate it themselves because of sickness or old age. Both andē and reciprocal labor exchange thus stood in strong contrast to employment for a cash wage, which as late as the 1950s was still considered antithetical to the ethics of kinship.

Because their own holdings of paddy land were insufficient the people of Kukulewa also worked land on andē in neighboring villages that were more prosperous, where their landlords were usually members of the Goyigama caste. The material terms of andē were the same in such cases as when landlord and tenant were fellow villagers, but they were evaluated very differently, especially by the landlords. The Goyigama people looked on their Vedda tenants as hereditary status subordinates who were performing their traditional labor service by cultivating Goyigama fields on andē. For their part, however, the Kukulewa people were unwilling to acknowledge their inferiority and were more inclined to extend the intra-village understanding of andē as an egalitarian relationship of mutual aid to include their dealings with their Goyigama landlords. But despite these conflicting interpretations Veddas and Goyigama were agreed that they belonged within the same hierarchical community and that consequently the provision of services between them should be compensated in kind and not cash.

Thus the particularistic norms attached to agrarian relations constrained economic action by inhibiting the free development of markets in land and labor at the same time as they gave ethical force to the distinction between the people of Kukulewa and their neighbors. Likewise agrarian practices not only sustained the village materially but also, by providing recurrent occasions for action that expressed communal norms, continuously recreated the very idea and experience of community. The recognition that certain agrarian relations that were appropriate between kinsmen were inappropriate between members of different villages, and vice versa, and the more intricate interpretation of materially identical relations as being, in the case of andē, an expression of communal solidarity when the parties were members of the same village, but an expression of hierarchical domination when they belonged to different varigas, served to reinforce a sense of identity that was centered on membership in the village community.

The simple reproduction of the village community was severely disrupted by a series of exogenous changes that swept through Anuradhapura District after the 1950s, the most general effect of which was to reduce the control that villagers exercised over their means of livelihood and to increase their dependence on economic and political processes external to the village.

One of the most fundamental developments was the accelerated rate of population growth. Starting at a little over a hundred in 1900, the population of Kukulewa doubled during the next forty years and then, from the 1940s onward, began to grow more rapidly. By 1970 it had reached 552, and in the next thirteen years it increased a further 67%, from 552 to 910. Almost all this growth was natural increase, since immigration and emigration, which were largely confined to marriage, more or less balanced one another. Up until about 1970 population growth was matched by the expansion of irrigation facilities, and the mean per capita holding of paddy land in 1970 was 0.3 acres, which is what it had been in 1931. But a good deal of the land that was brought under paddy cultivation in the 1960s was only marginally irrigatable. After 1970 very little further expansion was possible, and by 1983 the mean per capita holding had dropped below 0.2 acres. No less decisive was the increasing pressure on unirrigated cultivation, which led to a reduction of the chena cycle and a scarcity of land that had lain fallow long enough to give the best yields for traditional crops. Under these conditions the people of Kukulewa were forced more and more to go outside the village to obtain the means of livelihood, and they did so increasingly as wage laborers.

Between 1954 and 1968, in association with a significant increase in the proportion of the rice crop that was marketed rather than consumed at home, and doubtless also affected by legislation intended to promote the security of established tenants, andē was largely replaced by wage labor throughout Anuradhapura District, especially where landlord and tenant were members of different varigas (Brow 1978b). This freed the people of Kukulewa from the taint of status inferiority that attached to their traditional employment as the andē tenants of their Goyigama neighbors, but it simultaneously jeopardized their claim to their landlords' paternalistic protection, which was also associated with andē tenancy. Many Kukulewa people continued to appeal to hierarchical norms, claiming the right to be employed as wage laborers in the fields they had formerly worked on andē, and they continued to evaluate their new employers as they had their former landlords (who were not infrequently the same individuals), that is, in terms of their generosity and concern for the welfare of those who worked for them. For their part many Goyigama landlords were not averse to such appeals and remained willing to extend their patronage, which both provided them with a retinue and reinforced their sense of status superiority (Brow 1981a).

By 1970, if not earlier, wage labor had become the principal source of income for most Kukulewa villagers (Brow 1978b). By that time payments of cash wages had also become acceptable within the village. Only among very close kin, such as full brothers or father and son was there still a strong revulsion against offering or taking a cash wage. Indeed a different, and in some respects opposite, sentiment was already being expressed that by 1983 had become widespread. It was said that villagers who were in a position to hire wage laborers should first offer to employ their kin. In this way kinship was still accorded an economic privilege, even as the norms of behavior that expressed it were reversed.

Opportunities for wage labor within the village were, however, severely restricted, as most people were able to do the bulk of their own paddy cultivation using only unpaid household labor. In 1969–1970 Kukulewa villagers performed nine times as much wage labor outside the village as they did inside it (Brow 1978b:455). Most of this work was done within a few miles of Kukulewa, in the paddy fields of neighboring but better endowed villages. But already in the late 1960s it was not uncommon to find groups of men, mostly young and unmarried, who would leave the village for two or three weeks at a time to work at some distant location.

This trend was intensified after 1977, when the newly elected UNP government introduced its "open economy" policy, the central aim of which was to promote the free play of market forces. Aspects of the policy that affected peasant agriculture included the encouragement of large-scale capital investment, much of it based on foreign aid, liberalization of import regulations, reduction or removal of controls over the distribution of agricultural products, and legislation designed to restructure land tenure (Gunasinghe 1986). Kukulewa was not directly incorporated into any of the government's major projects, but it was affected by them. The massive Mahaweli Development Project provided new opportunities for wage labor upon which male villagers became increasingly dependent, especially in the early 1980s, when successive years of deficient rainfall severely reduced the scope of paddy cultivation in the immediate area. Kukulewa women also entered the labor market on an unprecedented scale during the same period. Encouraged by the new policy of economic liberalization, outside entrepreneurs whose political connections sheltered them from prosecution began to convert large tracts of officially protected jungle and forest land to cash crop production. Once this land had been cleared by men, many of the entrepreneurs chose to cultivate it with the cheaper and reputedly more docile labor of village women.

Within the village unirrigated, or dry-land, cultivation remained relatively free from market influences until the late 1970s. Attempts to grow a cash crop of gingelly or chilies in the off season (yala) were long established, but this was a significant option only for relatively wealthy villagers who could bear the risk of inadequate rainfall. In 1969–1970 the overwhelming majority of unirrigated farming was chena cultivation of the traditional kind, geared to the production of food crops for domestic consumption. By 1983, however, most villagers were responding to the market forces released under the "open economy" policy and were devoting at least some part of their dry-land cultivation to production for the market. In some cases the cash crops were ones that had long been grown for consumption at home, such as millet and pumpkin, but which traders now found it profitable to truck from the villages to the urban markets at Kurunegala and Colombo. But the most popular cash crops were ones that ten years earlier had either been uncommon or unknown, such as gram and cowpea.

Almost all Kukulewa households derived a significant income from wage labor, but most of them also undertook some dry-land cultivation. The way they divided their labor between these two activities and their preference within unirrigated cultivation for subsistence as against cash crops were determined mainly by factors of household demography and the amount and kinds of other resources they commanded. Households headed by young men, and others that contained only a single adult male, depended most heavily on wage labor. Their dry-land cultivation was often confined to their home garden (vatta), or to a small chena close to the village that could be tended with household labor even though the husband and wife were often absent doing wage labor. Millet was the principal crop, along with smaller quantities of other traditional chena crops intended for domestic consumption, such as maize, chilies, pumpkins, and gourds. Some also grew a little gram or cowpea for the market, but this was subordinate to the subsistence crops. The extent of their cultivation, however, was too small to meet their own consumption needs. Most felt that if they grew a chena large enough to provide their households with millet throughout the year they would not be able to seize opportunities for wage labor when it was available. And in order to be able to look after their chena they had to locate it close to home, where available land had lain fallow only for a short time and returns from millet cultivation were much reduced.

Households with grown sons, and others that contained more than one adult male, also grew millet as their subsistence staple, but the scale of their dry-land cultivation was usually greater, and a larger proportion of it was devoted to cash crops. These households also remained in the wage labor market, which their greater labor resources enabled them to do while simultaneously cultivating four or more acres of unirrigated land. This policy of diversification, in which significant contributions to household maintenance were made by the production of both cash crops and subsistence crops, as well as by wage labor, was further developed by those households, large or small, that commanded other resources beyond access to land and their members' labor power. If they controlled the necessary capital, villagers were tempted to branch out into other activities such as stock raising (cattle or goats), milk production, tobacco cultivation under contract with the Ceylon Tobacco Company, brewing liquor, and in a very small number of cases, money lending, shopkeeping, and labor contracting. For the most part these operations remained small, involving no more than an acre of tobacco, twenty or thirty goats, or ten liters of milk a day, but they were sufficient to raise those who undertook them above their fellow villagers. A few people, among them several of the twelve villagers who enjoyed regular employment outside Kukulewa, mostly as menial laborers in one government department or another, were also able to hire wage laborers to increase the scope of their agricultural production.

Production strategies were also affected by the increasing pressure on the land and by many villagers' reluctance to depend for their livelihood on market forces that were no more predictable than the monsoon rains. Everyone was well aware that yields of millet were severely reduced by shortening the fallow, but few were willing entirely to abandon production of their staple food, even though land suitable for traditional chena cultivation had become extremely scarce, especially in the areas close to their houses. Although they understood that successful production of the new cash crops, gram and cowpea in particular, was subject to much less stringent conditions, they nevertheless grew millet on readily accessible land that had lain fallow only for a few years, or even in the home gardens that they cultivated every year. This practice, which managed to limit involvement in the market only at the cost of reduced yields, was strongly criticized in some quarters, most vigorously by Wimaladasa, a villager who was more deeply engaged in market relations than most.

Wimaladasa: Anyone can easily cultivate one or two acres of gram or cowpea with the labor of his own family. He can even grow it in his home garden. But most villagers still grow millet, even though it doesn't do as well in gardens. Millet grows best on land that has been fallow for more than eight years, but there's very little jungle like that any longer. So villagers grow millet on land that has been fallow for only two or three years, where it doesn't yield much. If they were to grow gram or cowpea, which give good yields on land like that, they could use the money they made to buy all the millet they need.[3]

Very few villagers were prepared to risk such total dependence on the market. But equally few held to the opposite extreme and tried to avoid dependence on the market altogether. Appuhamy, whose cultivation did approach this latter extreme, provided a spirited defense of his practice.

Appuhamy: I have never cultivated gram or cowpea. I don't like them. I prefer millet, and when I have enough millet in my grain bin I relax. I don't need to worry about having enough food. I don't need to run all over the place looking for wage labor. Those who don't have any food at home have to go out for wage labor. And then they don't have time to cultivate a chena.

This brief account of household strategies reveals how little economic independence and security were left to Kukulewa villagers by 1983. It also suggests (but may also exaggerate, because the severe drought in the early 1980s restricted paddy cultivation to a minimum) that agricultural practices no longer forged powerful bonds among the households in the village. Most dry-land cultivation was done by households independently, while wage labor was mainly performed for outsiders. Likewise the marketing of dry-land crops linked villagers to external traders (*mudalālis*) rather than to one another. The few exceptions to this pattern involved only a handful of the more influential men in the village, who were able to bind their followers to them with ties of economic dependence. The careers of these men reveal more about the changing practices through which the ideal of the village community was used both to legitimate economic action and to mobilize political support.

Power and Enterprise

In Kandyan times authority within the village had resided mainly with the *gamarāla* (village chief), a hereditary official who was responsible for ensuring that the villagers performed their assigned services.[3] Certain plots of irrigated land, known as the *gamvasama*, were held by the gamarāla, who could call upon other villagers for assistance in cultivating them, but this privilege seems to have afforded little power, since the product of the gamvasama was largely dedicated to the support of collective ceremonies and the entertainment of visiting dignitaries.

British authorities took little notice of the gamarāla, and many of his responsibilities were transferred to the office of *vel vidāne,* which the colonial administration built up in the nineteenth century. The vel vidāne (irrigation headman) was formally charged only with the supervision of the village's irrigation system, in return for which he was entitled to a small percentage of the crop, but in many cases he was able to extend his influence into other areas of village life. As the sole representative of official authority resident in the village he became, in effect, the principal mediator between villagers and state officials. Villagers depended on him to bring their concerns to the attention of the administration, while officials relied on him as the most authoritative source of information about his village. This enabled the vel vidāne to intervene decisively in matters as varied as inheritance disputes, the acquisition of title deeds and licenses, and the distribution of welfare measures, all of which he could manipulate to his own advantage and the discomfort of his enemies.

These potentialities were dramatically illustrated in the career of Bandathe, who was appointed vel vidāne of Kukulewa in about 1930 and who made himself the dominant figure in the village for the next thirty years. Throughout Bandathe's tenure as vidāne, members of the Vanniya aristocracy continued to hold leading positions in the district administration, as rate mahatmayas and subsequently as divisional revenue officers, and the local bureaucracy retained its distinctively patrimonial style. Bandathe skillfully cultivated personal relations of loyalty and respect both at the rate mahatmaya's manor house *(valavva),* where his sister was married to a member of the household staff (and was herself reputed to be the rate mahatmaya's mistress) and at the government offices in Anuradhapura, where he successfully represented himself not just as vel vidāne of Kukulewa, but as the chief of the whole Vedda variga. With these connections and credentials he made himself the vital link between the village and the state, able to promote himself and reward his followers with the benefits he could secure by his mastery of the idiom of patrimonial politics. But Bandathe was also an indifferent rice farmer and, although he was able to acquire possession of several acres of paddy land, he failed to develop an agricultural enterprise that would bind his political followers with the further chains of economic dependence. Moreover, his arbitrary and over-bearing treatment of his fellow villagers provoked resentment, and the loyalty of many was more instrumental than personal. Some people even attributed the poverty of the village to the displeasure of the gods at Bandathe's violation of communal norms. Referring to what he charged was the vidāne's fraudulent acquisition of a plot of paddy land, Wannihamy, who became Bandathe's principal rival in his later years, claimed: "Whenever that land was cultivated there was a drought in the village that destroyed not only his paddy but everyone else's as well. This is the country of the gods, and the gods were angry with him."

The office of vel vidāne was abolished by the Paddy Lands Act of 1958, and although Bandathe's connections remained useful even after the act was implemented, much of his following faded away and attached itself to other prominent men in the village. He was a member of the first Cultivation Committee that took over his former responsibilities, but was not subsequently reelected.

One of his successors was Undiyarala, a man of Bandathe's generation who was widely respected in Kukulewa but not well known outside it. He was a man of moderate means who subsisted on his own chena and paddy cultivation and lived quietly in the center of the village, surrounded by many of his close kin. He was a knowledgeable source of traditional custom who was often sought out by his fellow villagers for his wise counsel and his skill in the judicious resolution of disputes, but he lacked the external contacts that he would have needed to be an effective broker in the larger political arena. He was, however, usually allied with Wanni-hamy, who did have such connections.

Wannihamy was the first native of Kukulewa to run a shop successfully in the village. He went into business in the late 1950s, at about the time that andē tenancy began to give way to the use of wage labor in paddy cultivation, and his success was undoubtedly attributable, in large measure, to the growing toleration of a cash nexus among members of the same community. Previous native shopkeepers had quickly gone bankrupt because they were unable to resist their kinsmen's demands for privileged treatment, and the most successful village shops in the district were run by outsiders, usually Muslims, Tamils, or Sinhalese from the Low Country (cf. Leach 1961:131). Wannihamy's business brought him into contact with more powerful traders outside the village, and in contrast to

Wannihamy, the village shopkeeper: "I am the only person who lends these people what they need."

Bandathe's patrimonial demeanor, he took on something of the trader's aggressively egalitarian manners and appearance. By the skillful advance of credit, by taking mortgages on villagers' lands, and by buying land when it came on the market, within a few years he made himself the wealthiest man in Kukulewa. From this base he was then able to extend his patronage to a large number of his fellow villagers who, as his debtors, tenants, and wage laborers, became also his following of dependent clients.

Bandathe remained a man of some influence until his death in 1976, but already by the mid-1960s Wannihamy was clearly the more powerful. The rivalry between the two men was expressed, among other things, in their connections with the major national political parties. Bandathe was a staunch supporter of the UNP in which, within Anuradhapura District, the Vanniya aristocrats were prominent. Wannihamy, on the other hand, supported the SLFP and was connected to the member of parliament for Anuradhapura until 1977, a cabinet minister in Sirimavo Bandaranaike's government from 1970 to 1977 who had kin and land in Mekichchawa, the Goyigama village immediately adjacent to Kukulewa.

Wannihamy's commercial success required him to subordinate his kinsmen's appeals for privileged treatment to an impersonal business ethic. He took paddy land into his own hands wherever possible, and advanced credit only to those he considered to be good risks. He preferred to lend to those who were regularly employed or who owned substantial amounts of paddy land or livestock. In times of scarcity, poorer villagers might have to wait until the government announced that there would be relief work before Wannihamy would allow them to take goods on credit. In 1983 he was advancing goods only to people who were willing to sell him their ration stamps, for which he paid two-thirds of their face value. Wannihamy saw his activities as providing a great benefit to his fellow villagers.

Wannihamy: I am the only person who lends these people what they need. I am the one who buys their ration stamps. Who else is going to advance them what they need? I take pity on these people. I help them in these ways. I lend to them because they are starving, and we are all human beings. I am of great service to them. But even so, they are not always grateful to me.

Wannihamy's views were shared by villagers who were in good standing with him. Appuhamy, who was one of his regular clients, offered a typical defence of his policies.

Appuhamy: I always buy from Wannihamy, and he gives me credit because he knows I am a hard-working man. He has never refused me. I borrow provisions from him, never money.

I know goods are cheaper in Sippukulama and Kahatagasdigiliya. That's where Wannihamy buys provisions. But you can't expect him to sell them for the same price at which he buys. He has to make a profit to stay in business.

It's wrong to go to Sippukulama to buy goods when you have money, and to try to borrow from Wannihamy when you don't. Wannihamy doesn't like that. I buy from him when I have money, and borrow from him when I don't. We have nowhere else to go to get credit. Is there anyone besides him to lend things to us? He is feeding the whole village. If it weren't for him most of our people would be starving to death.

It's true, however, that he only lends to those who will pay him back. He does not like people who are lazy. He prefers to lend to hard-working people. It is very difficult to do business with our people. If they can avoid paying back what they owe, they won't hesitate to do so. But they can't do that with Wannihamy. He knows how to recover his debts. People pay him back because they know him, and they know he's very tough. And the other thing is, if they don't settle their debts it will be very difficult to borrow from him the next time they're in trouble.

Wannihamy, however, was not without his critics, among whom was Wimaladasa, who seemed to echo Wannihamy's own words about Bandathe when he attributed the poverty in the village to the anger of the gods at the flouting of communal values.

Wimaladasa: I am Wannihamy's son-in-law *(bänä)*.[4] My sister is married to his son and my brother is married to his daughter. But when I borrow from him he charges me 20% interest every month. Isn't that exploitation? And if he treats me like that, what can other people expect from him? You could write your whole book about his dirty work.

Wannihamy gives credit and lends money to people who have paddy land, cattle, or a good chena. Then he begins to press them for settlement. Sometimes he goes to their houses, stands in their doorways, and hurls abuse at them. So they give him what they have to settle their debts.

All the people in this village are our kin (apē näyō). It's wrong to take away their possessions like that. It's because of people like my father-in-law that it doesn't rain here. The gods are angry at people like him and so they don't send the rain.

Wimaladasa's own rise to prominence took a different course from that of either Bandathe or Wannihamy. Like Wannihamy his success rested on his ability to exercise his entrepreneurial skills in a way that could sustain a reputation for communal responsibility without eliminating his profits, but he applied these skills to rather different activities. Where Wanni-hamy's following was mainly bound to him by the credit he could extend as a shopkeeper and by the andē tenancies and wage labor he could offer in his paddy fields, Wimaladasa made his way in the world by seizing the newer opportunities for commercial production of unirrigated crops and for contracting labor to work on projects outside the village. In the mid-1970s, when he was still closely allied with Wannihamy, Wimaladasa was involved in organizing the Kukulewa branch of the SLFP, and he was also able to find a job as a casual laborer with the Highways Department. After the 1977 election, however, he was threatened by the local leaders of the victorious UNP and found it prudent to leave the village for a while. Later he came back to live in Kukulewa and reestablished his contacts with officials in the Highways Department, for whom he began to organize contract labor. Under the new government's "open economy" policy a good deal of rural construction work, not only of roads but also of canals and other irrigation facilities, that previously had been done by government departments was given over to private contractors or rural development societies. Engineers and other officials of the Highways and Irrigation Departments were not allowed to take such contracts themselves, but Wimaladasa was willing to front for those who anticipated the profits to be made. He would use materials and equipment supplied by government officials and would take, say, 9,000 rupees to construct a mile of road, which he could do for an expenditure of 4,000 to 5,000 rupees. He hired his kinsmen and neighbors to provide the labor for these projects.

Wimaladasa: I only hire people who are prepared to work hard. I can only make a profit if they work hard and do the job in a few days. So I only hire people who I know to be good workers, and who I know are prepared to work long hours. Sometimes they work from six in the morning to nine at night, and for that I will pay them as much as forty rupees a day.

With the profits from his labor contracting Wimaladasa invested heavily in dry-land cultivation. In 1983–1984 he was involved in the cultivation of more than twenty acres of unirrigated land, fifteen acres of it on his own account and the remainder by means of andē arrangements. Andē in dry-land cultivation was unknown in the old days of subsistence chenas but was spreading with the development of cash crops. The standard arrangement was for Wimaladasa to provide the seed and pay the cultivator to clear the land and sow. Subsequent work, including protection of the crop, was the cultivator's responsibility, and the crop was equally divided between the two partners. This kind of arrangement was welcomed by villagers who wanted to undertake cash crop production but who were short of funds, and who would otherwise have had to cut back on their chena cultivation in order to look for wage labor.

Dinapala: If elder brother *(ayiyā)* Wimaladasa had not helped me I would have been in a lot of trouble. It is kind of him to help me cultivate my chena. There's nobody else in the village like that. He has helped me a great deal and I am indebted to him forever.

On the other fifteen acres of unirrigated land that he cultivated, Wimaladasa employed the wage labor of his kinsmen and fellow villagers. He also mobilized some unpaid household labor, but the scale of his operations was such that this was only a small proportion of the total. Altogether, between August and the end of October, he paid for more than 200 man-days of wage labor on this land.

Wimaladasa also lent money to his fellow villagers, mostly to those who worked for him as wage laborers. Unlike Wannihamy, he did not charge interest on these loans, and he recovered what was owed him by paying his debtors only half their wages when he employed them. One day Wimaladasa organized a *kayiya* (work party) to clear four acres of jungle. He claimed that he had been asked to hold the kayiya by those who worked for him so that they could make some return for the help he had offered them when they were in need. Forty men, most of them people who had been employed either in his other dry-land cultivation or in his contract work, came to the kayiya and worked all day to clear the jungle. Wimaladasa spent 750 rupees on food and drink for those who came to work, but he was well satisfied, for he reckoned it would have cost him 1,000 rupees to clear the land if he had employed wage labor, or 1,200 rupees if he had contracted with someone else to get the work done. He also recognized that there were less tangible benefits.

Wimaladasa: Villagers like to take part in a kayiya because they know they will be well treated. They also enjoy the good food. And a kayiya also helps to create a feeling of unity *(ekamutukama)*. When workers are hired for a daily wage, they do not work hard unless they are on good terms with the employer. The people who came to my kayiya are my wage laborers and the kayiya helps create unity with them because I work alongside them in the chena.

I never make a contract to get my chena cleared. People who work on contract try to get the job done as quickly as possible, and in their haste they leave weeds and bushes all over the place. I don't like to see a chena looking like that when the work is supposed to have been finished.

Wannihamy was scornful when he heard that Wimaladasa had held a kayiya to get his chena cleared.

Wannihamy: I never get my work done on kayiya. I pay people to work and get it done that way. People who come to a kayiya don't like to work hard. And you can't force them to work because they've come to help you and you're not paying them.

But Wimaladasa was even more contemptuous of Wannihamy.

Wimaladasa: Our people (apē minissu) only go to work for him because they need his credit. If he asks them to come to work, they can't refuse. If they did, he would retaliate. He would refuse to make loans to them. So they go to work for him, but only because they depend on him.

The people prefer to work for me because I pay them well and I give them good meals for fifteen rupees. I am the only person in the village who pays a man thirty rupees for chena work. I also pay women and boys twenty rupees a day. But Wannihamy only pays twenty rupees to a man, fifteen rupees to a woman, and twelve rupees to a boy. It's very unjust. People go to work for him only because they can't find work anywhere else. I can't employ them all.

Discussion

In the generation after independence, agrarian practices in Kukulewa, which had earlier been characterized by their relative autonomy and subsistence orientation, were fundamentally transformed by their steadily increasing incorporation within a larger economy that was predominantly governed by market principles. Unpaid household labor remained important both in dry-land and paddy cultivation, but other precapitalist forms of organizing agricultural work were largely replaced by the wage contract. And to the extent that agrarian practices were disengaged from the matrix of kinship and caste, economic relations among villagers became both more impersonal and more atomistic. This trend was mitigated only by the activities of those few influential men, like Wannihamy and Wimaladasa, whose enterprises joined a number of their fellow villagers to them by ties of economic dependence.

Equally decisively, and especially after 1977, as the new government's "open economy" policy began to take effect, the people of Kukulewa came increasingly to be bound at least as much by their economic connections to employers and traders outside the village as they were to one another. Kukulewa was not directly caught up in any of the larger projects set in motion under the new policy, but it certainly felt their effects. One of the most general results was for the function of the village in the regional economy to become ever more readily identifiable as that of a provider of cheap labor. This tendency was doubtless exaggerated by the virtual absence of paddy cultivation in the village in the early 1980s because of the drought, but paddy cultivation in their own fields had in any case come to provide only a small proportion of most villagers' livelihood.

Another discernable trend was that of increasing economic differentiation within the village. By promoting the free play of market forces, the "open economy" policy not only generated attractive opportunities for those with entrepreneurial skills, like Wimaladasa, it also created disparities between the better-off and the worse-off that were significantly more pronounced in 1983 than they had been in 1970.

The changes that occurred stemmed from a complex interplay between communal and economizing dimensions of social action, but their effect was to jeopardize the ability of agrarian practices to undergird and reproduce communal relations. The traditional economy assigned different practices to different social contexts, which they then served to define. Thus cash payments were held to be inappropriate between kinsmen and members of traditionally linked varigas, and so to offer someone cash wages was to deny him membership in one's own community. Correspondingly, the andē relationship was an affirmation that the parties belonged together, which itself served to recreate the sense of community. In some cases the same material relationship appeared in different social contexts, and was accorded different value according to that context.

Thus the material terms of andē were the same whether the parties were members of the same or different varigas, but in the former case the relationship was represented as one of reciprocity and mutual aid, while in the latter it was one of domination and service. In the absence of a material difference this communal distinction was not always easy to maintain, but it was reinforced in other areas by the ritual exchange of caste services, as well as by the permanently unidirectional flow of material appropriations. That is, it was always Veddas who worked as the andē tenants of Goyigama landlords, and never the other way around.

The penetration of capitalist relations of production introduced certain agrarian practices into social contexts from which they had previously been excluded, and allowed practices that had formerly been segregated to coexist in the same social context, where they now appeared as alternative forms of the social relations of production. This was accompanied, or shortly followed, by a change in the value that was accorded to the practices. Thus, on the one hand, the wage relationship acquired a range of meanings that varied, like the traditional andē relationship, according to social context while, on the other hand, it now became just one among several approved ways, along with andē, the gift of labor "for nothing" *(nikam)*, kayiya, and so on, of enacting community in agriculture.

These changes resulted in some ambiguity, and normatively disposed villagers were often uncertain which course of economic action was the proper one to pursue. But while traditionalists deplored the loss of firm guidelines, there were others who recognized the opportunities that the new situation afforded. It is difficult to determine with precision the intentions behind any particular set of actions, even in the absence of normative ambiguity. Habitual repetition of customary practice, active attachment to collective ideals, and cynical manipulation of norms to promote one's private interest were doubtless all involved to varying degree. But whatever the combination of conventionalism, altruism, and cynicism in particular cases, the general direction of change was clear. The social process through which a few men like Wannihamy and Wimaladasa were able to make themselves prominent and powerful in the village was the same process whereby wage labor and interest-bearing loans became almost unavoidable means to making a living. And it took no more than a generation for wage labor, the basic capitalist form of surplus appropriation, which had formerly been considered antithetical to the values of community, to penetrate and permeate the village economy. Those villagers who offered wages to their fellows, and thereby appropriated the surplus value they produced, came to be described as they described themselves, that is, as honorable men whose employment of their fellow villagers was evidence of their commitment to the spirit of community.

Nor was it irrational for villagers to describe those who exploited them as their benefactors. Short of water, short of land, and lacking other economic opportunities, almost any wage was better than none. And those who could attach themselves to a patron with employment and credit at his disposal did find it easier to secure their livelihood than did those who lacked such connections. Whatever their deepest convictions, it would have been imprudent of clients in this position to challenge their patrons' claims to ethical propriety.

Networks of dependency within Kukulewa, however, did not encompass all the households in the village, and in this sense, even if the new ethics of the wage sustained community as effectively as traditional practices had, there was some reduction in their scope. Not only Wannihamy and Wimaladasa themselves but also other villagers said that those to whom they gave employment and credit were all hard-working people. Cause and effect are hard to separate here. The manifestly greater poverty of some who lacked effective connections with a patron may indeed have resulted from their failure to work hard, but it may also have been the case that their poverty stemmed from their exclusion, which in turn was justified by the charge of laziness. In either case, however, it is notable that the personal characteristic of devotion to labor, so strongly emphasized by Max Weber in his classic account of *The Protestant Ethic and the Spirit of Capitalism* (1958), was now used to draw significant distinctions within the community of kin.

No less threatening to the maintenance of the village community was the declining number of agrarian practices that were either confined within it or excluded from it, but which in both cases served to define it. Where such distinctions were maintained the practice in question carried its communal message, so to speak, in itself. But where the distinction was abandoned, as with the universal toleration of wage labor, the communal meaning of the practice had to be separately asserted on each occasion.

Increasingly, agrarian relations between fellow villagers came to differ from those with outsiders only in the value that was attached to them and not in their material form. To the extent, then, that the sense of belonging together as people of Kukulewa had formerly been sustained by forms of relationship in agriculture that were now being discarded, the reproduction of the village community was placed in jeopardy.

Chapter 5   *Party Politics and Nationalist Rhetoric*

AT THE SAME time the people of Kuku-
lewa became deeply caught up in market relations, they also experienced increasingly vigorous interventions into their local affairs by state offi-cials. Inspired by the twin goals of raising agricultural productivity and re-ducing rural poverty, a vast array of government programs, ranging from the improvement of village irrigation works and the provision of credit, fertilizer, insecticide, and new strains of seed, on the one hand, to the grant of food rations and the construction of rural schools, hospitals, and dispensaries on the other, were either introduced or expanded in the period after independence. Not all these programs achieved their stated goals, although they certainly succeeded in ameliorating some of the most desperate poverty in villages like Kukulewa. But they did serve to reduce the autonomy of village society, and to the extent that the maintenance of the village community rested upon local control of village affairs, they threatened the basis of that community as well.

As government extended its control of the economy and official sur-veillance of village life became more intrusive, factional struggles within Kukulewa increasingly focused on the acquisition of resources at the dis-posal of the state. In the period after independence the allocation of state controlled resources passed from the hands of civil servants to those of elected politicians. And as an increasing proportion of these resources came to be means of individual rather than collective advantage, and politicians channeled them in directions that would reward their follow-ers and bolster their support, both the form and content of village politics were realigned. When village leaders of an earlier generation, like Ban-dathe, petitioned authorities for construction of a school, or improve-ments to the tank, or relief work in times of drought, they could plausibly claim to be acting on behalf of the whole village. But when their successors devoted their energies to influencing the individual distribution of jobs, or houses, or scarce agricultural inputs, they were quickly perceived by their fellow villagers to be acting in pursuit of purely personal or factional advantage.

Factional conflict had long been a prominent feature of life in Kukulewa, but only in the mid-1970s, when local branches of both the UNP and the SLFP were established in the village, did it become comprehensively organized within the framework of competition between the major political parties. The local branches of the parties were founded with the explicit goal, on the part of outside politicians, of mobilizing electoral support, and on the part of villagers, of enhancing their access to state resources. Their establishment brought about another shift in the character and style of village leadership, comparable to the difference between Bandathe and Wannihamy that was described in the previous chapter.

The new alignments of power in the village were revealed in the emergence of Jinadasa, who played the leading part in forming the Kukulewa branch of the UNP in 1975. Jinadasa's influence was not based on the credit or employment he could offer to his followers. It derived instead from his association with politicians outside the village. Jinadasa was the eldest son of Anthony Fernando, whose own parents had come from the Low Country and settled in Kukulewa in the 1920s. Anthony's mother had run a shop in the village, and Anthony too had made his living as a trader, as well as by working as a laborer for the village council, the administrative successor to the old *gamsabhāva* (village tribunal) that was responsible for such matters as the upkeep of minor roads. In the course of his business transactions a certain amount of paddy land had passed through Anthony's hands, but neither he nor Jinadasa was an experienced cultivator. Anthony found work for his son outside the village, and in 1973 Jinadasa was hired as a driver by the Ceylon Petroleum Corporation in Anuradhapura. There he made contact with workers for the UNP, which was still in opposition at the time, and in 1975 he returned to Kukulewa to set up a local branch of the party.

Politics and Nationalism

The intrusion of party political conflicts into everyday life came later to Kukulewa than to most other villages in Sri Lanka.[1] From the 1950s onward, rivalry between the factions of Bandathe and Wannihamy had sometimes appeared in the guise of party politics, but Jinadasa was the first to establish a formal party organization in the village. Wimaladasa gave an account of what happened.

Wimaladasa: Politics had nothing to do with our lives before 1977. But after that the village divided into rival groups. Even our own kinsmen became our political opponents. The only thing that Kukulewa people did before 1977 was to vote at elections. There were no branches of the political parties in the village.

At that time there were two rival factions in the village, that of Wannihamy and that of Bandathe Vidane. When the UNP candidate came to the village he would hold his meeting at Bandathe Vidane's house, and would go with the vidāne from house to house. Likewise the SLFP candidate would hold his meeting at Wannihamy's house. But after the election no one would try to destroy the supporters of the party that was defeated.

Before 1977 Kukulewa people who supported the SLFP became members of the Mekichchawa branch of the party. Kukulewa people had no education and didn't expect to get government jobs, so they took little interest in politics. The Mekichchawa people got them to join the party in order to show the MP that their local organization was strong and had lots of members. But Kuku-lewa people didn't benefit at all. It was the Mekichchawa people who gained the advantages. Kukulewa people were tied to their chenas and paddy fields and had nothing to do with politics.

In 1975 Jinadasa organized a branch of the UNP in Kukulewa. He had only eight people with him at first, so my brother Premadasa and some of his friends joined to help him make up the numbers. Then in 1976 a branch of the SLFP was also formed in Kukulewa, with Wannihamy as president and my brother Punchirala as secretary.

I was very friendly with Jinadasa in those days. We used to meet at his shop every evening to discuss the issues of the day. But after the big UNP rally in Colombo in 1976, he said that when the UNP came to power he would burn the houses of SLFP supporters. I got very angry when I heard that. I had also had enough of the SLFP government by then, but when I realized that Jinadasa and his people were planning to ruin us, I told him that I would support the SLFP and help organize its membership. But even after that we continued to go to his shop. We organized people for the 1977 election, and we got more supporters than the UNP did, but we still went to Jinadasa's shop to hear the election results on the radio. The UNP supporters were very happy when the election results were announced, and they drank to celebrate their victory.

The next day Jinadasa came to my father's house with a mob of about seventy people. They came into the house and threatened my father. They told him to put up the green flag of the UNP. My father told them that we had no flags. Then they threatened to burn our house and went away. They went next to my brother Punchirala's house and then to Wannihamy's shop, where they did the same thing. They planned to burn the houses down that night.

My brother Premadasa got angry when he heard about this. He gathered the other young men together and criticized Jinadasa's plan. So then Anthony, Jinadasa's father, went to some neighboring villages and asked the UNP supporters to come to Kukulewa and destroy our houses. But those people were friendly with us and wouldn't come.

According to Wimaladasa it was the UNP that first brought the threat of violence into the local political arena, but other villagers disputed this. Jinadasa's supporters, for example, admired him as much as anything for his courage in organizing a branch of the UNP in the village in 1975, despite the threats they said were made against him by officials of the ruling SLFP. There were also other interpretations of what happened in Kukulewa when the UNP won the 1977 election.

Anthony: There were political disputes in the village in those days, but we never tried to ruin one another. I supported the SLFP in 1970, but in 1977 I changed and supported the UNP. After our party won the election I asked Wannihamy to put up a green flag in his shop. I did that because he was my friend. UNP youths in Anuradhapura and other places were burning down the houses and shops of SLFP supporters, and I wanted to protect him from that kind of thing. I had no intention of harming Wannihamy, but he misunderstood me and took it as a threat.

Regardless of where they laid the initial responsibility, all villagers agreed that during the 1970s party political conflict became increasingly bitter and intense, exacerbated by the scarcity of resources and the undisguised bias of the ruling party in distributing them to their supporters. Under these conditions ideological differences between the two parties were not pronounced in Kukulewa. Nor were class differences the principal basis of party affiliation.[2] Political cleavages remained vertical rather than horizontal, as the more prominent and ambitious villagers used ties of patronage and dependence, bolstered by threats and intimidation, to forge shifting factional alliances that then dressed themselves in the colors of the two major political parties as they competed with one another for state controlled resources.[3] This emergent pattern of local politics was an uninterrupted development out of earlier forms of village factionalism. Nevertheless, to the extent that the enhanced significance of party organization fostered the idea that the allocation of state resources in the village should be based on party affiliation rather than in accordance with the principle of equity among kin, it also contained a potential new challenge to the ideal of the village community.

The absence of ideological differences between supporters of the UNP and the SLFP in Kukulewa did not by any means exclude ideological themes from the discourse of party politics. On the contrary, after the escalation of Sinhala nationalist rhetoric that accompanied S.W.R.D. Bandaranaike's successful campaign in 1956, the various programs of rural development were steadily subsumed within the burgeoning project of Sinhala Buddhist revivalism. Ideological competition also became increasingly sharp as each of the two major parties was driven by the claims of the other to assert that it was the more committed to nationalist aspirations.

Sinhala Buddhist nationalism is a complex and by no means unified phenomenon.[4] Its component features are derived from varied sources, and at different times in its development different elements have received the greatest emphasis. In the following description I concentrate on the popular forms in which nationalist ideas were officially propagated in villages like Kukulewa in the late 1970s and early 1980s. In these contexts nationalism achieved a simple but powerful coherence through its selective composition of a historic destiny that bound together the Sinhala people, Buddhism, and the island of Sri Lanka. Elaborating on the myth that the Buddha himself selected Sri Lanka as a place where his teaching should flourish, and that it is the unique mission of the Sinhala people to accomplish this goal, nationalist ideology was centrally constructed as a narrative of virtue, degeneration, and redemption. In the glorious days of the Anuradhapura kingdom the nation was believed to have been ruled by a succession of righteous and heroic kings, who protected the order of monks, preserved the doctrine, constructed tanks and monumental works in honor of the Buddha, and drove off foreign invaders. The corresponding social order was one of prosperous, contented, and largely self-sufficient village communities in which simple devotion to Buddhist precepts and harmonious cooperation in agriculture were the hallmarks of social life, and the basic unit of organization was the family farm. This social order flourished for more than a thousand years before eventually succumbing to foreign invasion and the imposition of colonial rule. But redemption was now believed to be at hand, as national virtue could be restored if contemporary rulers followed the example of the ancient kings by governing righteously and pursuing a vigorous policy of development that sought to revitalize peasant agriculture and restore the village community. Such a policy was possible because, since 1948, the nation had again been independent and its government, especially since S.W.R.D. Bandaranaike's electoral triumph in 1956, had become the people's government.

Sinhala Buddhist nationalism thus combined a number of apparently heterogeneous elements—for example, popular sovereignty and kingship, Buddhist precepts and economic development—into a "relatively unified ideological discourse" (Laclau 1977:102) that by the 1970s was being incessantly propagated both through the widespread apparatuses of government, which included most of the mass media and educational institutions, and through channels that were more or less independent of the state.

The peasantry occupied a particularly prominent place in this discourse. Much of what was expressed in state ceremonies, political speeches, and "rituals of development" (Tennekoon 1988) celebrated the peasant farmer and announced his restoration, under the tutelage of national leaders who had inherited the mantle of the Sinhala kings, to the dignity and virtue that he formerly enjoyed. This was not principally a strategy of euphemization (Bourdieu 1977:191–97; cf. Scott 1985:305–14) designed to mask the peasant's economic exploitation since, at least in the Dry Zone, peasants were not subject to surplus appropriation on a large scale. They certainly suffered from low output prices for their products, but they were also the substantial beneficiaries of numerous welfare and development programs (Moore 1985). Celebration of the peasantry had more to do with its electoral strength, which had often been decisive, and the nationalist rhetoric in which it was enveloped was, above all, a discourse of hegemony in terms of which those who controlled the Sri Lankan state both justified their rule to themselves and sought to educate the consent of those they governed. In this uneven and always uncertain struggle to induce a compelling sense of national identity and unity—a struggle that proceeded as much at the level of unquestioned assumptions as at that of rational assessment—official rhetoric served to paper over the cracks and cleavages that divided society and to bind the people together in the "imagined community" (Anderson 1983) of the nation. What was shared by all members of the nation was stressed, and represented as a homogeneous unity. Antagonisms of class, caste, and region were displaced and obscured by an insistent emphasis on the common interests that united all who belonged within the nation. Simultaneously, in order to gain the support of subordinate classes, images of the social order were disseminated that celebrated their contributions to the welfare of the nation. In this still largely agrarian society the peasantry was thus authoritatively placed at the moral core of the Sinhala nation, even as it was also implied that its regeneration required the guiding hand of dedicated and virtuous leaders.

But especially in a country like Sri Lanka where the peasantry exercised the right to vote, an effective hegemony that successfully articulated the interests of peasants to the project of their rulers also demanded that rhetorical concessions of this kind be accompanied by the distribution of real material benefits. In electoral terms the numerical strength of the peasantry made the struggle for its votes intensely competitive, and the UNP and the SLFP strove mightily to outdo one another not only in eulogizing peasants and promising them further benefits but also in actually channelling funds into programs of rural development. These programs thus served, at one and the same time, both as the means to realize the hegemonic unity of the nation and as tangible steps toward the nationalist goal of revitalizing peasant agriculture and the village community.

Sinhala nationalism, however, did not encompass every social group in Sri Lanka. It was fundamentally the ideology of Sinhala Buddhists, and it tended to repudiate groups whose members did not speak the Sinhala language or did not practice Buddhism. Nationalist practice was, then, as much a process of exclusion as of inclusion. Indeed the very notion of the Sinhala nation *(sinhala jātiya)* implied the existence of other peoples whose difference from the Sinhalas allowed the latter to define themselves. We have encountered this already in the distinction between the civilized Sinhalas and the savage Veddas, but by far the more prominent opposition was that between the Buddhist Sinhalas and the Hindu Tamils, the largest minority in Sri Lanka, whose different language, religion, and purported race stamped them as irrevocably other. Thus the process of homogenization, whereby differences among those who were included within the Sinhala nation were submerged and obscured, also entailed a related process of polarization whereby, as cultural heterogeneity was eroded internally, the more uniform Sinhala nation that emerged was brought into increasingly stark and unmediated confrontation with its Tamil other (cf. Tambiah 1986:120).

But if "homogenization" and "polarization" are useful terms with which to summarize the main tendencies of identity formation in Sri Lanka, they are not in themselves sufficient either to capture the full range of movement or to analyze the complex social processes of which they were the prevalent outcome. They adequately describe, for example, the tendency for previously salient distinctions between the Kandyan Sinhalas and the Low Country Sinhalas to be muted, and for the differences between the Sinhalas and the Tamils to be more pronounced, but they do not account for the contrasting experience of, on the one hand, Sri Lanka's Catholics, who had once formed a relatively unified community that was becoming increasingly divided between its Sinhala- and Tamil-speakers (Stirrat 1984) and, on the other hand, the mainly Tamil-speaking Muslims, who were officially defined as a separate ethnic community that was distinct from both the Sinhalas and the Tamils. Differences such as these indicate that, however prevalent they may have been, homogenization and polarization were not inevitable tendencies but the variable and contingent results of specific struggles in particular historical circumstances. In the case of the Veddas, evidence has already been presented of the contradictory tendencies to maintain the polar opposition between the savage Veddas and the civilized Sinhalas, while simultaneously incorporating the Veddas within an expanding Sinhala nation.

Nationalist Rhetoric and Village Culture

Despite their anticolonial thrust and distinctly Sinhala appearance, the images of the village community propagated in nationalist discourse derived as much from colonial observation and speculation as from the experience of Sinhala peasants.[5] While àlso drawing on nostalgic constructions of the rural past generated by the indigenous Buddhist revival, the nationalist imagination appropriated some of its most potent material from nineteenth-century debates among western scholars and administrators. These foreign observers, however, were never able to agree on the fundamental characteristics of the village community in South Asia, and the legacy of conflicting and often tendentiously imprecise definitions that they bequeathed afforded ample scope for subsequent ideological manipulation. Among the more influential European writers who addressed the topic in the nineteenth century, Metcalfe's famous assertion that "the village communities are little republics" (quoted in Dumont 1970:112) stressed political autonomy, while Maine (1906:272) gave priority to the collective landholdings of the kin-based "assemblage of proprietors." Other characteristics attributed to the Indian (or Aryan) village community at various times have included autarky, equality, democracy, cultural homogeneity, social harmony, and even material prosperity, and the implication has not been absent that, when the village community *really* existed, all these features were present at once. Descriptions of the village community have, moreover, often uncritically assumed the additional presence of that "sense of belonging together" that I have adopted as the defining characteristic of community. Thus variably constituted, the notion of the village community has served as a rich and volatile ideological concoction, and its evaluation and deployment in political practice have been extraordinarily complex and contentious (Dewey 1972; Samaraweera 1978). In the nineteenth century it was admired by conservatives for the social cohesion it displayed, condemned by laissez-faire liberals for the barriers it imposed on individual enterprise, and held up by radicals in exemplary contrast to the social devastation wrought by an unfettered market.

In all of this the ideological potential of the village community was only enhanced by the fact that, although there was little or no consensus about its definition, almost everyone came to agree that it no longer existed. It is true that, as late as the 1870s, some remote villages in Anuradhapura District were still described as "small agricultural republics" (Dickson 1873), and as I reported in the previous chapter, at that time they were indeed still largely self-sufficient, relatively unstratified, and culturally homogeneous, if not also harmonious or prosperous. However, for the most part the existence of the village community was fixed somewhere in the past (cf. Spencer 1992).

Colonial accounts tended to emphasize the structural features of village social organization, but at the beginning of the twentieth century, when images of the village community were carried over into the developing discourse of Sinhala nationalism, they came to be imbued with a new nostalgia for the precolonial past. Ananda Coomaraswamy's account, in his influential *Mediaeval Sinhalese Art,* originally published in 1908, even incorporated a romantic critique of commercial civilization that was clearly inspired by William Morris and the Arts and Crafts Movement. Elements of this romanticism, which celebrated the aesthetic pleasures of rural life, were to persist in nationalist discourse, but they were generally overshadowed by the more austere moralism of the protestant Buddhist revival.

As Samaraweera's studies (1973, 1977, 1981) indicate, however, the politically decisive incorporation of the village community into nationalist discourse did not take place for another twenty years. Earlier nationalist intellectuals had begun a muted protest against peasant landlessness, but it was not until the 1920s that the political leaders of the nationalist elite, who by then occupied positions of considerable authority and influence, vigorously embraced the cause of the peasantry. They directly attributed the disintegration of the village community to the growth of plantation agriculture and argued that peasants should have priority over capitalists in the distribution of Crown lands. This was an extraordinary move, not least because many of those who made it, most notably D. S. Senanayake, who was soon to become minister of agriculture and lands, had themselves greatly prospered from their involvement in the plantation sector.

It was also a move with enormous consequences. Samaraweera links it to the need of the westernized and predominantly Low Country Sinhala elite, against the skepticism of the colonial authorities, to strengthen its claim to represent the people of Sri Lanka as a whole. Expanding on this suggestion, it appears that the decision to champion the interests of the peasantry, even at some economic disadvantage to itself, was crucial to the process whereby the elite sought not only to achieve a rapprochement with the leaders of the Kandyan Sinhalas, who had experienced most directly the growth of the plantations, but also to bring together most of the Sinhala subaltern classes, including the peasantry, in an effective alliance of national-popular unity. Ominously, however, this alliance was only accomplished by the exclusion both of the Tamil plantation workers and of the Sri Lankan Tamils in the north.

This hegemonic manoeuvre set the course for much that followed. Samaraweera (1981:136) may be correct in doubting that the elite consciously adopted the cause of the peasantry in order to create a political clientele in the future, but after the introduction of the Donoughmore constitution in 1931 (against the opposition of many of the elite) that is precisely what the peasantry became, and a rural bias was established in national politics that persisted for the next fifty years. Subsequent agrarian policy consistently followed the general lines laid down by the Land Commission of 1928, which was dominated by members of the elite and which was convinced, above all, of the importance of preserving the peasantry (Moore 1985). After independence the commitment to promote the small peasant farm was increasingly integrated with the resurgent Buddhist ambition to recreate a virtuous society, so much so that by the 1970s the goals of material welfare and moral uplift had become thoroughly conflated in official policies and programs of rural development.

Although Sinhala nationalism drew on the culture of the villages as one of its sources, its elaboration into the dominant ideology was mainly the work of urban intellectuals. Its more explicit formulations were therefore experienced by villagers, in Kukulewa and elsewhere, principally as something presented to them from outside, which then confronted the less systematically articulated representations of the social world that they had always generated among themselves. This did not, however, present major problems of integration, because in many respects nationalist ideology was congruent with the popular culture of the villages.

In the first place, the nationalist image of the traditional village community concurred in large measure with villagers' own recollections of the past. It is true that many villagers recalled the past as a time of poverty, ignorance, and disease (cf. Spencer 1992:362), but that was a recent past, the time of their own or their grandparents' youth, not the glorious past of harmony and prosperity that was believed to have prevailed when the land was ruled by virtuous kings. Second, although the dominant ideology fostered a sense of Sinhala national identity, in contrast to the more local identities rooted in kinship and the village to which rural people had long been attached, that in itself generated no contradiction, because the nation was represented as a nation of villages. Third, while harmony and cooperation were by no means the universal, or even the normal, experience of village life, they were held up as ideals of village culture no less than of nationalist imagination. Fourth, just as the nationalist representation of the former village community accorded with villagers' memories of a prosperous past, so the dominant celebration of the small family farmer expressed many of their aspirations for the future. An increasing proportion of the rural population in fact depended on wage labor for its livelihood, but there was little evidence of a corresponding shift of attention from gaining possession of productive land to organizing in defense of a decent wage. Under prevailing demographic and ecological conditions a rural population organized into viable family farms may have been quite impossible to achieve, but it was an ideal that was still embraced from below as well as propagated from above.

Another important area of accord between nationalist ideology and the culture of the villages was that of the proper role of government. By presenting themselves as successors to the Sinhala kings, the leaders of post-independence governments assumed not just the majesty but also the responsibilities of traditional monarchy. At the very beginning of one panegyric account of J.R. Jayewardene's victory in the election of 1977, it was noted that "the annals of history record that in ancient Sri Lanka, on important occasions of state the rulers of our nation worshipped at the venerated Temple of the Tooth . . . and then addressed their subjects" (Dissanayake 1977:i).[6] The author then goes on to describe Jayewardene's visit to the temple after the election, and reports that

> when Prime Minister J. R. Jayewardene and his Cabinet, having fulfilled their religious obligations appeared on the. . . balcony of the Temple of the Tooth, over a million voices rent the air with their acclaim. Having repeatedly and unsuccessfully attempted to speak he found a moment of relative quiet and began thus: "My fellow countrymen, it is from here the kings of ancient times addressed the people and I thank you, the people of Sri Lanka, because it is you who gave me the opportunity to address the nation from here. I ask you please to extend to me your co-operation and assistance to give you the *righteous* government I promised" (Dissanayake 1977:ii; emphasis added).

The commitment to create *dharmistha samajaya* (a just or virtuous society) had been one of the most prominent pledges made by the UNP in the 1977 election campaign. It expressed a concern for social justice in nationalist discourse that was all too often obscured by the fierce rhetoric of ethnic chauvinism, but it was a theme that resonated strongly with villagers' understandings and expectations. The vision of a just society, in which the ruler governs righteously, protects valued cultural institutions, and provides for the material welfare of the common people, was one that was widely shared in Kukulewa. It sustained the villagers' claim to a right of access to the means of subsistence, which it was the responsibility of government to ensure. This claim was expressed in the assertion of the state's obligation to provide water for irrigation, land to cultivate, relief work in times of drought, and so on. During election campaigns villagers assessed the relative merits of the contending parties by asking which of them was better able, or more committed, to meet the standards of righteous government. In Kukulewa during the campaign of 1970 this had sometimes been addressed with reference to the personal piety of Dudley Senanayake (then leader of the UNP) and Sirimavo Bandaranaike (leader of the SLFP) and their devotion to the cause of Buddhism, but more often the issue was their commitment to the people's material welfare. The records of successive governments on such matters as relief work, the rice ration, and the improvement of local irrigation facilities were closely scrutinized and hotly disputed.

Despite their admixture with notions of popular sovereignty and electoral politics, these attitudes and expectations had much in common with what Hobsbawm (1965:118; see also Bendix 1969:54–57) calls "populist legitimism." In this understanding of legitimate authority the people possess certain basic rights, which it is the ruler's obligation to preserve and protect. The ruler himself "symbolizes. . . the people and its way of life" (Hobsbawm 1965:118) and "represents justice" (1965:119). Violations of the established order are typically attributed to lower-level officials and the locally powerful, and only exceptionally laid at the door of the superior authority, who, on the contrary, is normally idealized. As Hobsbawm describes the popular attitude, "if the king only knew what injustices were done in his name, he would not tolerate them" (1965:98).

Aspects of Sinhala nationalism penetrated the consciousness of Kukulewa villagers at various levels. Ideas about social justice and legitimate rule that were explicitly discussed were, in Giddens's (1979:5) terms, matters of " 'discursive consciousness', involving knowledge which actors are able to express on the level of discourse." Other elements of nationalism, such as the mythically endorsed association of Buddhism with the island of Sri Lanka, seemed to be lodged closer to the pole of practical consciousness, where they accumulated "as tacit stocks of knowledge" (Giddens 1979:5) that were taken for granted and went without saying (Bourdieu 1977:164–71). They might occasionally be endorsed in the recitation of myth, but were scarcely brought into question.

The hegemonic prospects of Sinhala nationalism were undoubtedly enhanced by its congruence with villagers' tacit understandings and unquestioned beliefs, as well as with their explicit aspirations and ideas of legitimate authority. But the pervasive reach of nationalism was not attributable solely to the successful education of consent. It was also the product of disciplinary constraint. As will be shown more fully in the next two chapters, the language of nationalism was thoroughly interwoven with that of development, and this conflated discourse was ubiquitous throughout the administration. During the same period that state officials came to intrude ever more directly into village life, official practices became ever more thoroughly permeated by the discourse of nationalism, to the point where villagers had little alternative but to position themselves within its terms. Adoption of nationalist discourse became virtually unavoidable for anyone who sought to gain access to state-controlled resources (cf. Woost 1994).

This combination of coercion and consent, of attraction and constraint, defined the scope of nationalist hegemony. But although there had been considerable movement toward what Williams (1977:110) describes as "a saturation of the whole process of living," hegemony was by no means complete. In part this was due to factors inherent in any struggle for hegemony, insofar as it is always at least partly conducted at the explicit level of discursive consciousness. Most fundamentally, the very criteria that both UNP and SLFP governments invoked to justify their rule established standards by which subaltern groups could legitimately make critical assessments of the actual performance of government. Thus nationalist discursive practices were marked, on the one hand, by superordinate assertions of legitimacy and attempts to neutralize social divisions and antagonisms by containing them within the unifying embrace of the nation and, on the other, by the efforts of subordinate groups to preserve and extend their legitimate rights by holding up to the dominant elite the critical mirror of its own ideological pretensions.

In the 1970s the vulnerability of nationalist rhetoric was aggravated by the growing disparity between the vision of rural society it promoted and the lived realities of village life. The image of a nation of self-contained villages composed of self-sufficient family farmers was always an idealization, but it contrasted much more starkly with the conditions of agrarian life in the Dry Zone in the 1970s than it did with what had obtained thirty or forty years earlier. The number of smallholdings may have increased (Moore 1985, 1992), but many of them were not self-sustaining farms, and as in Kukulewa, more and more rural households had come to depend for their livelihood on wage labor (Brow and Weeramunda 1992), which typically did not generate the diffuse and enduring bonds of mutual obligation and solidarity that underlay the older forms of exchange labor and sharecropping tenancy. Similarly, the competitive struggle to acquire resources controlled by the state, exacerbated by the establishment of party political organizations at the village level, made a mockery of the image of the harmonious village community. Under these conditions the dominant ideology might still be embraced by villagers, but its elements could also be used as tools of criticism directed back against those who were most vociferous in its propagation.

Chapter 6　　　　　*The Awakening Village*

SHORTLY AFTER the victory of the UNP in the general election of 1977 Ranasinghe Premadasa, who became prime minister after J. R. Jayewardene was elevated to the presidency under the new constitution, and who also served as minister of local government and housing, introduced his program of Gam Udava (Village Awakening). Premadasa's program drew on what had become part of the national elite's common-sense understanding of the traditional village community, but it was particularly inspired by the Sarvodaya Shramadana Movement, a flourishing nongovernmental organization dedicated to grassroots development that had received considerable international acclaim and support.[1] The Village Awakening Program derived a good deal both of its agenda and of its rhetorical style from Sarvodaya, whose goal was to achieve the spiritual and material regeneration of rural life through programs of self-help that would restore the village community to the condition of harmony, virtue, and prosperity that it was believed to have enjoyed in ancient times.

The particular program designed for Kukulewa was modelled on the prime minister's initial project in Kurunegala District, and its early formulation was ambitious.[2] A memorandum circulated by the GA (government agent, the chief executive officer) of Anuradhapura District at the end of July 1978 stated that it would include the development of agriculture and irrigation, roads and highways, health, education, postal and telecommunication facilities, transport, cooperatives, marketing and agrarian services, the supply of electricity, and the allocation of land and houses. Actually, however, much of this never materialized, because budgetary constraints dictated a severe reduction in the scope of the project. In the course of its implementation the project came increasingly to concentrate on housing, but even here the early plans had to be abridged. The original program had called for the construction of 180 new houses, but it was subsequently decided that only twenty-five would be built in the first stage of the project. These houses were to be built on what official documents referred to as "*attam* basis," adopting a term traditionally used for reciprocal labor exchange in agriculture. The idea was that the government would supply the materials for the houses and that unpaid labor would be provided by the eventual recipients, who would collectively do the actual construction. This plan, however, was itself soon modified, as the prime minister wanted the project completed within three months, and it was thought that the attam process would be too slow to accomplish this. It was then decided that the houses would be built directly by the government, using wage labor, and that the target should be fifty or sixty houses, the maximum number that government could construct in three months. Finally, officials settled on a goal of sixty houses, thirty of which would be built directly by the government and the other thirty by contractors.

The location of the new housing was also changed at this time. Originally it had been intended to build the houses more or less in the center of the existing village, in an area close to what was known as Kukulewa junction, where tracks branched off from the dirt road that ran through the village, on one side down to the main tank and on the other to the neighboring hamlet of Kuda Kapirigama. Instead of this plan, which would have required the demolition of a number of existing houses, a new site was chosen about a half-mile north of Kukulewa junction, in an area of scrub jungle used for chena cultivation. Thirty acres of land were to be surveyed there, cleared, and divided into half-acre lots for the new houses. The houses themselves were to be of uniform design, single-story concrete buildings twenty feet wide and thirty feet long, internally partitioned into three rooms with a lavatory attached at the rear. Each house would cost about 36,000 rupees to construct.

The modifications to the original plan were to have serious social consequences. The removal of the housing project to its new site implied that what was now contemplated was not so much the renovation of the old village as the establishment of a new settlement, physically separate from Kukulewa as it then existed. Moreover, the reduction of the number of new houses to sixty, at least in the first stage of the program, raised the question of how they could be equitably allocated among the 125 households in the village.

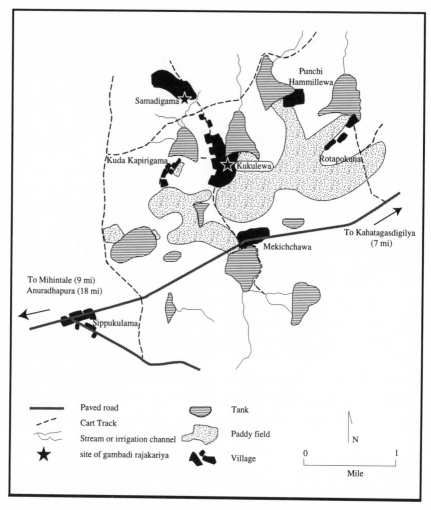

Kukulewa and environs

The construction project made slow progress at first. Although the prime minister had called in October 1978 for its completion within three months, it was the middle of 1979 before the land for the new houses was cleared of its jungle cover. Here again there was a change of plans. It had at first been decided to clear the land by means of *sramadāna*, "the gift of shared labor" donated by the villagers toward a collective goal, but as with the construction of the houses themselves, the political demand for quick results persuaded the government to hire the villagers as wage laborers instead. A resident engineer was sent to the village to take charge of the project, and under his supervision the contract to provide the necessary labor, first to clear the site for the houses and subsequently for the construction of the thirty houses that the Department of Housing was itself to build, was entrusted to Naidurala, a Kukulewa villager who had recently been elected president of its rural development society.

Construction of the Houses

Rural development societies were village-level organizations that had been set up with official assistance and encouragement to initiate local development projects such as cottage industries, well digging, and road repairs. The accomplishments of the Kukulewa rural development society (RDS) as an instigator of change were meager at first, but it became more active after the SLFP government of 1970–1977 began to use the societies as agencies through which to channel aid for development.[3] It appears that the officers of the Kukulewa RDS were able to work together quite amicably for a while, despite the fact that they were not all associated with the same political party, but by the time the plan for Village Awakening was put forward this had ceased to be the case. At a meeting of the Kukulewa RDS on September 9, 1978, Sumanapala, its president, who was also vice-president of the local branch of the SLFP, announced that he could no longer work with fellow officers who were dishonest and corrupt, and resigned his position. At its next meeting the RDS voted unanimously to replace him with Naidurala, who was already president of the Kukulewa branch of the UNP. Looking back on this incident five years later, Sumanapala made no mention of corruption, but stressed that after the UNP gained power it became impossible for him to work with UNP supporters such as Jinadasa and Wijeratne.

Naidurala had played a less active role then Jinadasa in the establishment of a UNP organization in the village, but his status was not tainted by the knowledge that his parents were outsiders. He was an industrious farmer whose father had been vel vidāne and he was widely respected for his skill in treating children's ailments. For these reasons he was elected to the prestigious position of president of the UNP, while Jinadasa contented himself with the less prominent but still powerful office of treasurer.

Naidurala's election to the presidency of the RDS made its leadership almost identical to that of the local UNP, with a single difference attributable to the fact that the latter organization also included the neighboring Goyigama hamlet of Kuda Kapirigama, which supplied the party secretary. Naidurala was now president of both the RDS and the UNP, and Jinadasa was similarly treasurer of both organizations, while Jinadasa's first cousin and close associate, Wijeratne, was secretary of the RDS and assistant secretary of the UNP. This alignment promised practical advantages that were well understood by all concerned. The RDS was poised to receive whatever benefits the government had to distribute to the village, and it could reasonably be expected that the local MP, who was a member of the ruling UNP, would be most likely to bestow his favors on an RDS whose officers were supporters of his own party.

Unity among the new leadership of the RDS, however, lasted only for a few months. Once work began at the site where the new homes were to be built Naidurala's control of the labor force, and the way he exercised it, soon antagonized his fellow officers. Mudalihamy, a UNP supporter, gave one version of what happened.

Mudalihamy: I was employed at the site when work started there in 1979. Naidurala was in charge of hiring the labor and at the beginning, before the engineer came to the village, he also supervised the work of clearing the jungle. Jinadasa and Wijeratne were not satisfied with that arrangement. They wanted to be in charge of the work themselves, and they wanted to give jobs to members of their families. But Naidurala hired only people that he knew to be good workers.

Wijeratne, on the other hand, turned the charge of favoritism back onto Naidurala, and added a political twist to it.

Wijeratne: When Naidurala took charge of the work at the construction site he gave jobs only to his own close kin. Those men were mostly SLFP supporters and even while working there they criticized the government.

Naidurala: I did the work of clearing the jungle on contract. I hired only people who worked hard. I was the contractor so it was my money that was involved. That's why I didn't employ lazy people. I didn't take any account of party political allegiance. Both UNP and SLFP supporters worked at the site. A resident engineer was sent out to the site when construction of the houses started at the end of June. He supervised the work and I helped him organize the labor. Thirty of the houses were built by contractors, and they hired whoever they wanted. But the thirty houses built directly by the government employed village laborers whom I hired in Kukulewa. I selected only obedient people who were prepared to work hard. Wijeratne worked for the contractors.

Naidurala's critics raised other charges against him.

Herathamy, a UNP supporter who subsequently turned against Naidurala: There was no government official at the site when the jungle was being cleared. Naidurala kept the records of labor attendance. Officials of the Housing Department came out to pay the workers, but they didn't pay them directly. They gave the money to Naidurala. And Naidurala gave them false figures. He claimed to have employed more people than actually worked there. And he kept the difference for himself.

Menikrala, another UNP supporter who turned against Naidurala: Naidurala took bribes from people who wanted to work at the site. And a portion of that money was given to the engineer. Naidurala didn't do any work himself, but he was paid a salary. The contractors also bribed the engineer. They supplied timber of very poor quality that wasn't even suitable for firewood. When people pointed this out they were fired from their jobs and banned from the site.

Jinadasa: Naidurala is a fool. He worked hard at the site for Samadigama. He worked very hard and helped that engineer make a lot of money. He didn't even allow Wijeratne and me into the work site. He conspired with the engineer against us. One time I tried to supply bricks and sand to the construction project. I hired five tractors and brought the materials to the site. The next day the engineer told me not to bring anything to the site again. Naidurala was jealous because I had made 150 rupees on that one day, and he told the engineer not to give me any more contracts.

Wijeratne: One day a lorry load of inferior timber was brought into the site to be used in construction of the houses. I complained about this to Naidurala, but he didn't listen to me. So I informed the AGA (assistant government agent), and he ordered the load to be sent back. That made both Naidurala and the engineer furious. I'm sure the contractors had bribed the engineer and that's why he allowed them to supply inferior timber.

So Wijeratne, Jinadasa, and their allies became estranged from Naidurala. But as long as Naidurala enjoyed the trust of the resident engineer they could make little headway against him.

Mudalihamy: Naidurala became very friendly with the engineer. He used to go hunting with him, and the two of them would drink together. Jinadasa and Wijeratne were antagonized because the engineer only hired people whom Naidurala recommended. And as Naidurala lost the confidence of the leading figures in the UNP he came increasingly to depend on the engineer. When Jinadasa and Wijeratne saw that they couldn't get anywhere they went to the MP and asked him to tell the engineer to hire UNP supporters. The MP gave letters to the members of Jinadasa's and Wijeratne's faction to show to the engineer, and after that the engineer employed them. But the new men who were hired on the MP's recommendation didn't work. The engineer found them drunk on the job. He saw them as a hindrance to the project and so he fired them. After that he didn't employ people who had been recommended by the MP. That made Wijeratne very angry and he complained to the MP that Naidurala was working against the UNP. But the MP didn't take any action, perhaps because the engineer told him that Wijeratne's faction was obstructing the project. But he did order the engineer to hold an enquiry to see whether the charges made against Naidurala were true. The engineer found Naidurala not guilty, and he got very angry with Wijeratne. He called him a trouble-maker and banned him from the site.

Wijeratne: Because Naidurala wouldn't listen to the appeals of UNP committee members we had no alternative but to complain to the MP and inform him that Naidurala was not giving priority to UNP supporters when hiring villagers for work at the site. The engineer in charge investigated our complaint, but because he was friendly with Naidurala he found him not guilty, and he ordered us out of the site. Jinadasa assaulted Naidurala that same evening as he was going home from work. It happened at Kukulewa junction. There were some other young men there as well who had also been mistreated by Naidurala, but only Jinadasa assaulted him, and it was only a slap.

Mudalihamy: Jinadasa assaulted Naidurala as he was going to the site for night watch duties. Naidurala had his gun with him. Jinadasa and Wijeratne and about ten young men were at the junction near Jinadasa's old house. When Jinadasa saw Naidurala he started to abuse him, and he grabbed Naidurala's gun. Then he grabbed him by the hair and pushed and pulled him about. Then he slapped his face. Naidurala couldn't do anything, and he didn't say a word. Then Jinadasa let him go, and gave him back his gun. Naidurala went on working at the site after that, but he had nothing more to do with the other leaders of the UNP.

Allocation of the Houses

For the time being Jinadasa and Wijeratne were frustrated by Naidurala's alliance with the engineer, but they continued to press their argument that party loyalty should be rewarded, and they began to apply it to a more momentous question than that of Naidurala's hiring policy. As the housing project moved toward completion the salient issue became the sixty houses themselves, and how they were to be distributed among the 125 existing households in the village.

Naidurala maintained that the houses should be allocated to the sixty "root families" *(mul pavul;* sing. *mul pavula)* in the village. The origins of this term remain obscure. It was not used in 1968–1970, when I did my original research in Kukulewa. Some villagers claimed that it was introduced by government officials when they first announced the housing project, but it was not then given a precise definition. "Pavula," which is usually translated into English as "family," has an even wider and more variable range of reference than "family" in its common English usage. At one extreme it may be used by a man to describe only his wife, or his wife and children, but at the other it may be extended to include all his relatives, everyone in the village, or even the variga as a whole. "Mul" has the sense of primary, original, and radical. Some villagers stressed the temporal dimension of the term, claiming that only those families that had been living in the village for many generations, or were descended from its original settlers, qualified as mul pavul. This served to exclude the few families (most notably including Jinadasa's) that had moved into Kukulewa in recent memory, but it did not solve the problem of allocating the houses, for many more than sixty households were left with unchallengeable claims to be considered mul pavul by this criterion. The more common interpretation of the term, however, was also more pragmatic. Most people agreed that while brothers and sisters in their twenties were still to be considered junior members of the mul pavula of their parents, even if

Kukulewa house built in the traditional style.

they had already married and established independent households, by the time they reached their forties and had grown-up children each had combined with his or her spouse to head a new mul pavula. Although the exact point of fission was never defined, this did provide a way to divide the population of the village into roughly sixty units, and Naidurala's supporters argued that distribution of the houses along these lines would be the most equitable procedure. Jinadasa and Wijeratne, on the other hand, worked to consolidate their support within the local branch of the UNP by urging that the houses be given only to supporters of the party.

James, Jinadasa's father's brother, a UNP supporter: At first, the MP planned to give the houses to sixty mul pavul. That idea was given to him by government officials, and Naidurala agreed with it. But other UNP people opposed it because it would mean that SLFP supporters would get houses.

Menikrala: Most of the UNP people were frustrated by that time. If the houses were to be given to sixty mul pavul, then some of us would not get houses while SLFP supporters did. So Wijeratne, Jinadasa, Anthony, James and I got together and united against Naidurala. We got the support of many members

House built under the Village Awakening Program.

of the UNP and organized them against Naidurala. As a result the Kukulewa branch of the UNP split in two. Most of us were against the allocation of the houses to sixty mul pavul. But some, like Naidurala and Tikiribanda, favored the mul pavul idea.

Wimaladasa, SLFP supporter: Naidurala didn't know how to organize people. He didn't know how to talk to the villagers or how to behave toward them in order to get their support. Nor could he win the MP to his side because he couldn't express himself well. Meanwhile Jinadasa and Wijeratne were very active and went to see the MP several times.

Wijeratne: The MP became angry with Naidurala when committee members of the UNP informed him that Naidurala was abusing his power as president of the Kukulewa branch. We told him that Naidurala was mistreating party members and that most of the sixty mul pavul to whom he wanted to give the houses were supporters of the SLFP. Naidurala was left with only four or five followers in the UNP. Most of the members supported Jinadasa. That was because of Naidurala's plan to give the houses to sixty mul pavul. If that had happened, some active members of the UNP would not have received houses.

Menikrala: As a result of our complaints the MP advised us to summon a meeting of the Kukulewa UNP, and he said that he himself would come out to settle the dispute. He also sent a message to Naidurala asking him to attend the meeting, but Naidurala didn't turn up.

James: The MP sent a jeep to the village with a message asking Naidurala to see him at his house. Naidurala said to the jeep driver, "If the MP wants to see me, tell him to come and see me himself." That made the MP very angry. In October [1979] the Kukulewa UNP met at the school. The MP came out and presided. I proposed that Naidurala be removed from the presidency and the members voted in favor of my proposal. After that Wijeratne became president.

Mudalihamy: There was a meeting at the school before the houses were allocated. The MP came to that meeting. He also sent a message to Naidurala asking him to attend, but Naidurala refused to come. He stayed away. I was there at the meeting when it was proposed to remove Naidurala from the presidency. I was against it, but I didn't say anything. I was afraid to speak in favor of Naidurala because I thought I wouldn't get a house if I stood against Jinadasa and Wijeratne. Besides, the MP was on their side. Most of the people at the meeting wanted to keep Naidurala as president. But the MP wanted to be rid of him, so we couldn't object.

Sellathe, UNP supporter: There was a meeting at Kukulewa school at which the MP removed Naidurala from the presidency and appointed Wijeratne in his place. We didn't want to get rid of Naidurala, but we couldn't oppose the MP. The people who did want to remove Naidurala—Wijeratne, Jinadasa, and Menikrala—got together with the MP to do it.

Naidurala's removal from office signalled the end of the plan to distribute the houses among the sixty mul pavul. There followed a hectic scramble to influence the new allocations.

Menikrala: A month before the houses were to be allocated the MP held a meeting with committee members of the UNP at his house. He had a list with him of the sixty families that were to receive the houses. That list had been prepared by government officials after consultation with Naidurala. The committee members objected to it. They pointed out that most of the people on the list were supporters of the SLFP, so it was revised to include only the names of UNP members.

James: The MP asked the leaders of the UNP to name the villagers who should be given the new houses. Jinadasa promised to prepare a list. As a result the original list prepared by government officials, which distributed the houses among sixty mul pavul, was set aside. The list prepared by Jinadasa was subsequently revised from time to time. Committee members used to go see the MP and get him to revise the list. Menikrala, Wijeratne, Anthony, and Jinadasa did that. They didn't all go together. They went one after the other to make false complaints against people who were on the original list. In that way they got houses allocated to their own close kin.

Sellathe: I remember the MP saying at a meeting that he was going to allocate the houses to the sixty mul pavul. If he had done so there wouldn't have been these disputes over the houses. But Wijeratne and Jinadasa conspired to get him to change his mind. They prepared a list of those to whom houses should be given and gave it to the MP. I have heard that both my own name and that of my son were on the original list. But after Jinadasa and the others went to see the MP to get more houses for their kinsmen, my son's name was taken off the list. It was not because we were SLFP supporters—the only time I ever voted for the SLFP was in 1956—but because those people wanted more houses for their kin.

Menikrala: Committee members of the UNP used to meet the MP from time to time to get the list revised. They added the names of their close kin such as daughters, brothers, sisters, and so on. I was originally allocated one house and I wasn't satisfied with that, but other UNP members were also given only one house each. Then Anthony went to meet the MP and got five houses for his family. When I heard about that I also went to see the MP and told him that some families were being given more than one house. He asked me how many houses I wanted. I told him I wanted four and he revised the list accordingly, to give me four houses.

Herathamy: When the MP asked the UNP branch to name the people to receive the houses, several members of the committee got together and made up a list. It was principally Jinadasa, Wijeratne, and Menikrala who did that. Menikrala was not satisfied with the allocations, but Jinadasa forwarded the list to the MP. The next day Menikrala went to see the MP, and Anthony went with him. According to Jinadasa's list only one house had been allocated to Menikrala's family, but several houses had been given to Jinadasa's brothers and sisters. Also, Jinadasa had not allocated a house to his father, Anthony, or to Anthony's second wife, Kaluhamy. Menikrala pointed out to the MP that if the allocations were made according to Jinadasa's list some SLFP supporters would get houses. Anthony said the same thing. The MP asked them for the names of SLFP supporters on the list, and that is how the names of Tikiribanda and Bandathe Vidane's widow came to be removed. Menikrala replaced them with the names of his sons and daughters. And Anthony was also successful in getting a house for his wife, Kaluhamy.

Muthubanda, UNP supporter and Samadigama householder: It would have been reasonable if the houses had been allocated to the sixty mul pavul, as Naidurala proposed. That way I would have got a house, but my sons would not. Anthony would have got a house, but there wouldn't have been one for everybody in his family. And James would have got a house, but not his sons. At the last moment Menikrala and Anthony went to the MP and got the list prepared by Jinadasa and Wijeratne revised. That's how Menikrala got four houses. And Dharmaratne, who is married to a daughter of Anthony's sister, got extra houses because of that connection. People got houses for their close kin. Party affiliation was also considered, but it was a matter of kinship as much as party. Right up to the day the keys were handed over only a very few people knew that the houses were going to be distributed like that. Even members of the UNP committee didn't know. It was Jinadasa and Wijeratne who prepared the list and they did so without telling us anything. Menikrala and Anthony were the other two involved. Some houses were even given to supporters of the SLFP in return for bribes of 200 rupees. That money was divided between them by Jinadasa and Wijeratne.

Herathamy: The day before the ceremonial opening of the new village the MP came with the list of people who were getting the houses and handed over the keys. The people moved into the houses that same day. Jinadasa was shocked to see that his list had been altered, at the instigation of Anthony and Menikrala, without him being told. It is said that he had to pay money back to people to whom he had promised houses. Kukulewa people who had hoped to live in these new houses were very angry when they saw one family getting as many as five houses. They thought the houses were going to be given to the sixty mul pavul. If that had been done every family would be represented in the new village. If the leaders of the UNP had summoned a meeting to decide how to allocate the houses, I would have asked for them to be divided among the mul pavul. I was a committee member of the UNP, but I knew nothing at all about the allocations.

Muthubanda: Naidurala was offered a new house, the one that Ranbanda is now living in. But he wanted the house that was eventually given to Nandasena, because he had personally supervised its construction and had made sure it was properly built. When he was not given that house he refused the offer.

Naidurala: Everyone in Kukulewa hoped to get a house in the new village—until the day the keys were handed out. That was the day before the ceremonial opening, and on that day the MP came out to the village and asked to see me. I went to the site of the new village, and he told me that I had been given a house. I asked him whether the houses were to be given to the sixty mul pavul, and he replied that they were being given to supporters of the UNP. So I said to him, "then give my house to any dog you like. I don't want a house." And after that I went home.

A Celebration of Development

Shortly before the new settlement was completed, E.L.B. Hurulle, the minister of cultural affairs in the national government and the MP for a neighboring constituency, proposed that it be given the name of Sannasgama, in recognition of an ancient rock inscription discovered near the site that recorded the grant *(sannasa)* of a tank to a Buddhist monastery. This proposal was rejected in favor of another name—Samadigama—which no less clearly expressed the Buddhist aspirations of the project's sponsors. *Gama* means "village" or "estate," while *samādhi*, which Gombrich and Obeyesekere (1988:26) translate as "absorption," refers to a state of intense mental concentration attainable through Buddhist techniques of meditation.

At the time of its official opening, in January 1980, Samadigama contained sixty new houses and two larger buildings, one designed as a community center to be operated in conjunction with the Sarvodaya Shramadana Movement and the other divided between a cooperative store and a post office. Much of the rest of the original project seems to have been quietly abandoned. The road into the village had been paved, and a bus service was even begun on the day of the opening, but it proved to be uneconomical and was soon cancelled. Minor repairs were made to the village's irrigation works, but no new sources of water were tapped. Electricity was supplied only temporarily, for the opening ceremony itself. No dispensary or health center was built, nor were the school buildings enlarged. Most of the eight wells promised to the village were not completed, and to preserve appearances at the ceremonial opening two of them had to be filled with water taken from the tank. Above all, as far as the villagers were concerned, no new opportunities for employment were made available.

Nevertheless, local officials mobilized all available resources to impress their superiors with the project's accomplishments, and they spared no effort to stage a pageant for the official opening that would be a worthy celebration of national development. According to the program, the ceremonies began with a formal procession into the new village, followed by the unveiling of plaques and flags, including the Buddhist as well as the national flag. Then there was the formal opening of the cooperative store, the post office, and the community center. After that the prime minister planted a sapling taken from the sacred bo-tree in Anuradhapura, one of the most venerated places of Buddhist worship in Sri Lanka. Finally there was a "People's Rally" that included the handing over of the keys to the new houses, speeches by the distinguished guests, a speech of thanks by one of the new householders, and a musical performance put on by the Ceylon Tobacco Company.

Since I was not in Sri Lanka in 1980 I cannot confirm that the actual ceremony strictly followed the official program, nor can I describe precisely what the visiting dignitaries said in their speeches. But I was assured later by those who were present that the ceremony was performed according to plan, and that the content of the speeches was very similar to the written statements that the prime minister, the minister of cultural affairs, and the MP for Anuradhapura East contributed to a souvenir booklet that was published to commemorate the occasion.

The prime minister's contribution to this booklet was taken from a speech he had made earlier at the headquarters of Sarvodaya. It did not, therefore, refer specifically to the Samadigama project but was a more gen-

The sacred bo-tree in Samadigama, surrounded by a low wall and a circle of fence-posts. The community building is behind it to the right, and the post office and cooperative store to the left.

eral statement of the aims of the Village Awakening Program that stressed his government's commitment both to end poverty and to create a just society. This, he argued, required the cultivation of habits of honesty, hard work, and self-reliance. Sri Lanka had once been a prosperous country whose people lived virtuously and worked together for common goals, but when the country lost its independence the people began to lose those qualities. Nevertheless, he maintained, they could still be found to some degree in the more remote rural areas but unfortunately, because of their material poverty, the people were unable to raise themselves up without help. The prime minister then presented his Village Awakening Program as an effort to address this problem, calling it a step toward the realization of his vision of a society that was "healthy, virtuous and independent."

A second contribution to the booklet was made by E.L.B. Hurulle, the minister of cultural affairs and the MP for Horuwopotana, the constituency that had included Kukulewa before electoral boundaries were redrawn in the 1970s. Hurulle was also a member of the old Vanniya aristocracy, and he still maintained his ancestral home at Morakava, about fifteen miles from Kukulewa. His statement began by recalling the patriarchal relations of a former era: "Morakava has long been a center for the people of Kukulewa and other villages in the district. For centuries it has provided them with shelter, comfort and refuge. My ancestors knew these people well."

Hurulle then went on to recount his own efforts to assist the people of Kukulewa, noting how he had been frustrated when the UNP was out of power between 1970 and 1977. He claimed, however, that under the new UNP government the village was back on the path toward development. Hurulle also reported that, in his capacity as minister of cultural affairs, he had instructed the commissioner of archaeology to investigate an ancient inscription that had been discovered on a rock near Kukulewa tank. According to the commissioner's report, he said, in the first century A.D. Kukulewa had been a sacred place of Buddhist worship, inhabited by Sinhala people who protected the national traditions and culture.

The third statement in the booklet was written by Yasapala Herath, the MP for Anuradhapura East, the electorate that had included Kukulewa since the late 1970s. Herath began by recalling the glories of Sinhala history. He described the ancient irrigation system that had enabled the people to overcome an adverse environment and create a splendid civilization, the literary and artistic achievements of which were inspired by Buddhism. Referring to the rock inscription, he pointed out that it recorded the gift, by the wife of one of King Amanda Gamini's ministers, of a tank she had constructed to a Buddhist temple that she had also built. This, said Herath, was evidence not only that ancient kings and chiefs had been committed to the development of the country and the welfare of the people, but also that women had formerly played a leading part in tank construction and the work of development.

Herath then went on to describe how, after the decline of the Anuradhapura civilization, the village had reverted to jungle. In the seventeenth century, however, it had been resettled by another group of people, known as Vannivaru, who came from farther south in search of the game, honey, and wild plants from which they made their living. Herath said that these new settlers, who were the ancestors of the present villagers, "were closely related to the Sinhala people. They were the descendants of King Vijaya and Kuveni." He then went on to say that "the people of

Kukulewa may be of mixed origin (but that) the beliefs, customs and mode of living of the aboriginal people cannot be found in Kukulewa. They have been integrated into the traditions of the Sinhala people."

Finally, Herath described the poverty in which the villagers had been living. They were, he said, an unfortunate and uneducated people. But now they had been brought under the prime minister's Village Awakening Program and had the opportunity to regain their self-respect and independence. The opening of Samadigama, he concluded, "brings to an end the dark era in which the villagers lived in fear among wild animals" and marks the beginning of their march toward development.

Discussion

In the early 1980s ceremonies similar to the one staged at Samadigama were being performed almost every day in one part or another of Sri Lanka. They were among the most frequently produced and widely publicized events that government agencies organized in their ceaseless efforts to promote and celebrate development. Until it was later displaced by concern with national security, development was itself the most prominent and pervasive theme of official ideological activity. As the ceremony at Samadigama showed, the discourse of development was centrally implicated in the imaginative construction of the Sinhala nation, to which it contributed by linking contemporary government programs to the glorious achievements of the past. The ancient rock inscription and the new plaque, the old tank and the modern houses, the planting of the bo-tree and the ruins of a Buddhist temple, all were articulated with one another and identified as part of the unified project that is the Sinhala nation.

In this respect the most potent of all the ritual actions performed at the ceremony was the planting of a bo-tree sapling in the center of the new settlement. The sapling was taken from the sacred bo-tree in Anuradhapura, which was itself believed to have been grown from a branch of the very tree under which the Buddha attained *nirvāṇa*. That branch had been brought to Sri Lanka in the third century B.C., when Buddhism was first introduced to the island through the conversion of King Devanampiyatissa by the monk Mahinda, son of the Emperor Asoka. Subsequently saplings from the Anuradhapura tree were distributed all over the island (Rahula 1966:58), and these plantings came to symbolize the establishment of Buddhism in the island. More specifically, the bo-tree was widely understood to represent the Sinhala people's special mission, maintained over more than two thousand years through all the vicissitudes of national fortune, to preserve and propagate the Buddha's teachings in Sri Lanka.[4]

Planting a sapling from the bo-tree at Anuradhapura was a central feature of the opening ceremony, not just at Samadigama, but also at other Awakening Villages elsewhere in the island. The prime minister's program thus aimed to repeat the pattern of planting bo-trees throughout Sri Lanka that had followed the arrival of the original sapling at the time of King Devanampiyatissa. This was a powerful demonstration of renewed commitment to the propagation of the Buddha's teachings, one that inscribed the mission of the Sinhala people in the very soil of Sri Lanka.

Connections between ancient virtues, present policies, and future aspirations were also stressed in the politicians' statements, among which that of the local MP, Yasapala Herath, was particularly insistent on the essential continuity of Sinhala culture over more than two millennia. The prime minister, R. Premadasa, for his part emphasized rather the need to recover values that had been lost under colonial rule. Combined with the various ritual actions, these statements served to modernize what was traditional and to traditionalize the modern. At the same time they also expressed not just a national memory of historical continuity but also an energizing sense of national destiny. "It is the magic of nationalism," writes Benedict Anderson (1983:19) "to turn chance into destiny," to which it might be added that, at least in this case, it was the sense of destiny that lent both dignity to the nation and legitimacy to the state's claim to be its "organ of moral discipline" (Durkheim 1957:72, cited in Corrigan and Sayer 1985: 5). The ceremony at Samadigama was thus a powerful assertion both of national identity and of the state's responsibility to protect and promote the moral code by which that identity was defined. In other words, the people of Kukulewa were authoritatively informed not only who they were but also how they should behave.

The politicians did not, however, speak in perfect unison. While the populist rhetoric of Premadasa and Herath expressed sympathy for the villagers' suffering, Hurulle's patriarchal preoccupations kept his attention fixed firmly on his own accomplishments. And while Premadasa's acknowledgment of the state's responsibility to ameliorate the condition of the poor was balanced by a call for moral regeneration through self-reliance, Hurulle's perspective on development was exclusively "top-down," entirely a matter of enlightened leaders struggling to bring the benefits of prosperity to the simple villagers. And on this issue Herath stood closer to Hurulle, attributing development mainly to the initiatives of party leaders whose vision and commitment promised relief from the dismal round of poverty, ignorance, and disease that he described.

The ceremonial opening of Samadigama was certainly a spectacular pageant of nationalism and development. But that is not all it was. It was also a ritual of incorporation, by means of which the place of a marginal community was authoritatively fixed within the boundaries of the nation of Sinhala Buddhists. The planting of the bo-tree reestablished the sanctity of a place that, as the rock inscription demonstrated, had once been devoted to Buddhist worship. And in a comparable move, principally accomplished in Herath's statement, the inhabitants of the village were located within the Sinhala national community. Hurulle's statement had left a vacant space between the present inhabitants of Kukulewa and the Sinhala Buddhists who had once lived and worshiped there, but Herath proceeded to bridge this gap. While recognizing the Vedda origins of the Kukulewa people, he also stressed connections between the Veddas and the Sinhala kings, and concluded that elements of aboriginal culture could no longer be found in Kukulewa. Although their origins were "mixed," the villagers had by now adopted Sinhala traditions and customs.

This formulation served to incorporate the people of Kukulewa within the moral community of Sinhala Buddhism, while simultaneously acknowledging an original difference. Complete homogenization was neither asserted nor required. The Veddas remained a very small and powerless minority that posed no imaginable threat to Sinhala domination. Rather, they embodied the lack of civilization that it was the historic destiny of the Sinhala people to supplant.

Whatever the success of these hegemonic maneuvers, however, the organizers of the Samadigama project signally failed to recreate the spirit of cooperation that was central to their vision of rural regeneration. At the end of the day, when the distinguished visitors departed, what they left behind was far from the harmonious village community of their imagining. It was, rather, a village in which factional hostility had been sharply exacerbated by the fact that the sixty new houses were all allocated to the local leaders of the UNP and their immediate associates.

Chapter 7

The Rise of the Fernandos

WHEN THE VILLAGERS who were most outraged at the way the new houses had been allocated claimed that the houses should have been distributed among the sixty mul pavul (root families) in the village, they used the term more as part of an appeal for equitable treatment than as the label for a clearly identifiable social group. Since other criteria were eventually used to determine the allocations, it never became necessary to define exactly what a mul pavula was, or where the boundary lay between one mul pavula and another. Critics were content to assert that there were sixty mul pavul in the village and that each of them should have received one house. Precise definition was less salient than the communal ideals of equity and justice with which the term was imbued. Nevertheless there was broad agreement on the principles by which the households in the village could be grouped into mul pavul, and there was equally wide recognition that at least half these mul pavul had been denied new housing.

Dissidents charged that this had come about through bribery and the exploitation of their influence by leading members of the local UNP. Justice was also said to have been violated by the grant of houses to two of the four Kukulewa villagers who had earlier been given land in the peasant colonization project at Maha Kanadarawa, as well as by the allocation of houses to two people who were not even residents of Kukulewa. These charges surfaced in a petition that a group of villagers had composed and sent to the prime minister in Colombo.

Malpractices in the Allocation of Houses: Kukulewa Model Village

The houses in the above model village have been allocated only to a very few mul pavul. Houses have even been given to unmarried men in these families.

There are sixty mul pavul in the village. We think it would have been fair if one house had been given to each mul pavula.

We have come to know that the secretary, treasurer and president of the UNP branch organization have taken bribes, of one hundred rupees in each case, for the allocation of houses. We invite your kind attention to these facts. We are prepared to prove that bribes were taken. Houses were also given to nonresidents of the village. Some people to whom the government gave land under the Maha Kanadarawa scheme have been allocated houses in Samadigama.

We invite your kind attention to these matters. We, the villagers of Kukulewa, are prepared to prove these malpractices. We humbly beg you to make an inquiry into these things and to allocate houses on a more just and reasonable basis. (signed) Kukulewa villagers.

A second petition that was sent at about the same time took a somewhat different tack. Whereas the first had opened with an immediate reference to mul pavul, the second accepted that the houses should have been given to supporters of the UNP but aimed to expose the corruption in the local party leadership. It was also more explicit in its appeal to the standards of "populist legitimism," lauding the national government while indicting its local agents, but also reminding it of its pledge to govern righteously.

Opening of Kukulewa-Samadigama

We hereby present you with the inside story of Samadigama, which was ceremonially opened by you very recently.

(1) Three families have had sixteen houses allocated to them. These are the families of the treasurer of the Kukulewa Rural Development Society, the secretary of the Kukulewa Rural Development Society, and Menikrala, committee member of the Kukulewa Rural Development Society.

(2) Sithawathie, the wife of Sellathe who has paddy land and dry land at Maha Kanadarawa, has been given a house. An unmarried son of Muthubanda, who has land at Maha Kanadarawa, has also been given a house.

(3) Dissanayake, an unmarried son of Kalubanda, has been given a house.

(4) Apart from the sixteen houses mentioned above, a bribe of one hundred rupees has been taken for the allocation of every house.

(5) There are cases where the hundred rupees was given back to people to whom houses could not be allocated. For instance, the money given by Podiya and Polin Banda was returned to them. They will testify to this.

(6) When the allocations were made, factors such as the size of the family, income, and other important matters were not taken into consideration. Houses were given to members of the party in return for money and support.

(7) There are poor people in the village who are ardent supporters of the party. But two houses were allocated to outsiders from Kuda Kapirigama and Mekichchawa without regard to the loyal members of the party within the village.

(8) A sum of twenty-five rupees was taken from Banda and Karunadasa for the allocation of houses to them. They were made to promise to pay the balance of seventy-five rupees after they received the houses.

Your attention is directed to these facts. It appears that the member of parliament may have participated in these matters. There is a rumour that part of the bribes went to the MP. When he was informed of this he promised to provide other houses in the future.

Jinadasa, Wijeratne, and Dinapala from Kuda Kapirigama are the people responsible. Please appoint a committee of inquiry or direct the CID (Criminal Investigation Department) to look into the matter. If it is not done, your reputation will be tarnished. We are telling you this because the President and you are not aware of the injustices and malpractices being perpetrated in the name of your righteous government.

For necessary action, please. Victory to the righteous government. Faithfully, A Group of Kukulewa Villagers.

The two petitions were forwarded by the prime minister's office to the GA, Anuradhapura, who passed them on for investigation by the AGA, Kahatagasdigiliya. The AGA's subsequent report supported a number of the complaints, but found no evidence of bribery.

Model Village Program–Anuradhapura
East Electorate–Samadigama Model Village

With reference to your letter dated 19/3/80 and the petitions attached to it, I made an inquiry and looked into the matters raised in the petitions. This inquiry was conducted informally. My findings are as follows:

(1) Kirihamy and Dayananda, to whom houses were allocated, are both unmarried men, as mentioned in the petition.

(2) In addition, the above mentioned Dayananda is a brother of Jayatilike, who also has a house in Samadigama. Both Kandathe and his son Somapala received houses in Samadigama. Wijeratne, Peter Fernando, Seelawathie and Piyadasa are three brothers and a sister, all of whom were given houses. Seelawathie's husband, Dharmaratne, is a brother of Upasena, who also received a house in Samadigama. And Jinadasa, Sugathapala and Malietana, brothers and a sister of the same family, have been allocated three houses. Francis and William are brothers who each managed to get a house.

(3) There is no evidence to prove that bribes were taken for the allocation of houses.

(4) A man named Dinapala from Kuda Kapirigama is not a resident of Kukulewa, but he has been given a house. Nandasena, a resident of Mekichchawa, also has a house. Neither of these two is occupying his house in Samadigama. One of the houses is occupied by the postmaster of Samadigama Post Office. It is difficult to know whether she pays rent to the owner of the house.

(5) The occupants of house number 23 and house number 16, Anthony Fernando and Sellathe by name, both have five acres of dry land and paddy land in Maha Kanadarawa settlement scheme.

The two petitions sent to me are returned herewith for necessary action. AGA, Kahatagasdigiliya.

The two petitions and the AGA's report were further circulated within the bureaucracy, but in the end no action was considered necessary, and no allocations were changed.

Jinadasa's Faction

The AGA's report was accurate as far as it went, but it did not indicate either the full extent to which a small number of families had benefited from the allocation of houses or the basis of their privileged treatment. In particular, it was discretely silent on the question of political influence.

The leadership of the local UNP was composed of five officers—the president, vice-president, secretary, assistant secretary, and treasurer—and a

Table 1   Allocation of Houses to the Kukulewa UNP Committee and Their Close Kin

Name	Office[1]	Relationship to Other Officers[2]	Close Kin Who Obtained Houses[2]
1. Wijeratne	president	WB of 4	self,B,B,Z,MD,WZ,MH
2. Dinapala	secretary	KK	self
3. Jinadasa	treasurer		self,Z,B,FW,FD
4. Dharmaratne	vice-president	ZH of 1	self,B,Z,Z,F,WB,WB,WB,WMD
5. Dissanayake	asst. secretary	B of 10	self,B
6. Dayananda	member	B of 15	self,B
7. Premadasa	member		
8. Herathamy	member	WF of 12	self,S,D
9. Menikrala	member		self,D,D,S
10. Siriwardena	member	B of 5	self,B
11. Seneviratne	member	B of 13	self,B,Z
12. William	member	DH of 8	self,B,WB,WF
13. Wijepala	member	B of 11	B,B,Z
14. Sirisena	member	KK	
15. Jayatilike	member	B of 6	self,B,WB,WB,WZ,WF

[1]Office held in 1979.

[2]B = brother, D = daughter, F = father, H = husband, M = mother, S = son, Z = sister, WD = wife's daughter, WB = wife's brother, etc.; MD and FD = half-sibling; FW = stepmother, MH = stepfather; KK = resident of Kuda Kapirigama.

committee of ten other members. In 1980 Kukulewa shared a local branch of the party with the small adjacent hamlet of Kuda Kapirigama, and the secretary and one other committee member were from that hamlet. As the housing project was intended to benefit Kukulewa these two men were not strictly eligible to receive houses, but Dinapala, the secretary of the UNP, did nevertheless obtain one, although he never moved into it.[1] Only two of the other thirteen party officials failed to get houses. Both were already alienated from the rest of the leadership. One was Wijepala, whose brother was also on the committee and obtained a house. The other was Premadasa, who had joined the local branch when it was started in 1975 but who was closely related to the most prominent supporters of the SLFP in Kukulewa. The eleven UNP party leaders in Kukulewa who received houses for themselves also obtained them for their close kin, here defined to include children, siblings, parents, parents-in-law and siblings-in-law. A total of thirty houses were given either to these eleven leaders or to their close kin (table 1).

In fact, the allocations were even more densely concentrated than this figure suggests, because a number of the party leaders were closely related to one another. Dissanayake and Siriwardena were brothers, as were Dayananda and Jayatilike, as well as Wijepala and Seneviratne. William was Herathamy's son-in-law. Jayatilike was married to a sister of Dharmaratne, who in turn was married to a sister of Wijeratne. Leaving aside more distant relationships the party leaders could be grouped into eight, or even as few as six, clusters of close kin that obtained thirty houses between them. Herathamy and his son-in-law William, for example, received four houses—one for each of them, a third for Herathamy's son, and a fourth for William's brother. And Menikrala secured houses for a son and two daughters as well as for himself.

The greatest concentration was among the principal officers of the party, several of whom were close relatives of one another. Not only was Dharmaratne, the vice-president, married to a sister of Wijeratne, the president, but Wijeratne and Jinadasa, the treasurer, were first cross-cousins, the children of a brother and sister. These three men between them obtained fourteen houses for themselves and their close kin. By this time Jinadasa and Wijeratne were unquestionably the most powerful men in Samadigama. Jinadasa had been treasurer of the UNP since 1975, and treasurer of the rural development society (RDS) since 1977. Wijeratne had been assistant secretary of the UNP from 1975 to 1979, when he became president, and president of the RDS from 1974 to 1977, at which time he became secretary. It was these two, both of them about age forty in 1980, who had organized and led the opposition to Naidurala and who had taken control of the local UNP at the critical time when allocation of the houses was being decided. Jinadasa in particular had worked hard on behalf of the party for several years and had established connections with a number of influential people outside the village. This had enhanced his access to politicians, in dealing with whom he showed greater sophistication than men like Naidurala, whose experience was largely limited to encounters with villagers like themselves.

Jinadasa: I am not like Naidurala. I went with Mr. Herath to all his public meetings before the 1977 election. I also took part in the demonstrations led by Mr. J. R. Jayewardene. I even went to Colombo to take part in the non-violent protests against Mrs. Bandaranaike's government. We were attacked by the police on that occasion. Naidurala never participated in those kinds of activities.

It was I who made Naidurala president of the UNP branch. It was I who asked our boys to vote for him to be president. But when he became president he forgot about all that and worked against us. I'm not angry with him, but I have to tell the truth. Naidurala is a good man but he has a bad mouth. He doesn't know what to say or when to say it. He doesn't know how to speak to people.

Mr. Herath, the MP, used to call him *ayiyā* (elder brother), and he used to call Mr. Herath *apē hura* (our chief, cousin [a term of familiarity]). Then after the election in 1977, when Mr. Herath became our MP, there was a reception for him at Rampathwila school. Naidurala, Wijeratne, and I went there. Before we went I told Naidurala not to address Mr. Herath as hura any more. I advised him to call him member of parliament. When Mr. Herath saw Naidurala he greeted him by asking "how are you, ayiyā?" And then Naidurala went up to him and embraced him and said, "*malli* (younger brother), we came here to celebrate your victory. How happy we are that you won." The MP was very annoyed, but he controlled his feelings and didn't say anything. I was embarrassed to see Naidurala behave like that, and I came home without him. That is why I say he doesn't know what to say or when to say it.

Jinadasa was unlike his fellow villagers in that he had spent most of his working life outside Kukulewa, and after the UNP was returned to power he was able to take advantage of his familiarity with the larger political world, and his sophistication in dealing with its representatives, by effectively brokering relations between the village and external power holders. But this also served to put some distance between him and other villagers, and thus reinforced another source of his distinctiveness that was not at all the product of his familiarity with the world outside Kukulewa. Jinadasa and his cross-cousin Wijeratne were both born and raised in Kukulewa, but the brother and sister, who were the father of one and the mother of the other, were not native members of the Vedda variga (caste). They were the children of Albert Fernando and his wife Millie, who had come to Anuradhapura District from the Western Province and were members of the Karava (Fisherman) caste.

The Fernando Family

Albert Fernando first came to Kukulewa in 1920 as an overseer in the Survey Department. When he retired from government service in 1924 he settled in the village and his wife opened a small shop. The Fernandos, who were a Catholic couple, had three children, two sons and a daughter, of whom the eldest was born in 1920. After their daughter was born in 1924, Albert's sister's daughter Podi Nona, a girl of about thirteen, also joined the household to help take care of the children while Millie ran the shop. A year or two later, Podi Nona began an affair with a young man in the village named Bandathe, with whom she went to live and whom she later married. The marriage violated the rule of variga endogamy, and many villagers shunned the young couple, who went to live three or four miles away in the small market center of Sippukulama. But after the birth of their only child, Tikiribanda, more amicable relations were reestablished, and the couple returned to Kukulewa. Bandathe went before the *variga sabha* (caste court) and won its approval to pay the fine of 550 silver coins that legitimated his marriage and guaranteed acceptance of Podi Nona's children as members of the Vedda variga.[2]

A few years later Bandathe succeeded to the position of vel vidāne (irrigation headman) and began to establish the autocratic power that was to make him the dominant figure in Kukulewa for the next thirty years. Throughout that time the Fernandos were among his closest allies and staunchest supporters.

Albert Fernando died in 1927, just before the birth of his second son. His widow remarried, but after a few years her new husband, who was an itinerant trader, moved to Trincomalee, where he was later joined by her elder son, Anthony. Millie herself remained in Kukulewa with her daughter and younger son, and continued to run the shop. In 1939 her daughter began an affair with a villager named Punchibanda.

Anthony: I was not in Kukulewa when that happened. I was living in Trincomalee with my stepfather. My mother told us that Rosalyn had gone to live with Punchibanda. She said that Rosalyn and Punchibanda had been carrying on an affair for some time. When she learned about it she warned Rosalyn against it, but Rosalyn left home and moved into Punchibanda's house, where she was accepted by his father. When my stepfather heard about this he came to the village and insisted that they get married. But there were objections. They had to get the approval of the variga court.

Kandathe: In those days, when variga rules were effective, there were restrictions on marriages outside the variga. Our men were allowed to marry women from outside, but they had to get the approval of the variga court. Our women, on the other hand, were never given in marriage to outsiders. Bandathe Vidane didn't have much difficulty getting the approval of the variga court when he married Podi Nona. That's because Kapuva, who was vel vidāne at the time, wanted Bandathe to be his successor. But Rosalyn's marriage was one that caused some trouble. Punchibanda's family was shunned for a while even though it had been one of the most respected families in the village. Then Punchibanda's father went to offer betel leaves to Seerala and Undiyarala Lekam, who were members of the court, and asked them to approve the marriage. He had to pay a fine of 550 silver coins and feed the whole village for three days, but that settled the matter.

Anthony: When a person was taken into the variga with the approval of the court no one could afterwards look down on him. If someone then said that he was an outsider he could complain to the variga court and the offender would be fined. The court's decision was final. But although Rosalyn was taken into the Vedda variga, others in our family were still treated as outsiders.

Thus Rosalyn's children, of whom there were eventually ten, were fully accepted as Veddas in a way that her brothers' children were not to be. Anthony married an outsider of mixed Buddhist and Catholic parentage and returned to Kukulewa in 1947 to take over the running of his mother's shop. He made no attempt to associate his own inherited identity with that of his neighbors, except in the playful sense of his favorite saying that Karava people hunt in the sea while Veddas hunt in the jungle. His younger brother, James, was somewhat more assimilated. Like other villagers James made his living from cultivation, and he married a woman who was Vedda by birth but who had been adopted and raised by a Goyigama family. The marriage was not brought before the variga court and its status remained uncertain, but many people who treated Anthony's family as outsiders included James's family in the category of apē minissu (our people).

In the 1950s Anthony began an affair with a married woman in Kukulewa, which offended some people but which others tolerated because of the support that Anthony provided. Ukkuhamy's husband was an epileptic who suffered the misfortune of falling into a fire during one of his seizures. His burns left him crippled, and he was never able to work again. Anthony took care of the family and fathered Ukkuhamy's next seven children. Eventually, after her husband's death in 1971, he left his own wife and moved in with her.

Liaisons that crossed variga lines became increasingly common after the 1940s, and there was less unanimity in opposing them.[3] Older villagers attributed the change to the decline of the variga court. Appointments to the courts of the different varigas had been made by the Vanniya aristocrats who regularly occupied the position of rate mahatmaya during the British administration, and the rate mahatmayas had used this privilege to bolster their authority in the district. But the office of rate mahatmaya was replaced in 1938 by that of a regularly appointed civil servant, the divisional revenue officer, and thereafter the Vanniya aristocrats gradually lost interest in maintaining the court system.

Kandathe: Members of the variga court used to be appointed by the rate mahatmaya, who always came from one of the old aristocratic families. The rate mahatmaya appointed both the members of the variga court and the vel vidāne.

On the day of his appointment a new member of the court was given his robes of office, which included a hat, a cane, and so on. The villagers received the new member, and he had to feast both the people in his own village and members of the court who lived in other villages. After the feast there would be a meeting at the new member's house at which other members of the court explained the powers that were now vested in the new member. They would say, "You people take care. Don't violate the laws of the variga. This man is a new cobra. His teeth are not broken. So don't you women run away with outsiders. He can tear your limbs, and he can punish you as he likes. So beware of him, and don't break the laws of the variga."

That was how they maintained the laws of the variga in those days. But when the rule of the rate mahatmayas was ended the variga court fell into decay. After that our women got married to men of other varigas, and our men got married to women of other varigas. At first the villagers opposed such marriages, but there was nobody to punish offenders.

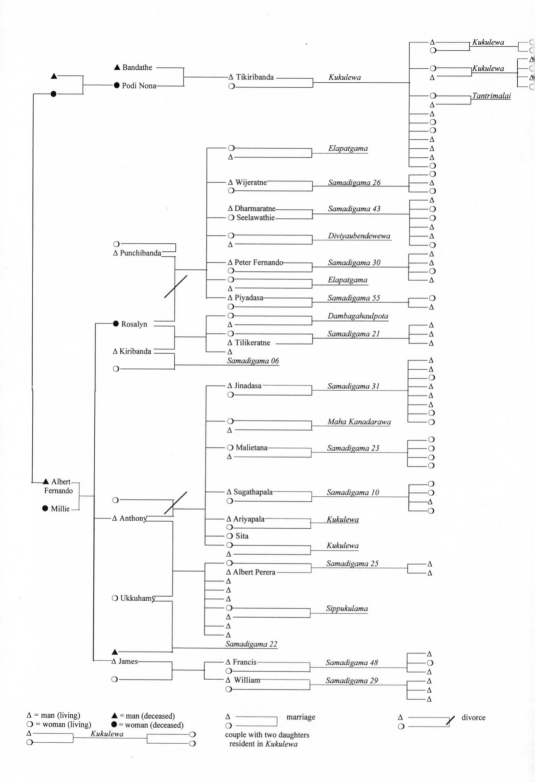

Δ = man (living)   ▲ = man (deceased)
○ = woman (living)   ● = woman (deceased)

Δ ——————� Kukulewa
○ ——————⎤   ⎡——————— ○
couple with two daughters
resident in Kukulewa

Δ ——————⎤ marriage
○ ——————⎦

Δ ——————／ divorce
○

One such marriage that stirred some opposition but no organized retribution was that of Anthony's oldest son, Jinadasa.

Kandathe: I went to sign the register as a witness to Jinadasa's marriage. Bandathe Vidane also went because his first wife was Anthony's *näna* (cross-cousin). But apart from Bandathe and Kiribanda, Rosalyn's second husband, I was the only person from the village to attend the wedding. Kalubanda was also invited, but he was afraid that people would look down on him, so he didn't go.

Anthony's recollections of the event were somewhat different.

Anthony: Jinadasa wanted to marry Tikirala's daughter, Anulawathie. When I came to know of it I asked Tikirala if he was prepared to give his daughter in marriage to my son. He said he had no objection if that was what the girl wanted. His wife agreed with him. Then they talked it over with their son and he also approved. Some villagers had a few things to say but most had no objection to the marriage. We held a big wedding ceremony and Vedda people came from villages as far away as Welewa and Elapatgama. No one boycotted my shop because of the marriage, and my business wasn't hurt in any way.

In the twenty years after Jinadasa's marriage the number of connections between the Fernandos and the Kukulewa Veddas increased sharply and, to some minds, alarmingly. Anthony's two oldest daughters married outsiders, but another daughter and two other sons besides Jinadasa married within the village. Six of Rosalyn's children also married within Kukulewa, although there was no question of impropriety in these cases, since Rosalyn's marriage had been legitimated by the variga court. And one of James's sons married a Kukulewa woman, while the other brought in a wife from outside.

Twelve Kukulewa villagers married other outsiders, unrelated to the Fernandos, during the same period, but these were isolated links that produced nothing like the dense network of alliances that connected the Veddas to the descendants of Albert and Millie Fernando. Nevertheless,

---

The Fernando family in Kukulewa and Samadigama. Names are given only for individuals mentioned in the text. Where Samadigama is the place of residence, the number given is that of the house allocated under the Village Awakening Program.

the number of these marriages suggests a greater tolerance of cross-caste alliances than had formerly prevailed, and indeed many villagers came to share the sentiments expressed by Ukkubanda.

Ukkubanda: Twenty or thirty years ago we never gave our women in marriage to outsiders. Occasionally our men married women from outside the variga, and for that they had to get the permission of the variga court. But after the court approved the marriage, the couple was accepted as belonging to the variga. Rosalyn's marriage was like that, and so her children are considered Veddas. But when the rule of the raṭe mahatmayas was ended all those regulations disappeared. Now we treat anyone who marries into our variga as belonging to the variga. After all, we're all human beings.

There are a few people who still hold to those old customs, but even among their children you'll find that some are married to outsiders. For example, Muthubanda opposed his daughter's marriage to Anthony's son Ariyapala. But he didn't object to his son's marriage to an outsider in Maha Kanadarawa. I am a Vedda myself, but I don't take those kinds of things very seriously.

On the other hand, there were still some families in Kukulewa in 1983 that refused to participate with the Fernandos in ceremonial events such as weddings and funerals. Kadirathe, whose daughter was married to one of Anthony's sons, claimed to have had nothing to do with his daughter for the past eight years, even though she lived less than a half-mile from him. Moreover, no one forgot where the Fernandos had come from, and since the demise of the variga court no formal sanctions were applied against them when they said so.

Kandathe: In those days, after the variga court had approved someone's marriage to an outsider, no one dared to scorn the couple. But now when there's an argument someone will say, "you bitch, you're married to a Karava man."

Thus, despite the number of marriages that connected them, some Kukulewa Veddas strove to hold the Fernandos at a certain social distance, and none forgot their foreign origin. But this may have stemmed less from a lingering inclination to maintain variga exclusiveness than from apprehension of a particular family. The Fernandos were more exposed to outside ways and urban manners than were most villagers, and much of their behavior did not readily conform to traditional Kukulewa standards of propriety. They were widely perceived to be ill-mannered, loud, violent, and immoral. Moreover, there were a lot of them, and in the struggle over the houses in Samadigama they had shown an unrivalled capacity for disciplined organization that had brought them tangible results. When the sixty houses were distributed, thirteen of them were allocated to direct descendants of Albert and Millie Fernando, and already there were the first stirrings of concern that what had been created was not a housing development for Kukulewa but a private estate for the Fernandos.

Chapter 8   *Life in Samadigama*

THE PEOPLE WHO moved to Samadi-
gama at the beginning of 1980 were proud of their new houses and had
great hopes of creating a new community. Not everything they had been
promised had been provided, and in particular the lack of new employment opportunities was keenly felt. However, there was always hope that
these would come later, and in the meanwhile there were sufficient public
facilities, besides the houses themselves, to lay the basis for the new community. The need for a post office may have been less than pressing, but
the cooperative store next door was a great convenience, making food-
stuffs and other small items readily available, as well as the ration goods
provided to welfare recipients. The bo-tree planted by the prime minister
became the sacred center of the village, and close to it stood the community building, with space for meetings and other collective activities. The
community building was constructed with help from the Sarvodaya Shramadana Movement, which also trained Jinadasa's youngest sister, Sita,
and sent her back to Samadigama to teach preschool classes and to act as
community organizer. Also much appreciated were the two deep tube-
wells from which water could be pumped even in the last months of the
dry season, when the older wells were often exhausted. But it was in the
houses themselves that the people found the greatest satisfaction.

Menikrala: I had no land, nothing in Kukulewa. May Prime Minister Premadasa
attain nirvāṇa! May the gods bless him! He gave us houses. We are happier
here.

Ranmenike, a woman of Samadigama: Our old house in Kukulewa was too
small. There wasn't room to move about in it, but we didn't have the money to
build a bigger place. This house is big enough for the whole family. I can use
one part to store millet, another to keep food and kitchen items, and another

as a bedroom. The old house needed repairs all the time. But even though we replastered the floor regularly we couldn't keep it clean. During the rainy season there were all kinds of problems. Water would trickle through the roof and the floor was always damp. White ants would destroy anything lying on the floor, and then there were snakes. There was no way to rest in those houses, even in our sleep, because they had no proper doors or windows. There was no security at all. But these houses are safe and easy to keep clean, and we don't have to repair them all the time.

Karunaratne, a young man of Samadigama: The roofs of the old houses have to be repaired every year, but now, without enough water for paddy cultivation, there's a shortage of straw. The people of Kukulewa are facing that problem, and so would we be if we were still there. But these new houses don't need that kind of repair. The only problem with the new houses is that it gets too hot inside them during the day. The old houses are better in that respect.

For several months after Samadigama was opened the hostility between those who had received houses and those who had been left behind in Kukulewa remained very intense. Families were split apart, and even close kin stopped visiting one another. Bitter resentment on one side was matched by jealous protection of the new assets on the other.

Wimaladasa: When Samadigama was opened the people left in Kukulewa were very upset, especially the UNP supporters who were not given houses. And SLFP supporters were angry because the houses were not distributed among the mul pavul. On their side the Samadigama people didn't allow the Kukulewa villagers to use either their wells or the cooperative store. Several times Kukulewa boys who went to buy things at the cooperative were assaulted. After that the Kukulewa people complained to the AGA, and he warned the leaders in Samadigama that he would have the cooperative closed if they didn't allow Kukulewa people to use it. "You can't have a cooperative just for sixty families," he said. "This cooperative is for both Samadigama and Kukulewa."

Appurala, a resident of Kukulewa: The people who moved to Samadigama were very proud of their new houses. They told us not to come to their wells for water. So we stopped going there. We were even harassed at the cooperative store. They said to us, "Why are you coming to the Samadigama cooperative? You can have your own cooperative in Kukulewa." When the MP heard that we were not allowed to use the wells he came to Samadigama and told those people off. After that we had no more trouble.

As time went on, the bonds of kinship began to reassert themselves and the level of hostility subsided. Ties were reestablished, and the people of one village began again to attend weddings, funerals, and puberty ceremonies in the other. Kukulewa people came to Samadigama to get water from the new wells, especially during the long dry season, and were no longer challenged when they did so. Members of the two villages began to mix more freely at the cooperative store and at the small private shops, as well as at work. Some people even came to believe that the anger and resentment were things of the past.

Karunaratne: When we came to Samadigama in 1980 it was as though we were all members of a single family. There was unity among us, and good feelings toward one another. But for a time we had nothing to do with Kukulewa people because those who were not given houses were jealous of us. Now we are again on good terms with the people of Kukulewa. Those little jealousies belong to the past and have been forgotten.

Trying to Make a Living

Because the Samadigama development project did not in the end provide any boost to production or any new jobs after its own completion, the residents of the new settlement continued to make their living much as they had done before the move. Those who held irrigated land in Kukulewa retained possession of it, but for three successive years the annual monsoon rains failed to fill the village tanks and paddy cultivation was minimal. The prolonged drought caused great hardship but was by no means unprecedented, and villagers knew better than to stake their livelihood on the uncertainties of irrigated agriculture. Chena cultivation, which produced a crop even in years of poor rainfall, was their first priority, and beyond that there was a demand for casual labor outside the village.

As described in chapter 4, dry-land cultivation was becoming increasingly commercialized in the early 1980s. Everyone still grew millet, the traditional subsistence crop, along with a mixture of vegetables, but those who could afford the investment also began to produce larger quantities of other crops, particularly legumes such as cowpea and gram, specifically for sale on the market. A few villagers also began to grow tobacco.

Almost every household sent some of its members outside the village to work for wages, either in commercial dry-land production or in the paddy fields of villages with superior irrigation facilities, or for construction work in one of the state's large development projects. This last was mainly an option for groups of young men, who would leave the village for two or three weeks at a time to find work in a labor camp. Similar gangs of laborers were occasionally also recruited for agricultural work under the big Mahaweli River Development Project.

At the same time there was a growing demand for female labor. Women had always worked as cultivators within the village, both in the chenas and in the paddy fields, but now they were also finding wage labor outside, although they did not go as far afield as the men. Unmarried women and others without the responsibility of small children were best able to seize this opportunity, and they began to translate their enhanced earning capacity into greater social independence, to the consternation of their parents, husbands and brothers.

Punchihamy, a young woman in Samadigama: I like to work as a wage laborer. I like very much to get away from home. I used to do wage labor before I was married. But my husband wouldn't allow me to continue. He used to come home drunk and beat me because I wanted to go for wage labor. That's why I left him.

I don't have those kinds of problems any longer. I am satisfied now. I can go to a place and work there for some time, and there's no one to order me about. I am free to do what I like.

Ukkubanda, a resident of Samadigama: It used to be that our women stayed home to take care of the children. They never went for wage labor. If they went to work in the chena they went with their husbands or grown-up children. Married women with children also used to go to reap the paddy harvest, but unmarried women never went. They stayed behind and looked after the house.

Now our daughters enjoy a lot more freedom. You see those girls in Samadigama. They're worse than young men. They go where they like and stay away from home for days at a time.

The change came after they started doing wage labor. Their parents can't control them when they're away. But parents have to let them go for wages because of their poverty.

It used to be expected that unmarried girls were virgins. But I doubt if any of these girls are virgins today. They know much more about life than their mothers.

James, resident of Kukulewa: Ten or fifteen years ago nobody in the village sent young girls for wage labor. Only women with several children did wage labor, either in Kukulewa or in neighboring villages. Mostly it was harvesting paddy in the fields and millet in the chenas.

Now you can see lots of young women going for wage labor. They go outside because there's not much work in the village. As far as I can remember this started about 1977. They are hired to work in cowpea, gram, and gingelly cultivation. Women can do that kind of thing because it doesn't involve heavy work like clearing jungle.

In those days it wasn't necessary for villagers to send their young women for wage labor. Chena cultivation gave good yields that were enough for the whole year. But as the population grew, more and more jungle was cleared for chenas, and eventually all the jungle was cut down. Now there's no jungle for chena cultivation and no water for paddy. That's why we have to go out of the village for wage labor.

Most employment remained tied to the agricultural cycle and in the drought years there were long periods when little work was available to either men or women. The government provided relief work at some of the hardest times, and most families in the village were eligible for welfare, but the struggle to sustain a family was unremitting.

Those who were best able to endure it were the seven men in Samadigama who were regularly employed. All seven had obtained their jobs through political influence, and five of them were members of the Fernando family. Jinadasa worked as a driver for the Ceylon Petroleum Corporation, his brother Sugathapala was a laborer for the Mihintale District Development Council, and his half-sister's husband Albert Perera, who had married into the village from the south coast, worked at the local depot of the Highways Department. James's two sons were also employed, Francis with the Highways Department and William as a platelayer on the railways.

Under these conditions even the monthly installment payment of thirty rupees that the villagers had to make on their houses came to be felt as a heavy burden. People recalled that when they agreed to the payment it was in anticipation that the government would also provide the jobs that would enable them to pay it.

Ranbanda, a Samadigama householder: Now we have the houses, but we don't have the rent money. If all sixty families got together and refused to pay they would have to take action against all of us. But those who have jobs have the rent deducted from their wages, so we all have to pay it. Otherwise we would be sent to jail.

We can't do anything together because there's no unity here. Before the election the MP told us not to pay the rent money. At that time we were paying thirty rupees a month. So on his advice we stopped making the payments. Now the Housing Department is demanding that we pay forty rupees a month.

We can't pay the rent because the government didn't do what it promised. It didn't give us the factory, the new lands, the collective farm, or the credit for animal breeding. So it's not our fault. I have seven daughters whom I have to feed, and there is no work for me to earn my living. How can they expect me to pay the rent money?

Disputes and Conflict

In the years after 1980 the faction led by Jinadasa and Wijeratne worked to consolidate its hold over the village. The local branch of the UNP was reconstituted in 1982, and separate organizations were set up in Kukulewa, where Naidurala reemerged as president, and in the Goyigama caste hamlet of Kuda Kapirigama, whose few inhabitants had previously belonged to the same branch as the people of Kukulewa and Samadigama.

This opened up the position of secretary, which had been held since 1975 by Dinapala of Kuda Kapirigama. At the meeting held in November to elect new officers for the Samadigama branch, Wijeratne (the former president) became secretary, Jinadasa (the former treasurer) became president, and Sugathapala, Jinadasa's younger brother, became treasurer. At the same meeting, and for the first time, the members also elected women to the committee. Two of the three women elected, Malietana and Sita, were Jinadasa's sisters.

Demons and Development

The UNP held another meeting two weeks later in preparation for the forthcoming national referendum. J. R. Jayewardene had been reelected president of Sri Lanka in October, and now a referendum was being held to vote on his proposal that parliamentary elections be deferred for five years. The president had warned UNP members of parliament that he would hold by-elections in any constituency that did not vote affirmatively on the referendum issue, and the effort to secure the vote was vigorous. Jinadasa told the meeting in Samadigama that the people should be grateful to the government for the benefits it had provided them and that to ensure government assistance in the future they should vote for the lamp, the symbol for an affirmative vote. Afterward the sign of the lamp and the green colors of the UNP appeared on all the houses in Samadigama.

Jinadasa's leadership, however, was increasingly being experienced as tyranny. Villagers complained that in the past he had been willing to listen and discuss things with other people but that now he and his allies, especially Wijeratne and Sugathapala, made all decisions on their own and then imposed them on everyone else. They were able to do this because of their superior organization and because they were willing to use violence. Suspicions also grew that the party leaders were misappropriating funds. Feeling excluded and oppressed, a number of those who had earlier been Jinadasa's firm supporters withdrew from village politics and even began to look wistfully back to Kukulewa.

Herathamy: Jinadasa led the fight we had with Naidurala so we elected him president of the UNP. That made him more powerful. But in those days he would still listen to us, and when we came to Samadigama in 1980 we were all like members of a single family. Our kinsmen in Kukulewa were against us then, and we were closely allied to Jinadasa's family.

But Jinadasa and Wijeratne took advantage of their power and got up to all kinds of corruption. They collected money from villagers telling them it would be used to get more benefits, but then they didn't do anything with it. When we realized what was going on, we took no further interest in party political activities.

I remember one occasion when Menikrala criticized Wijeratne about the use of funds collected from the villagers. Menikrala had so many problems after that. Jinadasa ordered him to get out of his house. And he was expelled from his position as a member of the UNP committee.

James once criticized Jinadasa for not giving him a house. Jinadasa hit him with a brick, and James's injuries were so bad he had to be admitted to the hospital.

I am not on good terms with Jinadasa now. Nor are most of the villagers. But we can't do anything about it because he has the power. The MP believes what Jinadasa says, and if the MP tells us to get out of the houses we will have to go. So we keep quiet.

Menikrala: Jinadasa and his gang are rogues. They collect money from the villagers for their expenses, saying they're going to discuss things with the MP in order to get more benefits for the village. But then they don't go to meet him. In fact they can't go to meet him. They're afraid to go because the MP knows what they're doing here. They're simply robbing people of their few coins.

I remember once we organized a meeting that we invited the MP to attend. The UNP branch decided to collect some money from the villagers for the meeting, and Wijeratne and I were appointed to collect it. Then the MP told us that he wouldn't be able to come, so we cancelled the meeting. I gave the money I had collected back to the villagers, but Wijeratne kept what he had collected and spent it on himself. He collects dues from the villagers every month. That's the way he keeps his family alive.

At the beginning we helped Jinadasa become leader of the UNP because we were against Naidurala. But now we can't get rid of him. His family is well organized. If we speak against him at a meeting it ends up in a fight. Before a meeting they decide who will be president, who will hold this or that position, and so on. And their decision is final. We are powerless. We can't criticize them.

I don't go to branch meetings anymore. I have no connection with them whatsoever. But I have nowhere else to go. If I had somewhere else to go I would leave this place.

Mudalihamy: I used to go to the meetings that Jinadasa's people organized in the community building. But I stopped going after Wijeratne misused party funds. He collected money saying he would use it to go to meet the MP in order to get more benefits for us. But it turned out in fact that he didn't go. I don't like living in Samadigama. Kukulewa is much better.

By 1983 social relations in Samadigama had seriously deteriorated. Disputes were frequent, and the evening quiet was often disturbed by the sounds of fierce argument and personal abuse. Members of Jinadasa's faction were often at the center of these affrays.

Sumanadasa: My brother and I both had houses along the road beyond Samadigama. Then my brother sold his land and house to Jinadasa's brother Ariyapala and moved to Tantrimalai. I didn't want to be living near Jinadasa's people, so I sold my house and land as well and built a new place behind my father-in-law's house.

When Jinadasa heard about it he came to my father-in-law, Menikrala, and told us off. He threatened us and said that I couldn't build a house in his village without his permission. He said, "You wait. I will inform the GA and he will do what is necessary. Get ready to leave."

Menikrala: We would be much happier here if it wasn't for Jinadasa. When I was on good terms with him I had no trouble, but now he's angry with me. He says, "This is my village. These are my houses. I gave you these houses. You must get out if I say so."

It's true that Jinadasa did a lot for Samadigama. It was at his request that the MP built the houses here. But I don't think the houses belong to him. The houses and the land in Samadigama belong to the government. Jinadasa has no right to order us out of the houses. I'm going to ask the MP if the houses belong to Jinadasa.

Many of the disputes focused on the behavior of the young women in the village, among whom Malietana and Sita, Jinadasa's sisters, were particularly prominent. Malietana was thirty-one years old in 1983, a divorced woman with four children. She had been married to an outsider, a man from Matara on the south coast, but the couple had separated soon after their first child was born. Malietana had then found work as a domestic servant in Anuradhapura, but had returned to Kukulewa when she became pregnant. She made her living in the village as a wage laborer, but was also reputed to supplement her income by entertaining a succession of paying lovers, by whom she had her two youngest children. In early 1983 she was carrying on an affair with Heratbanda, who was trying to run a small shop in Samadigama.

Her sister, Sita, was eighteen years old and unmarried, but she lived on her own in the small room at the back of the community building, where she was employed by Sarvodaya to conduct preschool classes and organize other community activities. Her private room and her need to travel to Anuradhapura to visit Sarvodaya's regional headquarters afforded her unusual freedom of movement for a woman of her age, and she was said to take full advantage of her situation. Her half-brother Somaratne claimed that she was having an affair with a wealthy man in Anuradhapura who also came occasionally to visit her in Samadigama. But in early 1983 it was Heratbanda, her sister's lover, whom she was supposed to be about to marry.

The rivalry between the two sisters came to a head in late February when they fought one evening outside Malietana's house. Sita left the village the next morning and was gone for ten days, during which Malietana resumed her affair with Heratbanda. But one night, on her way back to her house from Heratbanda's shop, she was attacked and beaten by Heratbanda's uncle, who was angry at her disruption of his nephew's marriage to her sister.

A few weeks later there was a wedding in the village at which a number of young men became aggressively drunk. One of them was Gunatilike, a native of Kukulewa who claimed to have earlier enjoyed an affair with Malietana, but who had moved with his wife to the village of Tantrimalai. Amid the drinking and brawling Gunatilike went several times to Malietana's house and demanded to be let in. But Malietana locked the doors and sent her children to a relative's house, while she herself went to spend the night with Heratbanda. Gunatilike was accompanied by his sister's husband, who boasted loudly that Malietana was attracted to him but would not have him because he was not a *mudalāli* (trader, shopkeeper).

By early May, Heratbanda had gone broke and was no longer able to run his shop. This seemed to spell the end of his affair with Malietana, who now planned to go to Colombo to resume work as a domestic servant. Meanwhile, Sita was again absent from the village. According to her half-brother, she was trying to get an abortion. She returned, very sick, the same day that Malietana left. Her mother said she was suffering from a severe stomachache, but others who visited her said she was bleeding badly and suspected the effects of an incompetent abortion. The next day she was taken to hospital, where she was kept for several days.

The behavior of Malietana and Sita did nothing to enhance the reputation of the Fernandos among the more conservative villagers. But James was inclined to put most of the blame on the women's father (his brother,

Anthony), who had left his own family to live with Ukkuhamy and who was now trying to establish a shop in Sippukulama, three miles away on the main road from Anuradhapura to Trincomalee.

James: My brother is a very immoral man. He can't even walk upright. He is terribly weak and he can barely see anything, but every night he gropes his way from Sippukulama to Samadigama to sleep with Ukkuhamy. Sita is now at the right age to be married. But my brother isn't doing anything about it. So she's running about all over the place like a young man.

Anthony was in fact no longer coming home to Samadigama every night. He spent most of his time at his shop in Sippukulama. Jinadasa was also away from the village a good deal, staying mostly in Anuradhapura, close to his work at the Ceylon Petroleum Corporation. But he returned at the weekends to visit his family, and then he would spend long hours sitting on the bench near his house in the center of the village, where people continued to greet him respectfully. On these visits, apart from occasional outbursts, the resentment against him and his kinsmen was contained, and the conversations were usually amiable.

With Jinadasa absent from the village much of the time, Wijeratne, still secretary of the RDS and now also secretary of the UNP, assumed day-to-day leadership in the village. It was Wijeratne who supervised relief work in Samadigama, until the AGA accused him of including the names of dead people on the rolls, after which he was replaced by his half-sister's husband, Gunapala. But increasingly within Samadigama it was Jinadasa's brother Sugathapala, the treasurer of the UNP since 1982, who became the most feared agent of the Fernandos' power and rage.

Early in May a few men who had come together on a relief work party complained that Sugathapala was not taking proper care of his cattle but was allowing them to wander into other people's gardens where they were eating the crops. The next night Sugathapala got drunk and set out on a brawling tour of the village. His first stop was at the tube well, where he heard someone bathing in the dark.

Sugathapala: Who's the fucker washing at the well? This water is for drinking only, and I won't allow any son of a whore to bathe here. This well is in my charge. I am responsible for it. If anyone dares to wash at this well he'd better be superior to my father. I don't even let my father wash here. I don't care who you are. Even if you're a king, this is my law: don't use this well for washing.

Afterward Sugathapala went around the village making other threats. He stopped at the houses of Herathamy and Upasena and challenged them to come out and fight him.

Sugathapala: I will not let my cattle stray. I will not sell them. I will tie them to trees and let them starve to death. But you people remember not to come to the well to wash.

Speak out if you dare. Come out if you dare. This is our village. These are our houses. I am not a good man. I will interfere in anybody's business. I will poke my fingers into the affairs of all the villagers. Come out. Come out and fight.

No one came out and in the morning, when the area around the well was usually crowded, no one came to wash. Then about midday some members of Jinadasa's family came to the well and washed themselves. Sugathapala made no attempt to stop them. But his sister Malietana scolded Ausadhahamy's daughter for having washed at the well, and when Ausadhahamy heard about it he got into an argument with Malietana. Malietana went home to pick up a stick, and then headed toward Ausadhahamy's house to assault him. But she was intercepted and restrained by cooler heads.

Herathamy: Sugathapala's cattle come into our compounds and eat all our garden crops. They destroy our manioc plants, and we have to put up with it. We have to watch his cattle grazing in our gardens. That's what he wants.

We didn't bring our own cattle to Samadigama. We sold them before we came because there's not enough room in this village to raise animals. There are no fences. Sugathapala is the only person who brought cattle here. And now he's threatening us because we told him his cattle are straying and damaging our property. He's very angry. You heard how he abused us the other night. And then Malietana went to Ausadhahamy's house and challenged him to a fight. This village has three leaders now—Jinadasa, Sugathapala, and Malietana. We have to obey their orders. Are we going to have to put up with this forever? One day this village will be a field of blood.

It's not because we're afraid of them that we keep quiet. We have to consider our families. If we fight with them it will end in murder. We would be sent to jail and our children would starve. I'm not going to support the UNP anymore. I'm going to collect as many people as possible in Samadigama and join up with Wimaladasa in Kukulewa. After all, his people are our people.

And I want to tape record what Jinadasa and Sugathapala say when they get angry. Then I'll send the tape to the prime minister. He'll soon say whether the houses belong to Jinadasa or to the government.

Herathamy's sentiments were shared by others. Many people who had backed Jinadasa and Wijeratne against Naidurala, who had loyally supported the UNP, and who had enjoyed the reward of a new house, now turned against their former leaders. But they were afraid of Jinadasa and his henchmen, afraid both of their violence and their political connections, and they were scared their houses might yet be taken from them. So they chose to stay away from Jinadasa's meetings, rather than oppose him publicly, and they kept their resentment to themselves.

Jayaratne: Here in Samadigama I keep company only with two families, those of Ausadhahamy and Mudalihamy. I go to other people's houses only when it's absolutely necessary, for a funeral or wedding. But I have nothing at all to do with Jinadasa and his relatives.

When my children got into an argument with Jinadasa's children, he picked a fight with me. "Hand over the keys to my house and get out," is what he said. If I had any land in Kukulewa I would go there. Most of the people in Samadigama are fed up with all this and want to go too. If the government gave us some land we wouldn't hesitate to leave this wretched place.

We don't go to their meetings anymore. We have nothing at all to do with them. Jinadasa's people treat us like slaves and expect us to obey them whether what they do is right or wrong. But our people are not united and don't know how to organize. That's why we can't do anything against them.

Ausadhahamy: The Fernando family lived like dogs when they were in Kukulewa. They didn't dare threaten other people then. It's only since they came here to Samadigama that they have started to behave like kings. If I had a house in Kukulewa I would go back there.

Mudalihamy: Sugathapala is now making threats against people who won't allow his cattle to graze in their yards. But if his cows come into my yard I'll shoot them. And if those people come to fight with me it will be the end of them.

Life in Samadigama

Life has become very hard in Samadigama because of Jinadasa, Wijeratne, and their families. I keep company with Sellathe and Kapurāla and people like that who are our kind of people, our kin. I would prefer to live in Kukulewa with our relatives. The only good thing about this place is that the houses don't need repairs and are more comfortable when it's raining. But we can't eat the houses!

Life in Samadigama had indeed become very difficult. For the third successive year the monsoon rains had failed to fill the village tanks, and very little paddy cultivation was even attempted. Chena cultivation was rather more successful, but yields were less than normal; by April most households' stocks of millet were already running low. The showers that sometimes fell in April and May might have permitted an off-season crop of chilies or gingelly, but they too were insufficient, and with few opportunities for wage labor during the long dry season the villagers faced several months of very lean rations. The fortitude and equanimity with which they customarily confronted such familiar hardship were still evident, but the sense of communal solidarity that otherwise helped sustain them was seriously jeopardized by all the quarrels and resentment. On top of that, and perhaps even provoked by it, there occurred several manifestations of supernatural activity that now translated concern with social relations among the villagers themselves into an examination of their relations with the gods and demons.

Chapter 9   *Gods and Demons*

THE WORLD VIEW and ethos of Kuku-
lewa villagers were fundamentally shaped by the teachings of the Buddha.[1] Although there was no Buddhist temple *(vihara)* in the village, and
no resident monk *(bhikku),* and although most adults in 1983 were still
illiterate, all were familiar with the basic tenets of the Buddhist tradition
(Buddhagama). The villagers inhabited a morally informed universe in
which, in accordance with the law of *karma,* virtue would eventually receive its reward and vice would sooner or later be punished. They understood that *dukkha* (suffering, imperfection) was the result of attachment
to the sensual world and that the way to escape it was by means of ethical conduct, mental discipline, and the acquisition of wisdom, following
the path to nirvāṇa (release, enlightenment) that the Buddha had identified. Given the magnitude of the task, Kukulewa villagers did not expect
to complete this journey in their present lifetime, but they did aspire
to live virtuously enough to be reborn next time into more favorable
circumstances.

Release from worldly attachments, however, while unchallenged as the
supreme goal of the religious life, was often pushed into the background
by the more immediate imperatives of everyday existence. The ultimate
goal of tranquil detachment was thus commonly deferred, eclipsed by
more urgent efforts to ameliorate the pressing conditions of ordinary life.
These efforts often took the form of attempts to influence the supernatural
powers of gods and demons.

The Pantheon in Kukulewa

Just as in the Sinhala Buddhist pantheon described in Obeyesekere's
(1966) influential account, which was based on research in the Central
Province, the gods and demons of the Kukulewa Veddas composed a hier-

archy in which both merit and authority were concentrated at the top. The most powerful gods were also the most virtuous. They were benevolently disposed toward men and women, and for the most part only afflicted them when punishment was deserved. But these powerful gods were also as remote from the villagers' everyday lives as were the senior government officials with whom they were sometimes compared. Even Lord Buddha, who occupied the presidential position in the pantheon but who had delegated his authority to the gods, was present only in his exemplary teaching and his sacred relics. Having attained nirvāṇa, Lord Buddha was no longer involved in the world, and consequently one did not seek his active intervention in one's own mundane affairs.

Some of the virtuous gods *(mahatma deviyō)*, however, were more readily accessible than others. The great Kataragama was one such powerful god with whom the people of Kukulewa and Samadigama maintained an intimate association. Indeed they even claimed kinship with him, for Kataragama's consort Valliamma was born of a deer and raised in the jungle by Veddas until the god abducted her. Such were the high-handed ways of powerful gods (and powerful men as well), but they carried also an obligation, which Veddas invoked when they claimed that Kataragama was their *massina* (brother-in-law). Shrines dedicated to Kataragama were common in the Vedda villages of Anuradhapura District, and the majority of Vedda kapurālas (priests) were his servants.

Kukulewa villagers nevertheless ranked Kataragama, the protector of human beings from demons and sickness, below the elephant-headed god Pulleyar, the lord of the jungle. Each of the major gods was associated with a certain region of the country, within which his authority was particularly enhanced, and whereas Kataragama's principal shrine was in the southeast of Sri Lanka, Pulleyar was held to be lord of the irrigation tanks and jungle that composed the North Central Province. Moreover, Pulleyar, who protected chenas from wild animals and cattle from disease, was Kataragama's older brother and held his superior rank on that account alone. But if it was Pulleyar to whom the greater respect was due, and to whom offerings were therefore made even before Kataragama, it was the latter who was considered the more powerful in practical matters. Pulleyar was somewhat passive. Villagers described him, drawing on the parallel with secular authority, as being like a treasurer *(baṇḍagarika)*. He looked after things, and watched over the investments that people made in their chena cultivation. By contrast Kataragama was more active and willing to intervene in human affairs, to grant favors or to punish wrongdoers. And it was from Kataragama rather than Pulleyar that the inferior gods and demons, with whom villagers most frequently interacted, derived their delegated authority and license *(varam)*.

Two other gods whose protection was regularly sought were Ayiyana-yake and Illandari. Many people in Anuradhapura District regarded Ayiya-nayake, the lord of the tanks, as the supreme god of the region, but the villagers of Kukulewa and Samadigama, who gave priority to the jungle over the fields, awarded that place to Pulleyar. They made vows to Ayiyanayake and Illandari for the success of their paddy cultivation and offered them food at collective ceremonies, but otherwise afforded them scant concern.

Below the major gods, and deriving their authority from them, were a number of lesser gods who frequently involved themselves with local matters and thus received the attention that such proximity both invited and compelled. The status of several of these gods was ambiguous and uncertain. In the abstract, the categories *deva* (god; pl. *deviyō*) and *yaksa* (also *yakā*, demon; pl. *yakku*) were distinct and even mutually exclusive, but some individual beings moved back and forth between them, or were indifferently defined now as deva, now as yaksa. Kambili was one who was called both Kambili deva and Kambili yaksa. Likewise, Bahirava, the guardian of buried treasure, was sometimes identified as a yaksa, at other times as a deva who despatched his subordinate yakku, also called Bahirava, to do his work. The most versatile of all was Kadavara, who was often described as a yaksa but who was represented in myth as none other than the younger brother of Pulleyar and Kataragama.

Kalubanda told the story with great relish: The great gods Isvara and Umayangana had no children. Umayangana was very worried about it. But one day, as she went to take a bath, she felt like producing a child, and so she used her divine powers to create a beautiful prince about sixteen years old.

Isvara was very jealous of his wife because of her great beauty. He suspected that she might have lovers, so he mounted his elephant and went to the river where she was bathing. To his amazement he saw a young man sitting near the clothes that his wife had taken off in order to bathe. This made him very angry and without a moment's hesitation he dismounted, drew his sword, and cut off the young man's head, which fell into the river.

When Umayangana came to look for the prince she saw, to her horror, only his headless body. Then she saw Isvara and realized what had happened. "You have killed my son, my only son whom I created with my divine powers. Give him back his life. Give my son life or I will kill myself by jumping into the river," she threatened.

Isvara looked for the prince's head but could not find it. So he cut the head off his elephant and placed it on the body. He fastened it to the body with his divine powers, and then the prince came back to life. He was named Pulleyar.

Isvara then challenged his wife to use her powers to create more children. So she created seven more princes. When he saw them Isvara embraced them with fatherly affection. But one of the seven broke away. Six of the princes joined together in Isvara's embrace and became Kataragama, the god with six faces and twelve hands. The one that broke away was Kadavara.[2]

As this story intimates, Kadavara was something of a trickster. His appetites were less controlled than those of the virtuous gods, and he could not be relied upon always to act on the side of justice. In these respects he was more like a demon than a god. Villagers said that unless they made regular offerings to him he would ignore their requests and was likely to provoke all kinds of trouble. Kadavara's mischievous, unreliable, and somewhat amoral character jeopardized his status, and he was made subordinate to his brothers, Pulleyar and Kataragama, for whom he acted as watcher (murakārayā). But Kadavara did not even obey the god Kataragama unless he received his share of offerings.

There were two other gods, occasionally also described as demons, to whom the people of Kukulewa and Samadigama were especially attached. They were Deveni Pattini, or Second Pattini, the second of seven Pattinis according to local belief, and Kaludakada, the nephew of Minneriya deva. Kandappu, the famous anumätirāla (spirit medium) who died in 1978, was possessed by these two gods, and it was his intimate association with them as their vāhana kārayā (vehicle-man) that ensured the village's protection against the ravages of demons and disease. The two gods, along with their sacred ornaments (ābharana), had originally been brought to the village by Kandappu's father.

Kalubanda: Forty or fifty years ago Kandappu's father was just an ordinary villager like anybody else. Then, when he was about thirty-five years old, he was possessed (vāhila) by Deveni Pattini and became an anumätirāla. It is told that when he was in trance *(māyam)* the goddess possessing him said that the ornaments in Debalgala temple, near Moragahawela, belonged to her sister Lanka Pattini, and that she wanted to go there and bring them back to Kukulewa. When the Moragahawela villagers heard that Kukulewa people were coming to their village to take the goddess's ornaments, they asked the priest (kapurāla) of the temple to put them under lock and key. They said, "we will not give any ornaments to those Veddas. We will send them back with tortoise shells."

When the Kukulewa people arrived at Moragahawela, the kapurāla invited Kandappu's father to use his powers to open the door into the room that held the ornaments. The anumātirāla then went into trance and touched the door, which immediately flew open. There were seven caskets in the room, and he selected the one that belonged to Lanka Pattini.

The Moragahawela villagers were now afraid of the goddess and they knelt before her to ask for mercy. They were ordered to carry the casket to Kukulewa.

Those ornaments can be seen in their casket even now, in the *dēvālē* (shrine) in Kandappu's compound. As long as they remain there no one can send a demon against the people of Kukulewa. Demons are scared to come to Kukulewa. They know the power of Kaludakada and Deveni Pattini.

In addition to Kaludakada and Deveni Pattini, Kadavara, Kambili, and Bahirava, the people of Kukulewa and Samadigama acknowledged a number of other lesser gods, but for the most part they scarcely bothered to identify them. These gods could, however, manifest themselves at any time, for example in dreams, and then an attempt might be made to determine who they were.

Below the gods, and subordinate if not always obedient to them, stood a host of demons. These too often remained unidentified, although the names of some, such as Mahasona, the demon of the graveyard, and Reriyakka, the demon with the thirst for blood, were well known. Unlike the gods, who were well disposed toward human beings, demons were malevolent, and their attention was generally unwelcome. But it was also difficult to avoid, because demons actually lived around the village and were a much more immediate presence than the superior gods.

Assault by a demon was a constant hazard of village life. But if the risk of attack could not be entirely eliminated, it could at least be minimized, by behaving cautiously at the times of day when demons were known to be most active and by avoiding, as far as possible, the kinds of places where they liked to lurk, such as graveyards and the vicinity of the tank bund. Amulets and magical spells (*mantras*) also provided a measure of protection, as did the company of others, for demons were most likely to attack someone who was alone. Both men and women might be visited by demons, but it was women who were more susceptible, especially during their menstrual periods, which attracted the demons' lust for blood. Painful menstruation, miscarriage, and difficult childbirth were all commonly attributed to demonic attack, and a high proportion of the rituals performed in the village were attempts to deal with problems of this kind.

Demons operated under the license (varam) of superior gods, who did not usually punish people unjustly, but their own actions were amoral, and the fright, sickness, and even death that could result from their appearance might seem to be inflicted quite arbitrarily. Demons had a voracious appetite for certain foods—especially fried foods, meat, and blood—and it was said that their main reason for attacking someone was the prospect of the offerings that would subsequently be made to them.

Kalubanda: Demons enjoy the offerings that are made to them. They like that food and get angry when it isn't given to them. If somebody makes an offering to a demon one year, he has to make it every year after that. Failure to do so makes the demon angry, and if the demon is angry he may possess the person concerned or make him ill. The demon doesn't care whether that person is virtuous or not. What he wants is his offering.

The appetite of demons suggests the usual way in which their attacks were treated. The victim consulted an appropriate specialist, who tried to determine what kind of offering would assuage the demon and persuade him to desist. The task was made easier if the victim could be induced to go into trance, for his movements were then believed to be the demon's movements and any words that he uttered were the words of the demon. This made it possible for a skilled practitioner to deal directly with the demon and negotiate the terms of an agreement.

Dingiribanda, the principal kapurāla in Kukulewa: When a woman is attacked by a demon she falls ill. She stops doing the work she usually does. She doesn't eat and she neglects her children. She suffers fever, chest pains, and dizziness.

We try to make her go into trance. If she is possessed by a demon he will ask for offerings. He will promise to leave her if an offering is made to him every year. He will also tell where he first saw her, how he possessed her, and so on.

When the offering is made the demon leaves the woman's body, but he doesn't leave her house. He stays there to look after her interests. But if his annual offering isn't made he will make the whole family sick.

There are some demons whose victims don't go into trance at all. They possess people but don't make them dance or speak through them. Only a *kaṭṭāḍiyā* (exorcist) can cure people who are under the influence of demons like that.

Demonic attacks were sometimes compelled by sorcery *(hūniyam)*, in which case the services of a kaṭṭāḍiyā were again required.

Mudalihamy: Demonic attack may be the result of sorcery. A person can make an offering to a demon and ask him to attack his enemy. The demon will do so without any concern for justice. A kaṭṭāḍiyā is needed to get rid of such demons. A kaṭṭāḍiyā can chase away demons with his magical powers, by chanting spells and invoking the aid of more powerful gods.

The lowest level of the pantheon, below even the demons and less powerful than them, was occupied by a final class of spirits, or ghosts, known as *prētas*.

Wannihamy: People who are miserly and don't spend money even for their basic requirements, like food and medicine, are destined to become prētas when they die. Such people have too much attachment to material wealth and don't gain merit by spending money on alms-giving.

Prētas are filthy. When someone is possessed by a prēta he stops washing. He goes around in rags and behaves just like a prēta himself.

A Charge of Sorcery

Demonic attack was not an everyday occurrence in Kukulewa and Samadigama, but it happened often enough to be accepted as one of the normal hazards of life. What excited unusual interest when Seelawathie was afflicted in June 1983 was the suggestion that her attack was the result of sorcery being practiced by the people of Kukulewa against the people of Samadigama.

Seelawathie was a thirty-five year old woman with six children, a daughter of Punchibanda and Rosalyn Fernando. She had been about eight years old when her parents separated, after which she was raised by her father and his parents. When her father moved to Diviyaubendewewa, to settle in the village of his new wife, Seelawathie stayed in Kukulewa and went to live with her mother and her stepfather, Kiribanda. She said that she was deeply attached to her mother, who, she claimed, loved her dearly, but Kiribanda did not like her coming to live with them. She married Dharmaratne when she was seventeen, and shortly afterward her mother died. Her married life was not satisfactory to her, and she described Dharmaratne as a man who came home drunk at night and beat her.

Seelawathie was closely related to several of the key figures in the struggle over the Samadigama houses. Naidurala was her father's younger brother, Wijeratne was her brother, and Jinadasa was her mother's brother's son. Dharmaratne, her husband, became vice-president of the UNP in 1979. Seelawathie was thus at the center of the cluster of close kin who had benefited most substantially from the housing project. Three of her brothers and a half-sister all received houses, as did her husband, one of his brothers, two of his sisters, and his father.

Seelawathie: One day in May I went out to the jungle to collect firewood and saw an *avatāra* (apparition, manifestation of a supernatural being). I got frightened *(baya unna)*. A few days later I fell ill with chest pains and felt faint. I took treatment at Tammanawa hospital, but that didn't make me any better. Some time later I went into trance, and my husband thought I might be possessed by a demon.

Dharmaratne: After she was brought back from Tammanawa she fell sick again and became unconscious *(sihi nathi unna)*, so I decided to consult an anumätirāla. The anumätirāla went into trance and told me that my wife was possessed by a demon. He said that if I made offerings to the demon it would be satisfied and wouldn't trouble my wife any more. So we went to Elapatwewa to meet the famous kattädiyä there. My wife went into trance again, and told the kattädiyä, "I am a demon sent by the people of Kukulewa to ruin the village. I come from Kadurugahagama. People from Kukulewa went there and asked a kattädiyä to send me to Samadigama to ruin it. I will go from house to house and destroy the whole village."

The demon refused to leave my wife's body, so the kattädiyä thrashed her with a coconut flower. After that the demon agreed to leave, on condition that we make an offering to him every year.

For the next two days her behavior was normal. But then she again fell ill and went into trance. This time the demon came out with the argument that the ceremony had not been properly performed. He said that the kaṭṭāḍiyā had not done anything to protect the house from evil spirits. He had not buried charmed stones in the four corners of the house.

I was very distressed by all this and went to see Ukkurala, a man in Kukulewa who knows how to deal with demons. He said he would try to cure her. She went into trance again, but this time the demon said nothing about sorcery. Instead he said, "I am prepared to leave her body if satisfactory offerings are made every year." So I promised to make an offering this month.

Later she went into trance again and told me not to worry about the cost of the offerings. The demon said, "I know how to get money for the offerings. You stay at home. There's no need for you to go anywhere looking for money."

I felt that something was going to happen to our family even before my wife became possessed. We began to hear unusual sounds. There was tapping on the doors and windows, and we even heard someone walking on the roof, which rattled and cracked under the weight. When my wife fell ill I saw peculiar dreams. One night I dreamed that two black dogs sprang on me. The next day I felt ill. I couldn't stand up. My whole body was aching with the weight of those two dogs that jumped on me. It's not just our family that has suffered this kind of trouble. First of all Malietana became possessed. She recovered only after several attempts were made to treat her. Then Jinadasa's mother fell sick. She was ill for months and only recovered after offerings were made. The next victim was Piyadasa, Ukkuhamy's son. And after that my wife's sister who is married to Tilikeratne went into trance. Tilikeratne had to spend a fortune to get rid of the demon possessing his wife. All these people are closely related to my wife.

My wife told us in trance that the demon possessing her had been sent by Kukulewa people to ruin this village. Those people are very angry with us because they didn't get houses in Samadigama. We must all get together and do something about this. What is happening to me today could happen to someone else tomorrow.

All the people of Samadigama helped us a lot when we were in trouble. They sent us food and money and everything. Even the people who were not on good terms with us came here. Almost everyone helped us in one way or another.

Tilikeratne: My wife was attacked and made ill by a demon. After she recovered, her sister, Seelawathie, was attacked. When she was in trance the demon possessing Seelawathie said that he had been sent by Kukulewa people and was not going to leave the village. He has come to destroy the whole village.

You can see how he goes from house to house. Malietana was possessed by this demon two years ago. Then Piyadasa was attacked. Jinadasa's mother also fell ill under the influence of this demon.

We have to do something to send the demon back. Otherwise it will ruin us. I spent a lot of money to get rid of the demon that was possessing my wife. I don't know what's going to happen now.

The charge of sorcery was not universally accepted. The words of a demon speaking through the voice of his victim compelled close attention, but one could not be sure that they were truthful. Demons were evasive and duplicitous creatures who often tried to conceal their real identities and intentions. In other words, they might be lying. It was always prudent, therefore, to scrutinize their words and actions closely, to see that they were correctly in character and to check for inconsistencies. This always left room for interpretations of what was happening that differed from those offered by the demon himself.

In the persistent atmosphere of bitterness and resentment between the two villages, the charge that Seelawathie's affliction was the result of sorcery by people in Kukulewa was explosive. But many people were more concerned to heal the breach than to widen it, especially those with close kin and longtime friends in both places. Kandathe was one such person. A respected *vedarāla* (doctor) and *uḍäkki kapuvā* (ritual drummer), he was strongly identified with the local UNP, of which he had been a committee member until 1979. He had been given a house in Samadigama, as had one of his sons and one of his sons-in-law, but he had not moved to the new village. His house there was occupied by another son, while he himself remained at his old place in Kukulewa, close to other kin and old neighbors. Kandathe was not convinced that sorcery was at work. He was more concerned to emphasize both its immorality and the fact that Kukulewa and Samadigama were a single community.

Kandathe: I myself was present when Seelawathie went into trance. The demon who is possessing her must be a powerful one. It may be Kadavara, who takes his authority from god Kataragama. I'm sure it's a powerful demon because he didn't obey the kaṭṭāḍiyā who performed the ritual. He was making all kinds of demands. I think Kadavara is angry with the people because they haven't made offerings to him for three years. That's why a demon has come to possess this woman.

It's a very bad thing to practice sorcery. Some people do that kind of thing in order to bring ruin on others. But Dharmaratne is very poor. Why should anyone practice sorcery on him?

It's not easy to send a demon to attack someone. People send demons to take revenge or to retaliate for something. Suppose you were to steal my cattle. I might send a demon against you. Or suppose you do something that damages my reputation, or that of my family. I might send a demon against you. But I never heard that Dharmaratne did such things. I don't believe it's sorcery.

It's true that people in Kukulewa were very angry over the allocation of houses. For a time the people of Samadigama and Kukulewa were like enemies. But after all they are our people. They wouldn't send demons against their own kin. That demon in the woman was just making trouble. He was telling lies to make things worse because the man who performed the ritual thrashed him.

It was a long time ago that Malietana was possessed. If it had been a demon sent by someone he wouldn't have been satisfied just to make her sick. He would have killed her in no more than a day or two. This talk of sorcery is all nonsense. Seelawathie is possessed by a very powerful demon and they must make offerings to satisfy him. That's the only way out of this trouble.

Kalubanda, also a ritual drummer, and a close observer of the gods and demons: It is Reriyakka who has made Seelawathie sick. At the ceremony (dāna) last year Dharmaratne threw away the rice that was given him, saying it wasn't enough. He doesn't know the power (balaya) of gods Kataragama and Kadavara. They were annoyed. Kadavara has sent Reriyakka to Dharmaratne's house to punish them for being disrespectful to Kataragama.

That's all there is to it. People send demons against rich people to make them poor. But why send a demon against the people of Samadigama who are already poor?

Seelawathie's demon had not identified the particular individuals in Kukulewa who had sent him, but one of the most prominent families to be excluded from the distribution of houses in Samadigama, and hence one upon which suspicion might easily fall, was that of Dingiribanda, the father of Wimaladasa. Dingiribanda had long been the principal kapurāla in the village. He looked after the small shrine, dedicated to Kataragama, that had been built in his compound, and he made many offerings to the powerful god on behalf of the village as a whole as well as for individual clients. Dingiribanda was also prominently identified with the SLFP. Two of his sons had been secretary of the local branch, and he was closely allied with Wannihamy, the shopkeeper who had been the village's leading advocate and organizer for the party for twenty years.

Dingiribanda was also the sister's son of Ukkurala, the old and respected kattāḍiyā whom Dharmaratne had called in to treat his wife, and Dingiribanda had accompanied his uncle when he went to see Seelawathie. His comments on the dangers of sorcery focused less on the moral threat, which Kandathe emphasized, than on the risks of counterattack. But he did also raise the moral issue in his subtle suggestion that it was because the people of Samadigama knew that the allocation of houses had been unfair that they were afraid of sorcery. Dingiribanda also had his own interpretation of the source of the trouble.

Dingiribanda: When Dharmaratne asked my uncle to try to cure his wife, my uncle invited me to go with him. I had heard that Seelawathie had said in trance that we Kukulewa people had sent a demon to Samadigama, and I wouldn't have gone there if Ukkurala hadn't asked me. She went into trance during the treatment, but she didn't say anything about a demon sent by us. Instead she said that the man from Elapatwewa who performed the earlier ceremony had failed to protect the house, and that was the reason why the demon had returned. I have my doubts. A real demon wouldn't say such things. A demon who wanted to come to the house wouldn't tell them that he was able to come because the house wasn't protected.

Many women in Samadigama have been possessed, but none of them before this has said it's because of a demon sent by us. Suppose somebody makes an offering to a demon to send it to attack a village or a man. The villagers, or the man, may make a better offering and send the demon back against the one who sent it in the first place. The demon may return to ruin those who originally sent it. It's very dangerous to send a demon against people. It may come back. If the Samadigama people believe that we sent that demon they may try to send it back against us.

When I was at Dharmaratne's house that day I didn't hear anything about a demon being sent against them by the people of Kukulewa. That is something they made up themselves. I think they suspect us of doing it because they know very well that the allocation of houses was unfair.

Why would we send demons against the Samadigama people? If someone had sent a demon they would all have been destroyed by now. Demons don't go somewhere just to live with the people and make them dance. They go to kill them.

It's not because of a demon sent by us that the women of Samadigama fall sick and go into trance. Before the houses were built Samadigama was nothing but jungle, and I know very well that there's treasure buried there. The treasure is guarded by demons like Bahirava, and the demons are angry because those people are living there. Nobody can live in an area guarded by Bahirava without making offerings to him. That's why the women fall ill. Bahirava is sending his demons to make them ill. I don't think Bahirava is going to let the people of Samadigama live in peace.

The idea that Bahirava was responsible for Seelawathie's affliction was challenged in its turn. Samadigama villagers argued that Bahirava would not attack just because there was buried treasure at the site of the village. He would attack only if someone actually tried to dig up the treasure, and no one had done that. So the discussions continued, but as time went on, and under the influence of respected and knowledgeable men like Dingiribanda, Kandathe, and Kalubanda, who had little interest in aggravating the enmity between Kukulewa and Samadigama, the charge of sorcery became less prominent, and suspicion of it was muted.

Meanwhile Seelawathie was herself redefining her possession. She was now going into trance several times a day, and was acquiring a reputation for curing and clairvoyance. People came to consult her in order to find things they had lost, to discover whether their houses were haunted by prētas, to learn what the future held in store, and to seek relief from various ailments. It began to seem to some that she was possessed by a benevolent deity rather than a demon.

Nevertheless the sudden flurry of sorcery accusations and denials had served to focus attention on the still strained relations between Kukulewa and Samadigama and on the question of their mutual community. And this happened during the weeks immediately preceding the performances of the village-wide ceremony called *gambädi rājakāriya,* which directly addressed the same communal issues of collective identity and solidarity.

Chapter 10   *Offerings to the Gods*

GAMBÄDI RĀJAKĀRIYA was held annually in late July or early August and was the principal collective ceremony conducted in Kukulewa and Samadigama. Its performance in Samadigama in 1983 was described in chapter 1.

The name of the ceremony, the complete but rarely used version of which was gambädi deva rājakāriya, is difficult to translate succinctly. "Gambädi" refers to the village *(gama)* and its environs *(bädi)*. "Rājakāriya" is a term that is deeply embedded in the structure of precolonial Sinhala society. It literally means "king's work," and was used to describe the obligatory services that a person owed to his traditional lord (Gunasekara 1978). The prefix *deva* (god) indicates that in this case the duties were owed to gods rather than kings.

Ukkubanda, the kapurāla who performed gambädi rājakāriya in Samadigama from 1981 on, said that the ceremony was intended to win the blessings and protection of the gods. His fellow kapurāla Dingiribanda, who conducted the ceremony in Kukulewa, indicated how this was accomplished.

Dingiribanda: Gambädi rājakāriya is held in order to make merit in the name of the gods. Making offerings *(dāna)* is itself meritorious, and when it is done in the name of the gods the merit is passed on to them. All the virtuous gods are waiting to become Buddhas, and the merit helps them to become Buddhas when the time comes.

There was also a sense that if gambädi rājakāriya was not performed the consequences for the community would be severe. The virtuous gods might not themselves punish the people, but gods like Kadavara, who watched out for their interests, might get angry and allow the demons to attack.

150

Gambädi rājakāriya was simultaneously a feast to be enjoyed by the people themselves. Dingiribanda explained how this was authorized by the god Kataragama.

Dingiribanda: Valliamma was adopted by Veddas and was brought up by them. But god Kataragama took her away from them by force. He fought with her brothers and defeated them. Valliamma felt very sorry for her brothers, the Veddas, and pointed out to god Kataragama that they had no opportunity to hold a feast on the day she married him. So at her request god Kataragama gave the Veddas permission to enjoy five celebrations. Gambädi rājakāriya is one of those five kinds of ceremonies, a *maha dāna* (major offering) at which many people are fed.

All members of the village community were expected to participate in the performance of gambädi rājakāriya. So when the people who moved to Samadigama in 1980 organized a separate performance of the ceremony, their decision indicated how serious was the social rift that now divided them from their kinsmen back in Kukulewa.

Ceremony in Samadigama

Kiribanda: We used to perform gambädi rājakāriya in Kukulewa. But after we moved to Samadigama in 1980 we had to hold the ceremony here. There were political disputes between the two villages and arguments over the way the houses had been distributed. Our kinsmen in Kukulewa were very angry and broke off all relations with us. They didn't even come to funerals in Samadigama. That is how it happened. We had to organize a separate ceremony because the Samadigama people didn't want to go to Kukulewa for it.

The first year we were here we couldn't find a kapurāla to perform gambädi rājakāriya for us. Dingiribanda was not on good terms with us then. Ukkubanda was also still living in Kukulewa, and he refused to come. So we invited a man from Welewa to perform the ceremony for us.

Dingiribanda: Up to 1980 there was only one annual performance of gambädi rājakāriya in this village. But after the people went to Samadigama they wanted to hold a separate ceremony. Those who got houses there are UNP supporters, and there were political differences between us. The differences are not very important now, but in 1980 the Samadigama people and the Kukulewa people were real enemies. They didn't even go to each other's funerals and weddings.

In 1980 they organized a separate performance of gambädi räjakäriya in Samadigama. They didn't invite me to conduct the ceremony. They wanted to, but they thought I would refuse. Actually, if they had invited me, I might have put aside the political disputes and done it anyway.

Ukkubanda was invited to act as kapuräla, but he refused to go. He was living in Kukulewa in those days, and he was very angry with Wijeratne, who is his son-in-law, for not giving him a house. So they had to get a kapuräla from Welewa.

Ukkubanda did, however, later move to Samadigama, where two of his other married daughters, besides Wijeratne's wife, were living. He did not acquire a government house but built his own hut at the edge of the village, on the side farthest from Kukulewa, clearly expressing thereby his new affiliation. And from 1981 on he was invited to act as Samadigama's kapuräla in the performance of gambädi räjakäriya.

Responsibility for organizing ceremonial activities in Samadigama was rotated annually among the sixty households, ten of which were entrusted with this duty each year. In 1983 it was the turn of the families occupying the houses numbered 11 to 20 to make the arrangements for gambädi räjakäriya. In fact, however, the principal organizers were Wijeratne, Dissanayake, and Malietana, none of whom lived in any of these houses. Rather, they represented the dominant Fernando faction in the village. Wijeratne was secretary of the local UNP, while Dissanayake, its assistant secretary, was a more intimate supporter of Jinadasa than anyone else who was not closely related to the Fernandos. Malietana was Jinadasa's sister and also a member of the UNP committee.

Villagers who were already distressed at what they perceived to be the tyranny of Jinadasa and Wijeratne were further alienated by this presumption. Menikrala, Ausadhahamy, Kiribanda, and Sellathe, four eloquent if not always outspoken dissidents, were even tempted to evade their responsibility to participate in the ceremony. They criticized the way that contributions were collected and did not take part either in the construction of the shrine and its altars or in the preparation of the feast. They and their families did eventually appear for the main offerings in the afternoon, but they remained at the edges of the crowd and slipped away before the end of the proceedings, without joining in the communal meal. If, then, they even heard Wijeratne's god appeal for harmony within Samadigama, they were hardly ready to respond.

In fact, however, Wijeratne's god directed his remarks not at them but at the women of the village who had approached the sacred bo-tree during their menstrual periods. This conventional attribution of social malaise to the anger of the gods, themselves displeased by the improper behavior of the people, seemed to be aimed specifically at Jinadasa's younger sister, Sita, who took care of the community building and regularly swept the area around the bo-tree, which stood in front of it. In a way, Sita had been acting almost as the custodian of the bo-tree, but she was also the subject of scurrilous gossip and rebuke for her promiscuous sexual behavior. If the leap was made from menstruation to sexual activity, and then extended from Sita to those of her friends whose reputations were no less tarnished, Wijeratne might have expected an active response to his god's criticism, for there were many people in the village who were offended and outraged by the blatant sexual independence of Sita and her associates. Moreover, many of the fights that had troubled the village in preceding months had indeed been connected with the behavior of these women. But three days after the ceremony, when Wijeratne and Dissanayake began to build a fence around the bo-tree, as the god had directed, only Sugathapala and three other young men turned out to help them.

Wijeratne's god's pronouncements also provoked some sharp theological criticism. The god had referred to the sacred bo-tree in Anuradhapura as the abode of Kaludeva, the Black God, but it was also a favored site for orthodox Buddhist worship, and it was this aspect that was seized upon by Kalubanda, a devout believer but always also a critical interrogator of messages from the gods.

Kalubanda: What Wijeratne's god said about the bo-tree has nothing to do with Buddhism. Lord Buddha never told women not to come to worship during their menstrual periods. Lord Buddha spoke about purity of mind, not about purity of the body. It's true that we should be clean when we perform ceremonies for the gods. But Lord Buddha was very sympathetic toward women. Any woman was allowed to approach Lord Buddha whether she was clean or unclean. Many women used to come to Lord Buddha for advice and guidance. Do you really think he asked them whether or not they were menstruating?

This god doesn't know anything about Lord Buddha or Buddhism. There's no need to build a fence around the bo-tree. Anyone who goes there should be allowed in. I don't have any respect for a god who doesn't make sense. And I'm not afraid of gods who don't know anything about our customs and beliefs.

On the whole, what Wijeratne's god had to say about the lack of harmony within Samadigama excited much less interest than his call for unity between Samadigama and Kukulewa. The plea itself was universally applauded, but the obstacles to its attainment were also clearly recognized. Some people, like Sirimalhamy in Samadigama, thought that the god's expressed wish for a single ceremony was in itself enough to compel obedience.

Sirimalhamy: The god wants the people of Kukulewa and Samadigama to perform gambādi rājakāriya together. If that's what the god wants we have no alternative but to do it. But it will be very difficult to bring all the people together.

After we came to Samadigama in 1980 we performed gambādi rājakāriya here. But we don't have a tank or paddy fields in Samadigama, and even though the village has its own name we all come from Kukulewa. So I think the best thing to do is to hold gambādi rājakāriya in Kukulewa. In any case, that's what the god wants.

The appeal for unity was also welcomed in Kukulewa, but many people demanded that the Samadigama villagers first take further conciliatory steps. Wannihamy, the shopkeeper and staunch supporter of the SLFP, was one of them.

Wannihamy: It's good that the god said he wants unity between the two villages. After all, we are all kinsmen. The people of Samadigama are our relatives. There's no point in having two performances of gambādi rājakāriya. But we won't go to Samadigama to hold the ceremony there. Those people will have to come here. Samadigama isn't even a village. It has no tank, no paddy fields, no land. Do you think we should go there? They are the ones who left us to go there. Let them come back here if they want unity.

Some of the ritual specialists raised other problems.

Kalubanda (drummer): The two villages will never be united. You can call me a dog if that ever happens. When a god comes to live in a village he lays down its boundaries. The god who used to live in Kukulewa did that, and he chased the demons out of the village.

Samadigama does not lie within the boundaries he established. It was thick jungle in those days, and now it's a separate village as far as the god is concerned. So it's not correct for Wijeratne's god to try to bring the two villages together.

A very powerful god might be able to unite the two villages, but I don't think such a god would come here. The people are very bad. They are not virtuous. So the gods won't look favorably upon us.

The Samadigama people started to hold gambädi rājakāriya separately in 1980. If they don't continue to do so now the gods may get angry. I will cut my hair and become a monk the day the two villages are united. Kukulewa people will never come to Samadigama to perform gambädi rājakāriya, and the people here will never go there.

Ukkubanda (kapurāla): It isn't possible to hold a single ceremony for both villages any longer. Offerings have been made to Kadavara in Samadigama for the last three years now, and Kadavara is not like other gods. If offerings are made one year he expects them to be made every year.

It's easy to satisfy Pulleyar or Kataragama, even without making offerings here in Samadigama. But Kadavara won't listen. He won't listen if his offerings are not made. There'll be a lot of trouble if he doesn't get them. He'll send all his demons to Samadigama to ruin it. Kadavara is a demon who doesn't even listen to god Kataragama if he's not given his offerings.

Kukulewa and Samadigama are two different villages. Samadigama doesn't fall under the divine protection of the god who used to live in Kukulewa. That god is still there. But because there is no one virtuous enough to be his vehicle-man he doesn't possess anybody.

Samadigama used to be jungle, and it was into that jungle that the Kukulewa god drove the demons that were troubling the village. So Samadigama doesn't have the god's protection. If we want to avoid trouble here we'll have to hold our own separate ceremony.

The true identity of the god possessing Wijeratne was also vigorously debated. Wijeratne's claim that he was a watcher sent by the god who had formerly possessed Kandappu anumätiräla, and that the god himself wanted to return, was not accepted by everyone. It posed a threat to those who feared that the god might try to remove his sacred ornaments, which in themselves afforded protection to the people, from Kukulewa to Samadigama. But at the same time it also suggested a test.

Dingiribanda: When Kandappu's father was still alive, we asked him what we should do when he died and the god no longer had a vehicle-man. He told us not to worry, and said the god would select someone suitable to carry his messages to us. And he said that even if that didn't happen we would still enjoy his protection as long as we brought his ornaments to the place where gambädi räjakäriya is performed.

Sirimalhamy: The god who used to live in Kukulewa went away after Kandappu's death. But his ornaments are still there in Kukulewa. If that same god now comes to Samadigama we can bring his ornaments here. But Kandappu's sons are refusing to open the doors and will not hand them over.

If Wijeratne is possessed by the same god he can go to Kukulewa in trance and take them himself. He can use the god's power to open the door without a key. If he can do that they'll have to let him keep the ornaments.

Those ornaments are very powerful. At times of sickness we wash them and drink the water in which they've been washed. That protects us from sickness.

Every year the ornaments are brought to the place in Kukulewa where gambädi räjakäriya is performed. But since we came to Samadigama we haven't had the benefit of those sacred ornaments. The Kukulewa people don't allow us to bring them here for our ceremony. That's because they weren't given houses in Samadigama. And after all, what Jinadasa and Wijeratne did was wrong. They should have distributed the houses among the sixty mul pavul.

Kalubanda: If the god is the same one that used to live in Kukulewa, he should go there to fetch his ornaments and weapons. I don't see any reason for him to send his watcher. He can go himself to get his ornaments. It's true that I'm a blind man, but I don't believe stories like this. If he's the same god he must know what kinds of ornaments he has there in Kukulewa. He must be able to say that he has so many necklaces, so many rings, so many bracelets, and so on, and he must fetch those things. People are not going to give the ornaments to Wijeratne until he proves that he's now the vehicle-man of the same god that used to possess Kandappu.

Malhamy (Kandappu's son): Those ornaments are in our charge. We keep them under lock and key. If this god is the same one who used to possess our father, he will be able to open the door with his divine powers and take the

The shrine in which the sacred ornaments of Kandappu's god were kept.

ornaments away. But we're not going to give them to Wijeratne just because he shakes his limbs up and down. Our grandfather brought these ornaments from Moragahawela, where they were locked up. He was able to open the door with his divine powers, by just touching the door. Wijeratne must show that he can do the same thing. If it's a true god, he will be able to open the door without a key.

Some young men in Kukulewa seemed to relish the occasion for legitimate violence that this test might provide.

Jayasena: If they come here to take the ornaments to Samadigama, we'll demand that they open the door of Kandappu's shrine without the key. If Wijeratne can't do it, they won't get away without a sound thrashing. This time they'll really learn their lesson.

Thus many people remained unconvinced that Wijeratne was already possessed by a powerful god, or even that he would be in the future. There were various grounds for skepticism. Wannihamy appealed to general principles.

Wannihamy: I don't believe that either Wijeratne or his sister is possessed by a god. It may be demons. Powerful gods don't enter into such intimate relations with human beings. And they never take possession of women. These so-called gods in Samadigama are really demons.

It was Wijeratne who broke off relations with us. It may be that the god in Kukulewa sent a demon to force him and the others into unity with Kuku-lewa. That would make sense. But I don't believe these stories about gods in Samadigama.

Kalubanda's skepticism, on the other hand, referred to Wijeratne's state-ment, made in trance, that he was more virtuous than the other people whom the god had tried earlier but found wanting.

Kalubanda: This god doesn't really want to make the two villages into one harmonious unit. If that was what he wanted he wouldn't have said that he previously tried to speak through seven other people. The god said that their minds were not clean, that they were jealous, and that kind of thing. Now those people are angry about it. They'll never believe that story. In what way is Wijeratne better than those seven other people? Is his mind pure? Is he not envious of other people? If it was a true god he wouldn't say things like that, which make people even angrier with one another. That's why I say this god doesn't make sense.

But Kalubanda was still ready to be persuaded. He recalled Wijeratne saying that the god himself would come if offerings were made on seven successive *kemmura* days, days on which the gods themselves convened and which were auspicious times for humans to approach them.

Kalubanda: I don't know what will happen in the future. He said he was a watcher for the god, and that the god himself would come later. We will see after the seven kemmura days.

Ceremony in Kukulewa

But before the seventh kemmura day the people of Kukulewa held their own performance of gambädi rājakāriya. Dingiribanda, who had con-ducted the ceremony in Kukulewa for many years, was old and sick, and a few days before the ceremony was due to be held he decided he could no longer continue as kapurāla.

Premadasa: My father is sick and cannot conduct gambädi rājakāriya this year, so he has asked me to take his place. He doesn't want outsiders to come and hold ceremonies in this village. Our family has been performing these ceremonies for generations. But my two older brothers have had mental problems and are still not in good health, so I am the only one left to do it.

I am willing to conduct the ceremony. The only problem is that I like to have a drink every day. My father has advised me not to take alcohol on the day of the ceremony.

Premadasa was willing, but also nervous. Inexperience could be dangerous, as Kadavara was likely to pounce on any mistake in the ritual and punish the offender. Dingiribanda agreed to supervise his son's performance closely.

The ceremony was organized by Tikiribanda, the son of Bandathe, the former vel vidāne, and two sons of Undiyarala, a former gamarāla (village chief), Sumanapala and Gunawardena. These three men directed construction of the shrine and the clearing of the ground around it, and also visited every household in Kukulewa to ask for a donation of a half-measure of rice, half a coconut, some chilies, and a few condiments, and one and a half rupees in cash. The arrangements were discussed by those who gathered near the shrine on the evening before the ceremony.

Dingiribanda, the old kapurāla, and the two uḍäkki kapuvās (drummers), Kalubanda and his pupil Somasiri, deplored the failure of the gamarālas to take the lead in organizing the ceremony. They also claimed that the gamarālas were supposed to provide a meal to those who had helped prepare for the festivities on the evening before the ceremony. This appeal to traditional custom raised questions that were both complex and arcane. The title of gamarāla belonged to those villagers who held, ideally by right of inheritance, one of the four plots of paddy land in the old field under the main village tank that were known as *gamvasama* lands. In Kandyan times gamarālas had been effective chiefs of their villages, but their authority had long ago been transferred to new officials, like the vel vidānes, who were either appointed by the government or elected by the people. All that was left to them were a few ceremonial privileges and obligations. It was believed to be the ancient custom that the villagers collectively cultivated the gamvasama holdings, in return for which the gamarālas undertook to meet communal ceremonial expenses in the village and to entertain important visitors from outside. In the late 1960s, however, while these traditional duties were remembered, none of them had actually been performed. But now the gamarālas were again being called upon to meet their customary obligations.

It was by no means easy, however, to identify the particular individuals on whom these obligations fell. Sumanapala and Gunawardena, two of the three organizers of the ceremony, undoubtedly had a claim, because their father, Undiyarala, had held one of the four gamvasama plots, even though he had not inherited it. Undiyarala and his brother Keerala had each bought one of the gamvasama holdings from men who had left the village at marriage. But Undiyarala and Keerala both died in 1981, leaving a number of heirs, and since there had been almost no paddy cultivation after that because of the drought, it still remained uncertain which of their heirs would finally take possession of the gamvasama lands. A third gamarāla was Kiribanda, who had moved to Samadigama and had in any case mortgaged his gamvasama holding. The fourth position was no clearer, for the previous holder, Menikhamy, had left several descendants who could still claim to be her successor.

All this was quite confusing, but one point was plain enough, even if it remained unspoken in the discussion at the shrine. Kukulewa was certainly different from Samadigama, which because it had no tank and no paddy fields had no gamvasama holdings either, and therefore also no gamarālas with traditional authority to sponsor gambädi rājakāriya.

Dingiribanda made the most of this difference, arguing that only those villagers who held shares (pangukārayō) in the main field were obliged to contribute to the ceremony, and that they should contribute in proportion to the size of their holdings. But in fact everyone had been asked to donate the same amount, and again the conduct of the gamarālas was deplored.

Dingiribanda: These gamarālas are now begging from widows and orphans who have no lands in the main field at all. How disgraceful of them! Next year we're going to do this work according to ancient custom. Gamarālas and pangukārayō will have to contribute more. Other villagers can contribute if they want to, but we're not going to press them.

Later in the evening, after Sumanapala had first worshiped the gods with a gift of betel leaves and a little money, made on behalf of the village as a whole, Premadasa approached the shrine to make his preliminary offerings. The uḍäkki kapuvās beat their drums and chanted praise of the gods, drawing their attention to what was going on, while Premadasa, under the watchful supervision of his father, made the offerings of un-cooked food—rice, coconut, betel leaves, and areca nuts—that served as an invitation to the gods.

Dingiribanda: This is a very important occasion, and it is necessary to invite the gods beforehand. It is a ceremony *(magula)* which no one will attend unless he is invited.

After the offerings were made, most of the people present went off to Ti-kiribanda's house. Several of them had been specifically invited: Dingiri-banda and his son Premadasa, the kapurālas; Seerala, the old and respected villager who had once been secretary of the variga court; Kapuruhamy, the elderly teacher of the two uḍäkki kapuvās and the kapurāla of Kandappu anumātirāla's shrine; and Kandappu's son Jothipala who was in charge of the god's sacred ornaments. Most of the young men who had worked all day to prepare for the ceremony also came along, but their appearance caused some embarrassment and provoked further discussion of the ga-marālas' duties.

Tikiribanda: We can't serve everyone. We can only serve those we specifically invited.

When they heard this most of the young men began to drift away. Tikiribanda was apologetic.

Tikiribanda: I'm sorry to have to talk like that, but I have to because no one else is prepared to treat them. You can see that I can't afford to feed everybody. But these days no one accepts the responsibility of treating these people on the night before the offerings. The gamarālas are supposed to do it.

This remark was heard by Wannihamy, the shopkeeper, whose wife was a daughter of Menikhamy and thus one of the possible successors to her position as gamarāla.

Wannihamy: I didn't know that. If I had known I would have contributed. Send someone around in the morning. I can give some more rice.

Demons and Development

After the meal a few people decided to join Premadasa in his kapurāla's vigil through the night at the shrine. Premadasa was still being advised by his father.

Dingiribanda: I am too old to perform the ceremony now. There's no one in our family who can take it on except you, so it's your responsibility. If you can't keep away from liquor you may drink. But don't drink while you're making the offerings.

Eventually the talk came around to the recent events in Samadigama, and what they might portend for the next day's ceremony. For some people in Kukulewa, Wijeratne's appeal for unity had turned into a challenge, and it was one they were prepared to meet.

Sumanapala: I've heard that the gods in Samadigama are threatening that if they're not invited to our gambädi rājakāriya they'll be very angry with us. Seelawathie's god has said there'll be trouble in Kukulewa. But we're not afraid. We have our own gods, Deveni Pattini and Kaludakada, to protect us.

Many people came to the shrine the next morning to help prepare the festive meal. Women and children hauled water and brought pots and pans, knives, coconut scrapers, and other cooking utensils. The rice and other provisions contributed by the villagers were carried in procession to the site of the ceremony, and the various tasks were divided according to established custom. The food to be offered to the gods, *kiribhat* (milk-rice) and *kavum* (oilcakes), was prepared by men, while the women cooked the food that the people themselves would consume.

Several of the Samadigama dissidents came to help, including Kiribanda, who was a gamarāla in Kukulewa, and two sons of Keerala, a former Kukulewa gamarāla who had been given a house in Samadigama but who died without having moved into it. On the other hand, one or two prominent Kukulewa villagers, who lived toward the end of the village closest to Samadigama and who had close connections with the Fernandos, did not appear, among them Kandathe, whose son was married to one of Jinadasa's sisters, and Muthubanda, whose daughter was married to one of Jinadasa's younger brothers.

It took several hours to prepare and cook the food, and it was midafternoon before everything was ready. Then a group of villagers went off to

Kandappu's shrine to ask permission to carry the god's ornaments to the ceremony. Sumanapala went into the shrine and paid his respects to the ornaments with a gift of betel leaves and a few coins. Then his younger brother Dayaratne, accompanied by Kapuruhamy, the kapurāla of Kandappu's shrine, and Jothipala, Kandappu's youngest son, carried the casket containing the ornaments out of Kandappu's shrine and led a procession back to the site of gambädi rājakāriya, where the ornaments were carefully taken out of their casket and placed on a table just in front of the shrine.

Now Premadasa, accompanied by the udäkki kapuväs, began to make offerings to the gods inside the shrine. First he approached Pulleyar, who was given rice, coconut, betel, oilcakes, milk-rice, plantains, and areca nuts. Next it was the turn of Kataragama and his consorts, who were offered the same foods but without the coconut. After that came Bahirava, who received the same presents but with a young coconut added. Turning away from the main altar Premadasa made further offerings to the other gods, Pattini, Ayiyanayake, Illandari, and the rest—eighteen gods in all. Then he stepped backward out of the shrine and placed offerings to Kambili and Muruthan Kadavara at the top and bottom of the arch that had been erected in front of the shrine. Muruthan Kadavara is the Kadavara who looks after the offerings made to Pulleyar and Kataragama. The other six Kadavaras received their offerings at an open place at the foot of a tree about fifty yards from the shrine.

As he approached Muruthan Kadavara, Premadasa began to tremble, and it seemed that a god was about to alight on him, but he recovered himself and continued with the offerings. Instead it was a young man in the audience who began to quiver and shortly afterward went into trance. This was Pinhamy, a resident of Samadigama and one of Keerala's sons, who had been similarly possessed on several previous occasions. He was in fact one of the unsuccessful candidates whom Wijeratne's god had said were not sufficiently virtuous to be his vehicle-man. Pinhamy jerked convulsively about for several minutes. Then he settled down, and a god began to speak through his voice.

Pinhamy's god: I am Kaludakada god. I have come here to explain something to you. There are two people in Samadigama who say they are possessed by me. They are threatening that because you did not invite them here they are going to make trouble for you. Do not believe them. I am here for your protection. As long as I am here nobody can harm you.

At this point Sumanapala, who was in the audience, interrupted in a loud voice.

Sumanapala: No, no, we're not afraid. We know that no one can harm us as long as god Kaludakada's ornaments are here.

Pinhamy then moved over to the table where the god's ornaments were displayed. He did not touch the ornaments, but asked Kapuruhamy, Kandappu's kapurāla, for some of the powder made from ground stone that kapurālas place on people's foreheads for their protection. Pinhamy applied the powder generously over the whole upper half of his body, and then turned to Premadasa to ask permission to enter the temple. This granted, he went inside, worshiped the god Kataragama, stepped back out, and began to speak again.

Pinhamy's god: The gods who speak through the brother and sister in Samadigama claim that the ornaments in Kukulewa belong to them. That is what they said at the ceremony in Samadigama. But I sent my Bahiravas there to prove them wrong. I sent the Bahiravas who are in charge of my ornaments to show that the ornaments don't belong to those two people in Samadigama. And the Bahiravas made the sons of my old vehicle-man go into trance. I did this as a protest.

When he had finished speaking, Pinhamy's god began to dance. For a while he danced around the large pots of food that had been prepared for the villagers, speaking briefly again to several of the women who were standing beside them. Then the god left, and Pinhamy lay down to recover. All the gods had now received their offerings, and the people turned to enjoy their own feast.

When they talked about the ceremony afterward, only a few people were convinced that it was the god Kaludakada himself who had possessed Pinhamy. Most were more inclined to think that it was some emissary of the god.

Kalubanda: You can tell it was not Kaludakada himself who appeared at the gambädi rājakāriya. You saw that he didn't even touch the ornaments. If they

164

had been his ornaments he would have worn them. Only the god to whom the ornaments belong can wear them. If someone is not possessed by that god he cannot touch them. They would burn him if he tried to. You saw how he got that powder from Kapuruhamy? He had to ask for it because it wasn't his.

Sumanapala: It wasn't Kaludakada himself who came to the gambädi rājakā-riya. It was the Bahirava who is in charge of the ornaments. Kaludakada sent him to give his message. We're not afraid of the threats made by Seelawathie's god.

But there were also other interpretations of what had happened. Muda-lihamy, who had remained behind in Samadigama, where he was assuming the role of Seelawathie's kapurāla, believed that Seelawathie's god was responsible.

Mudalihamy: The man who went into trance at the Kukulewa gambädi rā-jakāriya was made to do so by Seelawathie's god. She was possessed by her god on that day. The god was angry that Seelawathie had not been invited. Just before the offerings were made at Kukulewa, Seelawathie's god spoke through her voice and said: "I am going to the ceremony. I will catch somebody there and make him dance." After that Seelawathie came out of trance. She was conscious all the time that man was in trance in Kukulewa. It was obviously Seelawathie's god who went there.

These disagreements persisted. Many questions were still unanswered, and people wondered whether things would become clearer when Wi-jeratne's god made his promised appearance on the seventh kemmura day.

WIJERATNE WENT into trance on each of the six kemmura days prior to August 24, the seventh kemmura day on which the god possessing him had promised to appear. His sister Seelawathie, meanwhile, had been going into trance three mornings a week ever since the middle of July, and was attracting a growing number of clients who came to seek treatment and advice from her god. Her fame was spreading, and people were beginning to come to her house not only from Samadigama and Kukulewa but also from more distant villages. However, the identity of the god possessing her remained a matter of some controversy. Kalubanda, the uḍākki kapuvā, was at first skeptical. He could not overlook the fact that Seelawathie had entered the shrine at the Samadigama gambädi rājakāriya without first asking the kapurāla's permission.

Kalubanda: I don't pay attention to any god who doesn't know our customs. Any god who wants to pay respects to Kataragama must first ask permission of the kapurāla in charge. If not, the kapurāla will treat the possessed person as someone who is faking.

Ukkubanda, the kapurāla, recalled the same error but was also impressed by the god's apparent powers.

Ukkubanda: I'm sure that Seelawathie is not possessed by one of the virtuous gods. If she was, she wouldn't have entered my shrine without my permission. But her god can see things that are hidden beneath the surface of the earth. And her god can foretell things and cure people of their sicknesses. It must be a powerful god but not one of the virtuous gods. I say that because the god doesn't know our customs.

Yesterday, when Seelawathie was in trance, she said that she was Naga Pattini (Cobra Pattini). But I'm doubtful. I think she is possessed by Kali. When

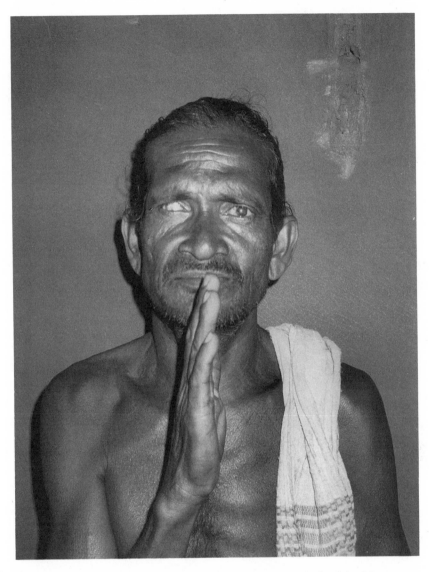

Kalubanda, ritual drummer: "I don't pay attention to any god who doesn't know our customs."

women are possessed by Kali they hide their faces with their hair. And that's what Seelawathie does.

Over in Kukulewa, Wannihamy the shopkeeper denied that it was a god at all, once again arguing from general principles.

Wannihamy: Gods never possess human beings. Only demons do that. Even Kandappu was possessed by a demon. Kaludakada is a demon, not a god. Pattini is a goddess, but people who go into trance and say, "I am Pattini" are telling lies. Demons never tell who they really are when they speak through their mediums. They don't like to reveal their true identity, but try to hide it.

Dingiribanda, the Kukulewa kapurāla, had a different opinion: Both gods and demons possess people and make them go into trance. But demons can't foretell things. They can cure sick people, but it's only gods who can foretell things. I hear that Seelawathie is curing people and foretelling things. If that is so, then she's possessed by a god. Only gods can do such things.

Others remained more aggressively skeptical. Jayasena, a grandson of Wannihamy, was away from the village for a while, and when he returned he learned that he had been accused of theft. Someone told him that Kandathe had gone to Seelawathie to find out who had stolen his goats, and Seelawathie had named him. Jayasena went to Seelawathie's house in a rage, and shouted at her from the road.

Jayasena: Don't tell lies, you bitch. You're just cheating these poor people and robbing them of their money. If you're really possessed by a god, do whatever you can to me. You're a liar. You're not possessed by a god. You should be sent to a mental hospital.

It was said that after Jayasena's outburst in front of Seelawathie's house her husband came home and beat her. The next morning Seelawathie told Ukkurala that her god would not stay long if people accused her medium of fraud and mistreated her in such ways.

Seelawathie in Trance

Despite such tribulations Seelawathie continued to go into trance. Two men became her constant attendants. Ukkurala, the old kaṭṭāḍiyā who knew mantras (magical spells) and other ritual skills, prepared charmed threads for her clients and performed the rituals she prescribed. Mudalihamy acted as her god's kapurāla, leading people in to see her and when necessary explaining to them what she said. These two men came three mornings a week to Seelawathie's house, where already by eight o'clock

Seelawathie dancing while possessed by her god.

she was preparing to go into trance. Sometimes Kalubanda, having over-come his early skepticism, also attended upon the god.

Her session on August 21 was typical. Seelawathie, dressed in white, sat on a mat in the inner room, with Mudalihamy beside her. Ukkurala and

Demons and Development

Kalubanda sat opposite her on another mat. Seelawathie's husband, Dhar-maratne, and other members of the household busied themselves around the house, as clients began to congregate in the outer room. Mudalihamy led one woman into the inner room and asked her to sit down in front of Seelawathie. She was holding a bunch of betel leaves which he instructed her to offer to the god. He told her to think only of the problem for which she wanted the god's help.

Seelawathie's fingers began to quiver, then her arms, and soon her whole body was trembling violently. She shook her head and her hair fell loose. Her breathing was fast and rhythmic, and a loud moan came from deep in her throat every time she exhaled. (Later, when a young man who was imitating this sound as he left one of Seelawathie's sessions was asked what it meant, he replied, "you're a married man; you should know"). Then the god began to speak.

Seelawathie's god: You want to know about a distant residence, don't you?

Mudalihamy (to the client): Speak up. Don't be silent.

Seelawathie's god: You want to know whether something is wrong at your residence, and also why you have so many troubles, isn't that so?

Client: Yes.

Mudalihamy (to the client): You must speak up. Say what's in your mind.

Seelawathie's god: Speak up and make my mind clear. You are the only person at your residence who is suffering from an ailment, isn't that so?

Client: Yes.

Seelawathie's god: You are always ill, isn't that so?

Client: Yes.

Seelawathie's god: There are no troubles at your residence, no problems caused by demons. Nothing is wrong as far as your residence is concerned. But your time is very bad. You help people but no one is grateful to you. Your mind is not at rest. You have so many problems, so many worries, isn't that so?

Client: Yes.

Seelawathie's god: Your children give you lots of trouble. You don't have a moment's rest because of them. And your neighbors also bother you, isn't that so?

Client: Yes.

Seelawathie's god: You are sick. You feel faint. You feel as though there is something heavy on your head, isn't that so?

Client: Yes.

Seelawathie's god: You feel something burning inside you. Do you?

Client: Yes.

Seelawathie's god: Have you made any vows to gods before this?

Client: No.

Seelawathie's god: There's nothing wrong with your residence. But there's something wrong with you.

Mudalihamy: What's that?

Seelawathie's god: It's caused by a kind of minor sorcery. All your children are doing well. Don't worry yourself about them.

Kalubanda: What kind of treatment shall we give her?

Seelawathie's god: Cut seven limes and put the sorcery away.

Kalubanda: Then bring seven limes, seven betel leaves, seven areca nuts, and a young coconut. And remember that you have to pay me for cutting the limes.

Seelawathie's god: Bring some gingelly oil when you come next time. I can cure headache with it.

The woman gave five rupees to Seelawathie and went away, apparently satisfied. Sometimes, however, the god's powers of divination were less acute.

Seelawathie's god: You want to know about something belonging to your residence, isn't that so?

Male Client: Yes.

Seelawathie's god: It's something inside your residence, isn't it?

Client: Yes.

Seelawathie's god: Is it about an illness?

Client: No.

Seelawathie's god: It's not an illness. But it is something inside your residence. It's about some object, isn't it?

Client: Yes.

Seelawathie's god: Is it jewelry?

Client: No.

Seelawathie's god: Is it something metal?

Client: No.

Seelawathie's god: Is it something made of silver?

Client: No.

Seelawathie's god: What is this then? Almost everyone who came here today was satisfied with what I said. None of them took their money back. Did you make some mistake? Do the betel leaves you gave me belong to someone waiting his turn to see me?

Mudalihamy: The time is not good. It's noon now. Come again in the morning and not at this time of day.

Seelawathie's god: Let me try again. I can see that you want to know about something that has been stolen from your house. I can see that it's something valuable. But I can't see what it is. Is it something made of bronze?

Client: No.

Seelawathie's god: Come again on another kemmura day. Don't think anything bad of me.

The man got up and left without leaving any money.

Wijeratne in Performance

While Seelawathie was struggling to establish her reputation, her brother was preparing for the seventh kemmura day on which his god had promised to appear. Small offerings were made to the gods on the six preceding kemmura days, and on each occasion Wijeratne went briefly into trance, but the god did not speak through his voice. Six villagers received special invitations to attend these rituals: Seerala, the Kukulewa village elder; Kapuruhamy, Kandappu's god's kapurāla; Tikirala, Kalubanda, and Kandathe, all uḍäkki kapuvās; and Kandappu's son Jothipala, who represented his father and his father's god. Apart from Jothipala, who came only on the first day, all of them attended the six ceremonies, at which they were fed by Wijeratne's family. All six of them, as well as many other villagers, also came to Wijeratne's house for the climactic seventh-day offerings.

A chair was made to serve as an altar, and on it were placed offerings of plantains, oilcakes, betel leaves, and areca nuts. Kandathe and Tikirala played their drums and chanted praises of the gods, inviting them to attend the ceremony. Kalubanda was also present, but he was sick and did not play or sing. Wijeratne stood close to them, dressed in a white sarong but naked above the waist. He remained motionless and silent for a long time. Suddenly he began to tremble, the movement starting in his fingers and then quickly spreading throughout his whole body. He thrashed about until Dissanayake restrained him, standing behind him and firmly holding his head. Then he broke free and began a spirited dance that continued for about fifteen minutes. Eventually he stopped, and turned to receive the invited guests, whom he welcomed individually. Then, after greeting the rest of the villagers, whom he addressed collectively as Kuveni's children (i.e., Veddas), he began to dance again. Now Seelawathie also appeared, went quickly into trance, and joined in the dancing. After a while Wijeratne stopped, and his god spoke.

Wijeratne's god: I am a powerful god. I have come here to help Kuveni's people. You can see that there is also a god here who has possessed the woman next door. That woman is the sister of my vehicle-man. She has cured people with the help of her god. She has shown divine insight into the truth and has told it correctly. But because of her husband's behavior the god is displeased and does not help her much. The god does not send people to her. That is because her husband spends his money on drink. He gets drunk and assaults the god's vehicle-woman. Tell him to come here.

Mudalihamy: Go and tell Dharmaratne to come here.

Dharmaratne came and stood beside Wijeratne.

Wijeratne's god: If you don't stay away from liquor the god possessing your wife will leave her. And the god will make you suffer for that. You must stay away from liquor and stop troubling your wife. You must take care of her and not make her angry.

Kalubanda: A wife should always be tolerant of her husband. She shouldn't get angry even when he does something wrong. The god should also be tolerant, because all humans make mistakes.

Wijeratne's god: The god possessing her has been very sympathetic toward him. The god gave him advice, but he didn't listen. This is my final warning to him.

Seelawathie's god: I want to speak. We two gods are brother and sister, just as this vehicle-man and this vehicle-woman are brother and sister. The god possessing him will be in charge of curing people's sicknesses. I will show my divine insight and put away sorcery.

Ukkubanda: If you gods don't demonstrate your powers to convince people who you are, they're not going to believe you. People are already laughing at us. We won't be able to face them if you gods don't show your powers and convince them.

Wijeratne's god: Wait and see. I can do that. Kuveni's people are divided into factions now. They hate one another. If they unite and have faith in us, we can help them. We can make them feel our presence and our powers.

Ukkubanda: If you convince them that you're powerful they'll come to you. They will believe in you. But they're not going to come to you just because you get hold of somebody and make him dance.

Kalubanda: Is there a place where I have not beaten my drum? I have beaten it behind every house in the village. I have beaten it at the invitation of all those who went into trance earlier. They all trembled and shook. I took them to be powerful gods and beat my drum for them to dance, but nothing happened. I am an old man now, and I have spent my whole life in the service of the gods. But since Kandappu died I have not seen anyone who can be called a real anumätiräla. The god who used to possess Kandappu was very powerful. He used to walk on fire. How sad I feel when I remember these things.

Wijeratne's god: I understand your sadness. Wait a while and see. I will do everything possible to please you and to make you happy.

Ukkubanda: Just saying so isn't enough. You have to prove that you're powerful. But since you say you are a true god who is acting under the authority of virtuous gods like Kataragama and Pattini, I will receive you.

Ukkubanda then offered some betel leaves to Wijeratne, who accepted them and put them on the altar.

Somapala: All these people go into trance and say they're Kaludakada or Pattini, but none of them has yet done anything to relieve our misery.

Jayatilike: I'm ashamed to go to work outside the village these days. People are saying that the gods only take possession of Veddas. They're making fun of us, saying that Veddas own nothing at all except the favor of the gods.

Wijepala's god: I know all that. I will make them come to me for help. I am a powerful god. I don't need any ornaments. I can do without ornaments. I can get those ornaments whenever I want them. Now I have said everything I came to tell you.

Someone then asked the god to heal Kalubanda, who was sick, and Wijeratne touched him with margosa leaves.

Seelawathie's god: The gods want to dance now to please the people.

The drummers began to play again, and Seelawathie and Wijeratne both danced for a while. Then Wijeratne suddenly stopped.

Wijeratne's god: Someone is blowing at me. I can feel someone blowing a *kalam* at me.

Wijeratne was referring to a magical means of challenging gods and demons. It was believed that if someone who knew mantras silently mur-

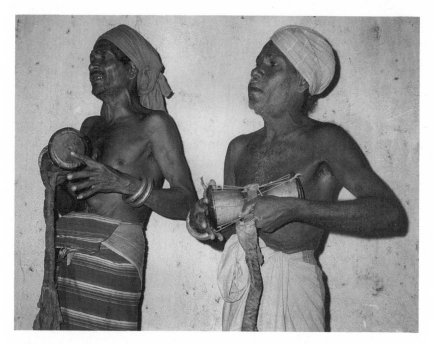

Kalubanda and Kandathe, ritual drummers, attending to Seelawathie's god.

mured the correct spell while blowing out his breath at a person in trance, the latter would fall to the ground unconscious. Since true gods were supposed to be able to feel the kalam, the technique could be used to test the authenticity of the possession.

When the accusation was made, two of Dingiribanda's sons—Premadasa, the new kapurāla in Kukulewa, and Wimaladasa, the SLFP organizer—moved quietly away to the edge of the audience. They knew that even if they had not blown the kalam they would almost certainly be suspected of it.

Ukkubanda: Gods should expect such things. People come to test the gods. Powerful gods can show their strength to those who come to test them.

Seelawathie's god: I want to dance. Beat the drum.

Ukkubanda: The uḍäkki kapuvās are tired and hungry. Gods may not get tired, but people do. We've had enough dancing. It's time for the gods to leave. Please be good enough to go. You can dance again on some other day.

The uḍäkki kapuvās then beat their drums and sang a final chant. Seela-wathie danced wildly, Wijeratne with more restraint. Soon the drummers stopped and the gods left. Wijeratne and Seelawathie lay down and were given water to drink, to help them regain their own senses. The ceremony was over.

So Wijeratne's god had once again raised the issue of social harmony, but the people turned the responsibility back to the gods. It was up to the gods to demonstrate their power. The villagers remained skeptical. Seela-wathie indicated that in future the two vehicle-people would concentrate on private practice, and the issues of collective identity and communal solidarity were allowed to fade into the background. Perhaps they would be raised again, and even resolved, at next year's gambädi rājakāriya.

In the meanwhile it was already late August, and there would soon be work again. Would the rains come and finally relieve the drought? Whether they did or not the chenas had to be made ready, for the villagers must try to make their living somehow. And with the blessing of the gods—how else?—they might even yet become prosperous.

Chapter 12   *Reflections*

AT THE OUTSET I stated that my intention was to construct a platform from which the voices of the Kukulewa villagers could be heard and understood. That ambition did not presume either that I could achieve a strictly objective account of events in Kukulewa or that my presentation of the villagers' discursive practices would escape its author's mediation. On the contrary, I am well aware that everything I have written contributes to a selective rendition of what happened in the village. Even in the later chapters, after enough historical background and cultural context has been presented to allow much of the narrative to be carried in the villagers' own words, my editorial hand has still been hard at work. My interventions may appear simply to have been linking one act or statement to another, innocently nudging the story along. But the previous and hidden work of determining which statements and events to include, and what patterns to impose on their presentation, was always shaping the material toward a particular interpretation of its significance.

It is time, then, for me to come out of the shadows into which, in the last few chapters, I have consigned myself. My first draft of this book ended with the previous chapter. At the time I wrote it, I thought I would undermine my whole project if, having opened up a space for the villagers of Kukulewa to tell their own stories, I returned at the end to take final command of the stage. To conclude by imposing my own interpretation of the events I have described would inevitably appear to reassert an authority I had otherwise struggled to disclaim. But now I see a greater risk that, by withdrawing my presence from the narrative, I might appear to be claiming that what I have reported is the "true" or "definitive" account of "what really happened" in Kukulewa, rather than a record of what I experienced and came to understand. I have therefore decided to conclude by offering an interpretation of the events described in the previous chapters that explicitly articulates a number of the more general themes in my account.

This will enable me directly to address the questions with which I started out. It will also serve to remind the reader of the always remaining difference that distinguishes the villagers whose lives I have tried to portray, from the characters who make up the cast of the ethnographic drama I have composed. It is perhaps too easy to lose sight of that difference. Indeed, it is not even clear to me any longer who—to borrow a trope from Kukulewa—has come to possess whom. The villagers maintain that gods and demons occasionally possess people and use them as the vehicles through which they communicate with human beings. An outsider, however, might be tempted to think that it is the villagers who occasionally take possession of their deities, whom they then use to lend authority to what they themselves have to say. Somewhat similarly, while I have constructed my text as a vehicle through which the voices of Kukulewa villagers might be broadcast, in doing so I have also inevitably appropriated them for my own purposes. With that caveat, I will first review the forms of community that used to prevail in Kukulewa, and will then go on to suggest an interpretation of the events that occurred after Kukulewa was selected for development as an Awakening Village.

The Former Basis of Community

As described in chapters 3 and 4, all the evidence suggests that through many generations the sense of belonging together in Kukulewa was principally articulated in the related idioms of kinship and caste. All those who lived in the same village were kinsmen who, as fellow members of the Vedda variga, enjoyed a strong sense of shared identity. Social relations within the village were governed by expectations of cooperation and reciprocity, as was appropriate among kin. These expectations were also extended to other villages in Anuradhapura District that were inhabited by Veddas, to whom the people of Kukulewa were connected by long established ties of kinship and marriage. But most of the villages in their immediate neighborhood were occupied by members of other varigas, with whom their interactions were structured in the hierarchical idiom of caste. The exact placement of the Veddas in relation to the Sinhala caste system was ambiguous, but the pervasive distinction between forms of interaction appropriate among kin and those appropriate between members of different varigas continuously reinforced the Kukulewa people's sense of their distinct identity, while the norms of reciprocity and mutuality that governed relations within the village no less continuously reproduced a sense of solidarity among them.

The sense of belonging together as Kukulewa people (Kukulewa min-issu) was doubtless fostered by the relative autonomy and economic self-sufficiency that the village enjoyed, as well as by the absence of any signifi-cant class distinctions within it, but it was not generated automatically by the material conditions of existence. On the contrary, it was the product of ceaseless cultural activity in virtually every facet of social life. It was constantly being created and recreated in the daily routines of agricultural cooperation, in the common use of kinship terms in mutual address, and in reciprocities between neighbors that normally "went without saying." It was also proclaimed on occasions of collective ceremony, such as gam-bädi rājakāriya, that explicitly identified the boundaries of the village community. Continuously reproduced in the course of these pervasive and unquestioned practices, there can be little doubt but that the ideal of the village community became deeply embedded in the local culture. This did not prevent sharp outbreaks of factional conflict within the village, but it did serve to contain them, for the idea that the village should form a community was taken for granted. It was a constituent component of the villagers' doxic common sense.

At the same time the village community was also a segment of the larger community of the variga, the experience of which was equally compelling and which was itself produced and reproduced in similar, indeed often overlapping, ways. In addition to the reciprocity expected between fellow Veddas, whether or not they lived in the same village, conventional prac-tices such as commensalism and endogamy within the variga also served regularly to reinscribe a firm distinction between those who belonged together and those who did not. This sense of shared identity was rein-forced by the belief in common descent from Vijaya and Kuveni, which served not only to define the character of the Veddas but also to establish how they were related to the Sinhalas. As the "children of Kuveni," Veddas asserted both their difference from the Sinhalas and their claim to be the original inhabitants of the country. At the same time, by emphasizing their descent from Vijaya, they could claim kinship, if not with all the

Sinhalas, then certainly with the earliest Sinhala kings. This enabled them also to affirm their royal status, despite their poverty. Moreover, their descent from Kuveni, who was known to command demonic forces, also identified them as a people with special connections to the world of gods and demons. Elsewhere in mythology this aspect of their identity was strengthened by the story of how god Kataragama chose as his consort Valliamma, who had been raised by Veddas. Some people in Kukulewa described the ceremony of gambädi räjakäriya as a celebration of their adopted sister's marriage to the great god, whose intimate affinal relationship to the Veddas was thus commemorated every year.

By such means the human community of Kukulewa was placed within a larger world in which people interacted not only with one another but also with gods and demons. One effect of this was to imbue the definition of the local community with a supernatural authority, for it was the village's tutelary deity who had laid down its boundaries and thus circumscribed its membership. No less important, norms of behavior among those who belonged together in the same community were ethically reinforced by the knowledge that the gods were pleased by virtuous conduct and angered by behavior that violated the norms of kinship. This in turn provided practical reasons for conforming to communal norms, since it was understood that, although the actions of the deities could not be precisely predicted, they were likely to bless the village when they were pleased, and to impose suffering and misfortune on it when they were angry.

Thus the people of Kukulewa inhabited a culturally constructed world in which their interactions with one another had immediate implications for their relations with gods and demons, and vice versa. In this context encounters with gods and demons, and statements about them, constituted a set of discursive practices that addressed fundamental issues of community. I do not mean to imply by this that the people of Kukulewa deceived themselves, or that they suffered from some form of "false consciousness." I am not suggesting that, although they may have *thought* they were dealing with gods and demons, they were *really* conducting a discourse about community. Crude reductionisms of that kind are as unnecessary as they are demeaning. No, they really were talking about gods and demons. But the idiom of gods and demons was extraordinarily rich and multifaceted, and its concrete imagery comprehensively encompassed the kinds of issues that I, as a social anthropologist, have been trained to address in the comparatively precise but more abstract language of concepts like "community," "identity," and "solidarity."

Imagining the Nation

In recent decades, in Kukulewa as in many other parts of the world, rapid and profound changes in the conditions of life have come to challenge the reproduction of culturally constructed worlds that were previously taken for granted. The commercialization of agriculture (chapter 4) and the steady intrusion of the state into village affairs (chapter 5) undermined established patterns of economic and political organization that had formerly helped to sustain the village as the central focus of community. But if the primordiality of established bases of community was thereby placed in jeopardy, vigorous efforts to substitute new ties of unquestionable attachment were scarcely less apparent.

The reorientation of village agriculture from subsistence to the market led agrarian practices that had previously helped to support the sense of community in Kukulewa to fall into decline. Social relations of production conducted in the idiom of kinship became less frequent, as villagers increasingly came to seek their livelihood through connections with traders and employers outside the village. Communal values, however, were not entirely displaced from agriculture. In fact, as illustrated by the claims of Wannihamy and Wimaladasa reported in chapter 3, their virtue was still loudly affirmed. But such assertions were scarcely more than a residual attempt to preserve some semblance of the communal relationships that had formerly permeated the practice of agriculture.

The impact of changes in political organization was, if anything, even more drastic, not only because they brought villagers into direct and open competition with one another but also because they introduced new ethical principles that claimed priority over that of mutuality among kin. Factional conflict in Kukulewa was frequent and often fierce; but only from the mid-1970s, after local branches of both the UNP and the SLFP were established in the village, did it become predominantly organized in terms of party political competition, and only after that did party loyalty come to present a serious threat to kinship as the primary basis of solidarity.

The incorporation of Kukulewa into national markets and the national polity was accompanied and facilitated by the vociferous propagation of a nationalist ideology that authoritatively constituted individuals as Sinhala Buddhist subjects. Sinhala nationalism, the general features of which were described in chapter 5, was a discourse of hegemony in terms of which those who wielded power not only justified their rule to themselves but also sought to win the consent of those whom they commanded. This discourse was both expansionary and exclusionary. It reached out to include marginal groups, such as the people of Kukulewa, who could be brought within the embrace of its imagined community, but it also punitively excluded those, most notably and tragically the Tamils, whom it could not absorb. At the same time nationalist discourse also homogenized those whom it addressed. Internal differences of caste, class, and region were suppressed in a barrage of interpellations that emphasized the single, unitary identity shared by all Sinhala Buddhists.

In recent decades vast amounts of labor have been invested in disseminating dominant images of the Sinhala nation. In the early 1980s the most spectacular occasions for this activity were ceremonial events like the opening of Samadigama (chapter 7), which were skillfully constructed to function both as rituals of development and as pageants of nationalism. Celebrations of this kind, the endless succession of which served ever more securely to articulate the discourse of economic modernization with that of religious tradition, were staged almost every day in one part of the country or another and had come to engage much of the time and attention of senior politicians (Tennekoon 1988). Alongside these spectacles the work of ideological propagation was also assiduously carried forward by other, less ostentatious means, to the point where nationalist discourse threatened to saturate social life, even in villages like Kukulewa that were remote from the centers of power. It informed virtually all projects of rural development, it permeated not only the mass media but also educational and religious practices, and it was even obligatorily invoked in villagers' encounters with politicians and government officials.

Thus although the people of Kukulewa were unaccustomed to the kind of official attention that was showered on them at the opening of Samadigama, much of what was said and performed on that occasion was already familiar to them. If they had not previously been treated to such a concentrated dose of nationalist rhetoric, they were nonetheless well acquainted with its principal ingredients. The ceremony at Samadigama may then have provided a privileged site for the dissemination of Sinhala nationalism, but the ritual assertions made on that occasion were marked more by the authority with which they were invested than by the novelty of their content.

Sinhala nationalism, however, was far from being a fully integrated and wholly coherent ideological formation, and some of its tenets were more readily accepted in Kukulewa than others. Certain elements of nationalism had long been part of village culture. Others were fully congruent with it and were easily absorbed, even coming to form part of the villagers' unquestioned assumptions about the world. Indeed, as it spread across the terrain of common sense, nationalist discourse presented relatively few challenges to the preconstructed subjectivities (Hall 1988:49) it sought to encompass. On the contrary, the local culture of the village provided fertile soil for the dissemination of an ideology that portrayed the Sinhala nation as a nation of villages and the peasant farmer as its most authentic representative. Within this framework, affirmation of one's identity as a member of the Sinhala Buddhist nation was perfectly compatible with continued attachment to membership in the village community. Even the notion that, despite their Vedda ancestry, the people of Kukulewa were to be included among the Sinhalas was hardly a radical innovation, since they already spoke Sinhala, professed Buddhism, and counted the founder of the Sinhala nation among their ancestors.

Nationalist penetration of the villagers' consciousness was not, however, accomplished solely by means of subtle persuasion, by infiltrating their common sense, articulating its points of congruence with nationalist discourse and covertly reshaping it in a nationalist direction. The struggle for hegemony was waged at the level of discursive as well as of practical consciousness, and some of its elements at times became matters of lively debate. Most prominent in this regard was that strand of nationalist ideology which, in appealing to the model of ancient kingship, raised issues of social justice and righteous government that were of abiding interest and immediate moment to the people of Kukulewa. Nationalist affirmations that rulers had the responsibility to govern virtuously, and thereby promote the moral and material welfare of the people, were warmly applauded in Kukulewa. At the same time villagers used this criterion of legitimacy as a critical standard against which to assess the actual performance of government.

Other elements of Sinhala nationalism seem to have exercised less appeal in Kukulewa. In my experience, for example, expressions of ethnic hatred were largely absent from the village, even in July 1983, when Tamils were being violently assaulted in many parts of the country. Perhaps it was continued attachment to their Vedda identity that inhibited the villagers' susceptibility to those more chauvinistic currents of nationalist ideology that emphasized the exclusive territorial claims and religious privilege of the Sinhala "race."

Although the ubiquity of nationalist discourse stemmed largely from efforts to educate the consent of subaltern classes, its presence was also an effect of power, as well as the product of the government's coercive determination that the language of Sinhala nationalism was to be an imperative means of access to the resources it controlled. For a villager to position himself inside this discourse, then, did not necessarily indicate either an unreflective adoption of nationalist ideology or a reasoned acceptance of its merits. It could just as well have followed the pragmatic recognition that use of nationalist discourse was indispensable to the acquisition of valued goods and services.

In combination, the education of consent and the threat of exclusion from state resources imposed a powerful discipline. But nationalist colonization of the practical consciousness of Kukulewa villagers had not yet become, by the early 1980s, comprehensively hegemonic. It had indeed occupied much of the terrain of their common sense, but it had not mastered and transformed the whole of it. Official rhetoric enveloped the village community in that of the nation, but the former still retained a measure of autonomy. The hegemonic sway of nationalist discourse was not total, nor was it beyond challenge. It successfully encompassed village culture, but there was no insistence on its formal precedence at every moment. It exerted definite pressures and set definite limits, but within those limits it left room to maneuver. Thus it was a matter of common sense among Kukulewa villagers that they somehow belonged within the national community of Sinhala Buddhism, as they were officially informed—or reminded—at the ceremonial opening of Samadigama, but they were not also obliged to surrender their identity as Veddas. They were not forced to choose between these two identities, and indeed, if somewhat uneasily and inconsistently, most of them maintained some attachment to both. Each of the two could then be adopted and asserted selectively, according to the circumstances at hand.

Thus, despite the congruence between the village community as imagined in Kukulewa and the village community as represented in Sinhala nationalism, the articulation of local and national discourses remained only weakly developed. The Village Awakening Program placed Kukulewa firmly within the Sinhala nation, but its location within the ideological configuration of the nation remained diffuse and imprecise. This reflected both the continued attachment of its inhabitants to their Vedda identity and their greater isolation, as compared to most Sinhala villagers, from the generative sources of Sinhala culture. There was no Buddhist temple in the village, and although it did contain a government school, much of its adult population was still functionally illiterate. Moreover, its school-teachers generally preferred to reside in neighboring villages that were better appointed than was Kukulewa. Consequently there was a notable absence from the village of the kind of cultural brokers whose role in linking local circumstances to nationalist discourse elsewhere in Sri Lanka has been convincingly demonstrated by Jonathan Spencer (1990a). Such local agents of nationalism—typically teachers, minor officials, and Buddhist monks—whose narratives connected local events to the larger story of the nation were not (yet) active in Kukulewa.

Under these circumstances the rhetoric of Sinhala Buddhist nationalism was unable to saturate the whole terrain on which the people of Kukulewa forged their identities and gave meaning to their lives. Many of them did, indeed, employ the discourse of nationalism when its adoption promised advantages, as when they approached politicians and officials in search of benefits controlled by the state. But when engaged in their own internal affairs they reverted to their own local idiom, which, despite the similarities and connections, was only marginally infused with specifically nationalist themes. In this small but significant space the cultural world they constructed, and the images of community it sustained, were neither wholly subordinate nor directly oppositional to the dominant nationalism. They constituted, rather, a still viable and at least partially autonomous, if also threatened, alternative. And it was principally with reference to this alternative cultural formation that many of them tried to deal with the crisis of community precipitated by the Village Awakening Program.

Crisis of Community

The Village Awakening Program was one of a number of initiatives launched by the UNP after its return to power in 1977 that were carefully fashioned within the framework of Sinhala nationalist discourse. Drawing on the unquestioned conventions of nationalist memory, its ambition was to awaken rural society from its slumber and restore it to the vitality it had reputedly enjoyed in precolonial times. The program thus looked backward as much as forward, envisaging the future development of rural society largely as the recovery of an imagined past.

At the same time Village Awakening was also designed as a mechanism for the dispensation of political patronage and the accumulation of political support. As events in Kukulewa were to show, however, this function proved incompatible with that of affirming the restoration of the village community as a central component of national revitalization. The intensity of competition between the political parties was such that appeals to village unity were unavailing. The threat erupted first in the disputes over labor at the construction site, later—and more decisively—in the question of how the houses should be allocated (chapter 6). Naidurala's stubborn adherence to the original policy of distributing them among the sixty root families in the village expressed his continued attachment to the principle of equity within the community of kin. But the supremacy of that principle was directly challenged when Jinadasa and Wijeratne argued that the houses should be given only to supporters of the UNP. Individual attempts to evade communal responsibilities were by no means unknown in Kukulewa, but in my experience such open and organized denial of their primacy was unprecedented. The shock was profound, and the anger and dismay that erupted appear to have been generated not merely by individual disappointment at the failure to receive a house, but also by collective outrage at the blatant disavowal of a moral principle that had not previously been brought into question.

Conflict over the housing allocations thus exposed a central contradiction in the nationalist project. Sinhala Buddhist discourse celebrated the nation as being composed of harmonious and cooperative villages, but it was largely propagated within an intensely competitive system of party politics that only managed to exacerbate factional conflict inside the villages. The Village Awakening Program was conceived as part of the hegemonic attempt to stitch together the nation into a single community, but its effect in Kukulewa was to tear apart the fabric of village unity. The contradiction was most nakedly exposed in the ceremonial opening of Samadigama (chapter 7), at which a pageant of Sinhala national unity was performed before an audience of villagers deeply divided by the project whose completion was being celebrated. On one side was a colorful display of the Sinhala nation, of its long-standing devotion to Buddhism, of the incorporation of the Veddas within it, and of its commitment to recuperate the values of the glorious past. On the other was the assembly of Kukulewa villagers, half of whom were outraged at the partisan distribution of the houses. What the project accomplished, in short, was not a reawakening of the village community but an intensification of cleavages within it.

The rift, however, was not pushed to the point of complete fission. The separate performance of gambädi räjakäriya in Kukulewa and Samadigama affirmed the distinct identity of the new settlement, but the two villages were so close, and their inhabitants so closely related, that despite all the anger and resentment it was hard to sustain an absolute disjunction. During the next three years social relations between the inhabitants of Kukulewa and Samadigama were gradually ameliorated. At the same time, however, a new rupture began to appear in Samadigama, provoked by what was perceived as the high-handed behavior of Jinadasa and his henchmen (chapters 8 and 9). By 1983 dissidents were pointedly referring to the alien origin of the Fernandos and the improper marriages with members of the Vedda variga that had allowed them to establish their power in the village. The Fernandos were also criticized for their arrogance and dishonesty, for their propensity to drink and fight, for their loose sexual behavior, and more generally for conduct that violated the local norms of communal life. These kinds of disruptive behavior were by no means restricted to the Fernandos, but many people believed that it was they who had introduced them into the village.

In this context, the charge of sorcery that was raised when Seelawathie was attacked by a demon served not only to focus further attention on the ethics of kinship but also to direct it back to the issue of relations between Kukulewa and Samadigama (chapter 10). This focus was further strengthened when, after Wijeratne also became possessed, his god demanded that "the children of Kuveni" bury their differences, reestablish the harmony appropriate to their mutual kinship, and in future hold only a single annual performance of gambädi räjakäriya that would reunite the people of Kukulewa and Samadigama (chapter 11).

These interventions were a forceful reminder that communal relations were subject to supernatural sanction. The definition and creation of community were not exclusively, or even primarily, a matter of human reason and discretion. On the contrary, communal relations were placed within an encompassing cosmic process in which social action was constrained by the exercise of superhuman power. Local communities were defined not only by ties of kinship but also by the regulations that gods had imposed. People could influence the behavior of gods and demons, but they were also at the mercy of these supernatural beings. They could neither avoid the attention of supernatural beings nor escape their bidding. And it was common knowledge that solidarity within the village and harmonious relations with its gods were mutually interdependent. If the people behaved toward one another with propriety, the gods would be pleased and would bestow prosperity on the village, but if communal norms were violated the anger of the gods would bring suffering, not only to the immediate offenders but possibly also to all their fellow villagers. Thus, assessment of the actions of both humans and deities was conducted simultaneously and within a single evaluative framework.

When Seelawathie was afflicted, for example, everyone quickly recognized that she had been attacked by a demon, but what kind of demon had attacked her, and why? Several different answers were given, each of which combined a specific recollection of how certain villagers had behaved in the past with a generalized knowledge of how gods and demons normally behaved. Perhaps the demon really had been sent to attack her by disaffected supporters of the SLFP. Or perhaps god Kadavara was expressing his anger at the villagers' failure to make offerings to him. Or perhaps Kadavara was punishing Seelawathie's husband for his disrespect. Or perhaps Bahirava and his demons were angry because Samadigama had been built at a site of buried treasure. None of these interpretations was implausible, but each carried different implications for the assessment of social relations within the village. Similarly, when villagers discussed whether Wijeratne was possessed by the same god that had formerly possessed Kandappu, they were arguing not only about the disposition of supernatural powers but also about the current state of communal relations.

Many of these discussions appealed to the authority of the past to determine what should be done in the present. This was strongly evident in the way villagers responded to Wijeratne's god's stated wish that Kukulewa and Samadigama be brought back together by holding a combined performance of gambädi rājakāriya in the future. On this issue both Kalubanda, the uḍäkki kapuvā, and Ukkubanda, the Samadigama kapurāla, were agreed that the prospect was virtually ruled out by actions the village's god had taken in the past. When a god took up residence in a village he laid down its boundaries, and subsequently he gave his protection only to those who lived within those boundaries. A village community, then, was composed of those who enjoyed the protection of the same god and who lived within the boundaries he had established. The scope of communalization in the present was thus restricted by divinely authoritative action taken in the past.

Nor was it only sacred tradition that was invoked in this way. When Dingiribanda, the Kukulewa kapurāla, asserted that the gamarālas, the village chiefs whose hereditary authority was linked to their holdings of particular plots of irrigated land in the main field, should properly take the lead in organizing the performance of gambädi rājakāriya, he was recalling a feature of Kandyan Sinhala social organization in Anuradhapura District that had long lost any practical relevance it might once have had. More than that, when he argued that pangukārayō (shareholders in the village field) should contribute to the ceremony in proportion to the size of their landholdings, he was evoking a form of moral economy that not only stood in contrast to the increasingly impersonal and market-oriented practice of contemporary agriculture, but was also one that it would have been impossible to institutionalize in Samadigama. The point was not made explicitly, but everyone was well aware that Samadigama had no paddy fields of its own, and therefore no one who could claim the title of gamarāla. It would not have been difficult then to draw the further inferences that no one in Samadigama was authorized to sponsor a collective ceremony such as gambädi rājakāriya and that Samadigama could not therefore constitute a village community.

These rhetorical mobilizations of the local past were paralleled at the higher level of discourse about the national community of Sinhala Buddhists. At the local level the village community was confined within the boundaries laid down by its protective deity. At the national level it was the mission of the Sinhala people to maintain Buddhist teachings within the area the Buddha had marked out on the three visits which, according to legend, he made to Sri Lanka. At the local level the village was constituted as a moral community in which the gamarālas and more prosperous pangukārayō were obliged to extend assistance to their poorer kinsmen. At the national level contemporary rulers willingly acknowledged the responsibility assumed by their royal predecessors to govern virtuously and provide for the welfare of the people. In such ways local constructions of the village community nestled comfortably within the embrace of Sinhala nationalist discourse.

In light of this it is perhaps worth remarking again on the meager extent to which some of the most central and widely propagated tenets of Sinhala Buddhist nationalism seem to have penetrated the discursive consciousness of the villagers. In 1983 the vexatious problem of restoring harmony within the village was still discussed in terms of winning the favor of the gods, rather than of following Buddhist precepts. Nobody mentioned the ancient rock inscription of which so much had been made at the opening of Samadigama three years earlier, and only Kalubanda linked the sacred bo-tree to Buddhist practices. For others the tree was the abode of the Black God, not a core symbol of the Sinhala Buddhist nation. No less revealing was the fact that, despite their subjection to the relentless bombardment of nationalist rhetoric, when villagers sought to recreate a sense of common identity with their fellows they still addressed them as "children of Kuveni" rather than as Sinhala Buddhists.

Persistent attachment to long established understandings, on matters ranging from the mutual obligations of those who belonged together as kinsmen to the characteristic dispositions of gods and demons, served both to constrain and to direct the actions of Kukulewa villagers by circumscribing what villagers thought they could do and at the same time instructing them in what they ought to do. And to the extent that these understandings saturated people's common sense, they also defined the limits of what was imaginable. But despite continued appeals to the authority of the past, these limits were not absolutely immutable. Some of the more conservative villagers might argue that Seelawathie must have been possessed by a demon rather than a god, because gods never did possess women, but others were persuaded by the evidence of what they had observed to relinquish this conventional wisdom. Most generally, while the villagers' cultural constructions imposed limits on how they would construe the events in which they were embroiled, they simultaneously provided an abundant treasury of familiar categories and conceptions that could be flexibly, selectively, and creatively deployed to interpret what had happened in the past, to make sense of what was happening now, and to shape what would happen in the future.

The Village Awakening Program had, however, thrown into serious question the adequacy of these discursive resources to deal with the rapidly changing conditions of social life. The strength of communal relations within the village had always lain in the consensual and unquestioned recognition of their ethical primacy. But the housing allocations had demonstrated not only that some villagers were now prepared to deny that primacy but also that they could do so successfully, with official endorsement and to their own material advantage. In 1983, under the influence of the god who was possessing him, Wijeratne was loudly proclaiming the virtues of the village community, but his leading role in ensuring that the houses were distributed along party lines had by no means been forgotten, and many villagers remained deeply suspicious of his intentions. Combined with his god's reluctance to demonstrate his miraculous powers, this did little to advance the cause he was advocating.

Nevertheless his god's repeated appeals for village unity and amity among kin were generally applauded. No alternative source of moral authority was as persuasive as that of the divinely sanctioned village community. Participation in the national community of Sinhala Buddhism remained diffuse, while party affiliation was more successful in providing access to material resources than in generating a sense of belonging together. It was still by reference to interactions between human and supernatural beings that the Kukulewa villagers could make the most intelligible sense of their lives, it was still the ethics of kinship that furnished the most convincing codes for conduct, and it was still the village and the variga that remained the most compelling focus for the definition of identity and the experience of solidarity. For my own part, however, as I contemplated the ways in which the villagers' lives were being transformed, I found myself speculating about a future, perhaps not so very distant, when such appeals to traditional ideals of community might be unable to summon up anything much more substantial than nostalgic yearning for an imagined past.

Notes

Chapter 2. Orientations

1. The principal texts are Leach 1960, 1961; Obeyesekere 1967; Tambiah 1958, 1965; Yalman 1960, 1962, 1963, 1967.

2. For a theoretical treatment of this issue, and a critical assessment of studies of agrarian classes in South Asia, see Brow 1981b.

3. For the results of this conference see Brow and Weeramunda 1992.

4. See Goonetileke 1984 for a bibliography of early accounts of the events of July 1983.

5. See especially Gramsci 1971. Besides Gramsci, I have been most influenced by the work of Raymond Williams (1977, 1980) and Stuart Hall (1979, 1980a, 1980b, 1986a, 1986b, 1988).

6. The relative priority of conditioning versus agency has been much debated in recent times, pitting "structuralists" against "culturalists" (Hall 1980b) and provoking such extravagant polemics as E. P. Thompson's (1978) sustained critique of Althusserian structuralism; see Perry Anderson's (1980) review. Thompson had earlier introduced his classic account, *The Making of the English Working Class* (1963:9), as "a study in an active process, which owes as much to agency as to conditioning." Pierre Bourdieu's influential *Outline of a Theory of Practice* (1977) is an attempt at theoretical synthesis, as are several of Anthony Giddens's works (1979, 1984). See also Ortner's (1984) account of the appearance of practice theory within anthropology.

7. These forces are what Durkheim (1964:10) called social facts, defined "by the power of external coercion" that they exercise over individuals.

8. This understanding of social determination as including both the setting of constraining limits and the exertion of constitutive pressures bears comparison with Foucault's (1977, 1980) insistence that power be considered not only as something external and restrictive but also as something internal and productive (cf. Mitchell 1991:xi).

9. Studies of hegemonic struggles to define the past that have influenced the present account include Alonso 1988a, 1988b; Bommes and Wright 1982; Comaroff 1985; Comaroff and Comaroff 1987; Corrigan and Sayer 1985; Turton 1984; Wright 1985.

10. Influential studies of popular resistance include Thompson 1963; Genovese 1974; Willis 1981; Scott 1985.

Chapter 3. Of Savages and Kings

1. For a more detailed analysis of ecological constraints on chena and paddy cultivation see Brow 1978a:92–104.

2. The historical summary presented in this and the next two sections draws on de Silva's (1981) general account, supplemented by other, more specialized studies by scholars including Rahula (1966) on the history of Buddhism; Gunawardana (1979a) on the early medieval period; Leach (1959) on irrigation; Pieris (1956), Dewaraja (1971), and Seneviratne (1978) on the kingdom of Kandy; and de Silva (1973) and Leach (1961) on the period of British colonial rule.

3. The segmentary organization of the precolonial Sinhala state is emphasized by Nissan and Stirrat (1987, 1990), drawing on the theoretical formulations of Anderson (1983), Gellner (1983), Stein (1983), and Tambiah (1976, 1977). Dirks's (1987, 1989) identification of royal honor rather than ritual purity as the discursive component that was most productive of hierarchy in South Indian kingdoms provides new perspectives on the operations of power and authority in the region.

4. Hocart (1970:117) long ago observed that "every petty feudal lord, every village chief in fact, copies on a small scale the royal state."

5. For the impact of plantation agriculture, see Bandarage 1983 and de Silva 1985. The effect of the plantations on peasant agriculture has been intensely debated. See Ceylon 1951; Sarkar and Tambiah 1957; Gunasinghe 1975, 1979; Shanmugaratnam 1980, 1983, 1985a.

6. This interpretation draws on the brief but characteristically incisive analysis in Leach 1961:19–20, 69–71, 76–78.

7. On peasant resettlement in the Dry Zone, see Farmer 1957 and Shanmugaratnam 1985b.

8. For accounts of agrarian change throughout Sri Lanka since independence see Abeysekera 1985 and Brow and Weeramunda 1992. Moore (1985) provides a valuable analysis of peasant agriculture in relation to state policy and national politics. Leach's (1961) exemplary study of kinship and land tenure in Pul Eliya, conducted at a time (1954) when the village was still largely turned in on itself, provides the benchmark for all subsequent analyses of agrarian change in Anuradhapura District. Readers who are familiar with it will recognize that I have drawn on it throughout my own narrative. More recent accounts of village life in the North Central Province, apart from my own work, include studies by Hettige (1984, 1992) and Perera (1985, 1992).

9. See chapter 5.

10. I analyzed Western representations of the Veddas—scholarly, administrative and popular—in Brow 1978a:3–40. The classic ethnographic study is Seligmann and Seligmann 1911. On the Tamil-speaking Coast Veddas see Dart 1985. For a critical review of some recent accounts of the Veddas see Brow 1991.

Chapter 4. The Village Community Confronts the Market

1. Analysis of kinship and marriage relations within the Anuradhapura Vedda variga is one of the principal themes in Brow 1978a.

2. For more detailed accounts of agriculture in Kukulewa, and of changes in its social organization up to 1970, see Brow 1976, 1978a, 1978b, 1980, 1981a.

3. For accounts of traditional authorities in the villages of Nuvarakalaviya see Ievers 1899; Codrington 1938; Pieris 1956; and Leach 1961.

4. Sinhala kinship terminology is of the Dravidian type, in which a man uses the same term *(māmā)* for his mother's brother and his wife's father and, correspondingly, the same term *(bänä)* for his sister's son and his daughter's husband. Consistently with this he uses the same term for his brother's wife's father and his sister's husband's father as for his own father-in-law. For an analysis of the way kin terms were used in Kukulewa, and of Dravidian kinship terminology more generally, see Brow 1978a:67–74 and passim.

Chapter 5. Party Politics and Nationalist Rhetoric

1. Robinson (1975) provides an account of village politics in Sri Lanka in the 1960s. More recent ethnographic studies include Spencer 1990a and Woost 1990a, 1990b, 1993, 1994. The topic is also addressed by several of the contributors to Brow and Weeramunda 1992, especially Silva, Gunasekera, Hettige, and Spencer.

2. This is not, of course, to claim that at the national level there was no association between class and party affiliation. For analyses that probe the class basis of competition between the UNP and the SLFP see Shastri 1983a, 1983b; see also Moore 1985.

3. The various parties of the left had no presence in Kukulewa, although they did have some supporters in the surrounding area, particularly among more urbanized and educated strata.

4. The historical development of Sinhala nationalism has been the subject of extensive scholarship in recent years, linked to the country's prolonged and devastating ethnic crisis. Important works include Gunawardana 1979b; Roberts 1979; Manor 1984; Committee for Rational Development 1984; Social Scientists Association 1985; Jayawardena 1986; Tambiah 1986, 1992; Kapferer 1988; Spencer 1990b, 1990c; Kemper 1992. By contrast, ethnographic studies of how nationalist ideology has been disseminated in the rural areas remain relatively scarce. But see Tennekoon 1988; Spencer 1990a; Woost 1990a, 1990b, 1993, 1994; and, for Tamil nationalism, Whitaker 1990.

5. For a study of the place of the peasantry in nationalist ideology, see Moore 1989, 1992. Spencer (1990a:138–64, 1992) gives an insightful account of various ways in which the village community has been represented by officials, scholars, and politicians.

6. The Temple of the Tooth is located in Kandy and contains the sacred tooth relic of the Buddha, which has long been intimately connected with Sinhala kingship. See Obeyesekere 1966; Seneviratne 1978.

Chapter 6. The Awakening Village

1. For accounts of the Sarvodaya Shramadana Movement see Goulet 1981; Macy 1985; Gombrich and Obeyesekere 1988:243–52; Woost 1993:506–7.

2. The following account is based mainly on documents held in government offices in Anuradhapura.

3. The account presented in this and the next two sections is based on the minutes of the Kukulewa RDS, the minutes of the Kukulewa branch of the UNP, and interviews conducted in 1983.

4. On the place of the bo-tree in the imagining of the Sinhala nation, see Nissan 1988:261; Gombrich and Obeyesekere 1988:388; Kemper 1992:passim.

Chapter 7. The Rise of the Fernandos

1. This was the first house that one passed on entering Samadigama from the old village. I was able to rent it in 1983, and Somaratne and I lived in it during the period of field research.

2. My account of the operations of the variga court, based principally on the recollections of Kukulewa villagers, is supplemented by the insightful observations of Edmund Leach (1961:70–74, 307–9). See also Pieris 1956:255–56.

3. For analyses of the extent of variga endogamy, and the frequency of extra-variga marriages, see Brow 1978a.

Chapter 9. Gods and Demons

1. My general description of religious beliefs and practices in Kukulewa is based on observations and discussions conducted in the village at various times since 1968. It has also been shaped by the substantial scholarly literature on Sinhala religion, much of which is of exceptionally high quality. Among the book-length monographs that treat religion in its social context are the outstanding Gombrich 1971; Malalgoda 1976; Seneviratne 1978; Obeyesekere 1981, 1984, 1990; Carrithers 1983; Kapferer 1983; Gombrich and Obeyesekere 1988; Stirrat 1992. Studies of demons and possession that bear comparison with the present work, although each of them develops a perspective distinct from that adopted here, include Obeyesekere 1969, 1970, 1975, 1981; Stirrat 1977, 1992; Kapferer 1979a, 1979b, 1983, 1988; Scott 1992, 1994.

2. For another version of this myth, also recorded in Kukulewa, and accompanied by an extensive analysis, see Obeyesekere 1990:105–39.

Glossary

Note on Transliteration

For the most part, Sinhala words have been given a plural form as if they were English words, by adding a final "s." In those cases where both singular and plural Sinhala forms appear in the text, both also appear in the glossary.

Terms

ābharana	ornaments, insignia	ekamutukama	unity, community
andē	sharecropping tenancy	gama	village
anumätirāla	spirit medium	gamarāla	village chief
apē hura	our chief, cousin (a term of familiarity)	gambädi rājakāriya	annual village-wide ceremony (see also rājakāriya)
attam	exchange labor, cooperative labor	gamsabhāva	village council, village tribunal
avatāra	apparition, manifestation of a supernatural being	Gam Udava	Village Awakening, a program of rural development introduced by the UNP government in 1977
ayiyā	elder brother		
balaya	power		
bänā	son-in-law; a man's sister's son; a woman's brother's son	gamvasama	plot of paddy land held by the gamarāla
bandagarika	treasurer	Goyigama	Cultivator caste
baya unna	became frightened	hēna	chena; shifting cultivation
bhikku	Buddhist monk		
Bodhisattva	future Buddha	hūniyam	sorcery
Buddhagama	Buddhist tradition	jātiya	kind, type, species, nation
cakravartin	world ruler, universal monarch	kalam	magical means of challenging gods and demons
chena	(Sinhala: hēna) shifting cultivation		
dāna	alms-giving, offering to the gods	kapurāla	priest of a god
		Karava	Fisher caste
dēvālē	shrine of a god	karma	law of moral causation
deva; pl. deviyō	god	kattādiyā	exorcist
dharma	teachings of the Buddha	kavum	oilcake
dharmistha samajaya	virtuous or just society	kayiya	work party
		kemmura	auspicious, appropriate day to propitiate gods
dukkha	suffering		

Glossary

kiribhat	milk-rice
magula; pl. magul	festival
maha	large, great; main cultivation season
mahatma deviyō	virtuous gods
Mahavamsa	the Great Chronicle
Mahaweli Development Project	(Sinhala: Mahaväli) massive development project including both irrigation and hydroelectric power
malli	younger brother
māmā	mother's brother; father-in-law
mantra	magical spell
massina	brother-in-law; male cross-cousin
māyam	in trance, possessed
minissu	people
mudalāli	trader, merchant
mul	original, primary
murakārayā	watchman
näna	sister-in-law; female cross-cousin
näyō	kin
nikam	for nothing, gratuitously
nirvāṇa	enlightenment, release from the cycle of rebirths, nonbeing
Nuvarakalaviya	province of the kingdom of Kandy; subsequently known as Anuradhapura District
pangukārayō	shareholders in village paddy field
pavula; pl. pavul	family
prēta	ghost
rājakāriya	service owed to a king or lord
rājaraṭa	land of the kings
raṭe mahatmaya	lord of a district in Kandyan times; senior local official under colonial rule
samādhi	absorption, mental discipline
Sarvodaya Shramadana	an influential grassroots development organization
sihi nathi unna	became unconscious
sramadāna	voluntary collective labor
Sri Maha Bodhi	the Great Bo-Tree in Anuradhapura
uḍäkki kapuvā	ritual drummer
vädda; pl. väddo	Vedda; reputed descendant of Sri Lanka's aboriginal population
vāhana kārayā	vehicle-man
vāhila	possessed
valavva	manor house
Vanniya	regional lord
varam	authority, warrant, license
variga	caste, subcaste
variga sabha	caste court
vatta	garden, yard
vedarāla	doctor
vel vidāne	irrigation headman
vihara	Buddhist temple
yakā, yaksa; pl. yakku	demon
yala	minor cultivation season

References Cited

Abercrombie, Nicholas, Stephen Hill, and Bryan S. Turner

1980   *The Dominant Ideology Thesis.* London: Allen and Unwin.

Abeysekera, Charles, ed.

1985   *Capital and Peasant Production: Studies in the Continuity and Discontinuity of Agrarian Structures in Sri Lanka.* Colombo: Social Scientists' Association.

Alonso, Ana María

1988a   The Effects of Truth: Re-Presentations of the Past and the Imagining of Community. *The Journal of Historical Sociology* 1:33–57.

1988b   "Progress" as Disorder and Dishonor: Discourses of Serrano Resistance. *Critique of Anthropology* 8:13–33.

Althusser, Louis

1972   *Politics and History.* London: New Left Books.

Althusser, Louis, and Etienne Balibar

1970   *Reading Capital.* New York: Pantheon Books.

Anderson, Benedict

1983   *Imagined Communities: Reflections on the Origin and Spread of Nationalism.* London: Verso.

Anderson, Perry

1980   *Arguments within English Marxism.* London: Verso.

Ariyaratne, A. T.

1970   *Sarvodaya Shramadana: Growth of a People's Movement.* Colombo: Shramadana.

Bandarage, Asoka

1983   *Colonialism in Sri Lanka: The Political Economy of the Kandyan Highlands, 1833–1886.* The Hague: Mouton.

Bendix, Reinhard

1962   *Max Weber: An Intellectual Portrait.* Garden City: Doubleday.

References Cited

1969   *Nation Building and Citizenship: Studies of Our Changing Social Order.* Garden City: Doubleday.

Bommes, Michael, and Patrick Wright

1982   "Charms of Residence": The Public and the Past. In *Making Histories: Studies in History-Writing and Politics,* edited by Richard Johnson et al. London: Hutchinson.

Bourdieu, Pierre

1977   *Outline of a Theory of Practice.* Cambridge: Cambridge University Press.

Brow, James

1976   The Impact of Population Growth on the Agricultural Practices and Settlement Patterns of the Anuradhapura Veddas. *Contributions to Asian Studies* 9:80–96.

1978a   *Vedda Villages of Anuradhapura: The Historical Anthropology of a Community in Sri Lanka.* Seattle: University of Washington Press.

1978b   The Changing Structure of Appropriations in Vedda Agriculture. *American Ethnologist* 5(3):448–67.

1980   The Ideology and Practice of Share-Cropping Tenancy in Kukulewa and Pul Eliya. *Ethnology* 19(1):47–67.

1981a   Class Formation and Ideological Practice: A Case from Sri Lanka. *The Journal of Asian Studies* 40(4):703–18.

1981b   Some Problems in the Analysis of Agrarian Classes in South Asia. *Peasant Studies* 9(1):26–39.

1988   In Pursuit of Hegemony: Representations of Authority and Justice in a Sri Lankan Village. *American Ethnologist* 15(2):311–27.

1990a   Notes on Community, Hegemony and the Uses of the Past. *Anthropological Quarterly* 63(1):1–6.

1990b   The Incorporation of a Marginal Community within the Sinhalese Nation. *Anthropological Quarterly* 63(1):7–17.

1990c   Nationalist Rhetoric and Local Practice: The Fate of the Village Community in Kukulewa. In *Sri Lanka: History and the Roots of Conflict,* edited by Jonathan Spencer. London: Routledge.

1991   Review of *The Vanishing Aborigines: Sri Lanka's Veddas in Transition,* edited by K.N.O. Dharmadasa and S.W.R. de A. Samarasinghe. *Ethnic Studies Report* 9(2):54–57.

1992   Agrarian Change and the Struggle for Community in Kukulewa, Anuradhapura District. In *Agrarian Change in Sri Lanka,* edited by James Brow and Joe Weeramunda. New Delhi: Sage Publications.

Brow, James, and Joe Weeramunda, eds.

1992   *Agrarian Change in Sri Lanka.* New Delhi: Sage Publications.

References Cited

Carrithers, Michael

1983   *The Forest Monks of Sri Lanka*. Delhi: Oxford University Press.

Ceylon, Government of

1951   *Sessional Paper XVIII (Report of the Kandyan Peasantry Commission)*. Colombo.

Clifford, James

1983   On Ethnographic Authority. *Representations* 1(2):118–46.

Clifford, James, and George Marcus, eds.

1986   *Writing Culture: The Poetics and Politics of Ethnography*. Berkeley: University of California Press.

Codrington, H. W.

1938   *Ancient Land Tenure and Revenue in Ceylon*. Colombo: Government Printer.

Comaroff, Jean

1985   *Body of Power, Spirit of Resistance: The Culture and History of a South African People*. Chicago: University of Chicago Press.

Comaroff, John L., and Jean Comaroff

1987   The Madman and the Migrant: Work and Labor in the Historical Consciousness of a South African People. *American Ethnologist* 14:191–209.

Committee for Rational Development, eds.

1984   *Sri Lanka: The Ethnic Conflict*. New Delhi: Navrang.

Coomaraswamy, Ananda K.

1956   *Mediaeval Sinhalese Art*. 1908. Reprint, New York: Pantheon Books.

Corrigan, Philip, and Derek Sayer

1985   *The Great Arch: English State Formation as Cultural Revolution*. Oxford: Basil Blackwell.

Dart, Jon

1985   *Ethnic Identity and Marginality among the Coast Veddas of Sri Lanka*. Ph.D. diss., University of California, San Diego.

de Silva, K. M.

1981   *A History of Sri Lanka*. London: C. Hurst & Co.

de Silva, K. M., ed.

1973   *University of Ceylon History of Ceylon*, vol. 3. Colombo: University of Ceylon.

de Silva, S.B.D.

1985   Plantations and Underdevelopment. In *Capital and Peasant Production*, edited by Charles Abeysekera. Colombo: Social Scientists' Association.

References Cited

Dewaraja, L. S.

1971   *The Kandyan Kingdom, 1707–1760.* Colombo: Lake House.

Dewey, Clive

1972   Images of the Village Community: A Study in Anglo-Indian Ideology. *Modern Asian Studies* 6(3):291–328.

Dharmadasa, K.N.O.

1990a   Veddas in the History of Sri Lanka: An Introductory Sketch. In *The Vanishing Aborigines: Sri Lanka's Veddas in Transition,* edited by K.N.O. Dharmadasa and S.W.R. de A. Samarasinghe. New Delhi: Vikas.

1990b   The Veddas' Struggle for Survival: Problems, Policies and Responses. In *The Vanishing Aborigines: Sri Lanka's Veddas in Transition,* edited by K.N.O. Dharmadasa and S.W.R. de A. Samarasinghe. New Delhi: Vikas.

Dharmadasa, K.N.O., and S.W.R. de A. Samarasinghe, eds.

1990   *The Vanishing Aborigines: Sri Lanka's Veddas in Transition.* New Delhi: Vikas.

Dickson, J. F.

1873   Report on the North-Central Province. In *Administration Reports,* Government of Ceylon. Colombo.

Dirks, Nicholas B.

1987   *The Hollow Crown: Ethnohistory of an Indian Kingdom.* Cambridge: Cambridge University Press.

1989   The Original Caste: Power, History and Hierarchy in South Asia. *Contributions to Indian Sociology* (New Series) 23(1):59–78.

Dissanayake, T.D.S.A.

1977   *J. R. Jayewardene of Sri Lanka.* Colombo: Swastika Press.

Dumont, Louis

1970   *Homo Hierarchicus: An Essay on the Caste System.* Chicago: University of Chicago Press.

Durkheim, Emile

1957   *Professional Ethics and Civic Morals.* 1904. Reprint, London: Routledge and Kegan Paul.

1964   *The Rules of Sociological Method.* 1895. Reprint, New York: Free Press.

Farmer, B. H.

1957   *Pioneer Peasant Colonization in Ceylon.* London: Oxford University Press.

Foucault, Michel

1977   *Discipline and Punish: The Birth of the Prison.* Translated by Alan Sheridan. London: Penguin.

1980   *Power/Knowledge: Selected Interviews and Other Writings 1972–1977.* Edited by Colin Gordon. New York: Pantheon Books.

Gamage, Siri

1984   The Destiny of Bintenne Veddas: Incorporation Perspectives and Problems of Re-Settlement. In *Incorporation and Rural Development,* edited by H. Heringa, U.L.J. Perera, and A. J. Weeramunda. Colombo: University of Colombo, Department of Sociology.

Geertz, Clifford

1973   *The Interpretation of Cultures.* New York: Basic Books.

Geiger, Wilhelm, trans.

1934   *Mahavamsa, or The Great Chronicle of Ceylon.* London: H. Milford.

Gellner, Ernest

1983   *Nations and Nationalism.* Oxford: Basil Blackwell.

Genovese, Eugene

1974   *Roll, Jordan, Roll: The World the Slaves Made.* New York: Pantheon.

Giddens, Anthony

1979   *Central Problems in Social Theory.* Berkeley: University of California Press.

1984   *The Constitution of Society.* Berkeley: University of California Press.

Gombrich, Richard

1971   *Precept and Practice: Traditional Buddhism in the Rural Highlands of Ceylon.* Oxford: Clarendon Press.

Gombrich, Richard, and Gananath Obeyesekere

1988   *Buddhism Transformed: Religious Change in Sri Lanka.* Princeton: Princeton University Press.

Goonetileke, H.A.I.

1984   July 1983 and the National Question in Sri Lanka: A Bibliographical Guide. *Race & Class* 26(1):159–93.

Goulet, Denis

1981   *Survival with Integrity: Sarvodaya at the Crossroads.* Colombo: Marga Institute.

Gramsci, Antonio

1971   *Selections from the Prison Notebooks.* Edited by Q. Hoare and G. Nowell-Smith. London: Lawrence and Wishart.

Gunasekara, Alex

1978   Rājakāriya or the Duty to the King in the Kandyan Kingdom of Sri Lanka.

References Cited

In *The Concept of Duty in South Asia,* edited by Wendy Doniger O'Flaherty and J. Duncan M. Derrett. New Delhi: Vikas.

Gunasekera, Tamara

1992 Democracy, Party Competition and Leadership: The Changing Power Structure in a Sinhalese Community. In *Agrarian Change in Sri Lanka,* edited by James Brow and Joe Weeramunda. New Delhi: Sage Publications.

Gunasinghe, Newton

1975 Production Relations and Classes in a Kandyan Village. *Modern Ceylon Studies* 6(2):116–39.

1979 Agrarian Relations in the Kandyan Countryside in Relation to the Concept of Extreme Social Disintegration. *Social Science Review* 1:1–40.

1986 Open Economic Policy and Peasant Production. *Upanathi* 1(1):37–67.

Gunawardana, R.A.L.H.

1979a *Robe and Plough: Monasticism and Economic Interest in Early Medieval Sri Lanka.* Tucson: University of Arizona Press.

1979b The People of the Lion: The Sinhala Identity and Ideology in History and Historiography. *Sri Lanka Journal of the Humanities* 5:1–36.

Hall, Stuart

1979 Culture, Media, and the "Ideological Effect." In *Mass Communication and Society,* edited by James Curran, Michael Gurevitch, and Janet Woollacott. Beverly Hills: Sage Publications.

1980a Race, Articulation, and Societies Structured in Dominance. In *Sociological Theories: Race and Colonialism.* Paris: UNESCO.

1980b Cultural Studies: Two Paradigms. *Media, Culture and Society* 2:57–72.

1986a Gramsci's Relevance for the Study of Race and Ethnicity. *Journal of Communication Inquiry* 10(2):5–27.

1986b The Problem of Ideology—Marxism without Guarantees. *Journal of Communication Inquiry* 10(2):28–44.

1988 The Toad in the Garden: Thatcherism among the Theorists. In *Marxism and the Interpretation of Culture,* edited by Cary Nelson and Lawrence Grossberg. Urbana: University of Illinois Press.

Hettige, S. T.

1984 *Wealth, Power and Prestige: Emerging Patterns of Social Inequality in a Peasant Context.* Colombo: Ministry of Higher Education.

1992 Agrarian Relations and the Seasonal Influx of Agricultural Labor in a Sinhalese Village in the Northcentral Province. In *Agrarian Change in Sri Lanka,* edited by James Brow and Joe Weeramunda. New Delhi: Sage Publications.

References Cited

Hettige, S. T., Jayanthi de Silva, and U. A. Chandrasena

    1993   *A Case Study on Veddha Community in Sri Lanka.* Kathmandu: UNICEF South Asia Regional Office.

Hobsbawm, E. J.

    1965   *Primitive Rebels: Studies in Archaic Forms of Social Movement in the 19th and 20th Centuries.* 1959. Reprint, New York: Norton.

Hobsbawm, Eric, and Terence Ranger, eds.

    1983   *The Invention of Tradition.* Cambridge: Cambridge University Press.

Hocart, A. M.

    1970   *Kings and Councillors: An Essay in the Comparative Anatomy of Human Society.* Edited by Rodney Needham. 1936. Reprint, Chicago: University of Chicago Press.

Ievers, R. W.

    1899   *Manual of the North-Central Province, Ceylon.* Colombo: Government Printer.

Jayawardena, Kumari

    1986   *Ethnic and Class Conflicts in Sri Lanka.* Colombo: Navagama Printers.

Kapferer, Bruce

    1979a   Entertaining Demons: Comedy, Interaction, and Meaning in a Sinhalese Healing Ritual. *Social Analysis* 1:108–52.

    1979b   Mind, Self, and Other in Demonic Illness: The Negation and Reconstruction of Self. *American Ethnologist* 6(1):110–33.

    1983   *A Celebration of Demons.* Bloomington: Indiana University Press.

    1988   *Legends of People, Myths of State: Violence, Intolerance, and Political Culture in Sri Lanka and Australia.* Washington, D.C.: Smithsonian Institution Press.

Kemper, Steven

    1992   *The Presence of the Past: Chronicles, Politics, and Culture in Sinhala Nationalism.* Ithaca: Cornell University Press.

Knox, Robert

    1911   *An Historical Relation of Ceylon.* 1681. Reprint, Glasgow: James MacLehose & Sons.

Laclau, Ernesto

    1977   *Politics and Ideology in Marxist Theory.* London: New Left Books.

Laclau, Ernesto, and Chantal Mouffe

    1982   Recasting Marxism: Hegemony and New Political Movements. *Socialist Review* 66(12:6):91–113.

References Cited

Leach, E. R.

    1959   Hydraulic Society in Ceylon. *Past and Present* 15:2–25.

    1960   The Sinhalese of the Dry Zone of Northern Ceylon. In *Social Structure in South East Asia,* edited by George P. Murdock. Viking Fund Publications, no. 29. Chicago: Quadrangle Books.

    1961   *Pul Eliya: A Village in Ceylon.* Cambridge: Cambridge University Press.

    1964   *Political Systems of Highland Burma.* 1954. Reprint, Boston: Beacon Press.

Macy, Joanna

    1985   *Dharma and Development: Religion as Resource in the Sarvodaya Self-Help Movement.* West Hartford: Kumarian Press.

Maine, Sir Henry

    1906   *Ancient Law: Its Connections with the Early History of Society and Its Relation to Modern Ideas.* 1861. Reprint, London: John Murray.

Malalgoda, Kitsiri

    1976   *Buddhism in Sinhalese Society, 1750–1900: A Study of Religious Revival and Change.* Berkeley: University of California Press.

Manor, James, ed.

    1984   *Sri Lanka in Change and Crisis.* London: Croom Helm.

Marcus, George E., and Michael M. J. Fischer

    1986   *Anthropology as Cultural Critique: An Experimental Moment in the Human Sciences.* Chicago: University of Chicago Press.

Mitchell, Timothy

    1991   *Colonising Egypt.* 1988. Reprint, Berkeley: University of California Press.

Moore, Mick

    1985   *The State and Peasant Politics in Sri Lanka.* Cambridge: Cambridge University Press.

    1989   The Ideological History of the Sri Lankan "Peasantry." *Modern Asian Studies* 23(1):179–207.

    1992   The Ideological History of the Sri Lankan "Peasantry." In *Agrarian Change in Sri Lanka,* edited by James Brow and Joe Weeramunda. New Delhi: Sage Publications.

Nissan, Elizabeth

    1988   Polity and Pilgrimage Centres in Sri Lanka. *Man* 23:253–74.

Nissan, Elizabeth, and R. L. Stirrat

    1987   *State, Nation and the Representation of Evil: The Case of Sri Lanka.* Sussex

Research Papers in Social Anthropology, no. 1. Brighton: Graduate Division of Social Anthropology, University of Sussex.

1990   The Generation of Communal Identities. In *Sri Lanka: History and the Roots of Conflict,* edited by Jonathan Spencer. London: Routledge.

Obeyesekere, Gananath

1966   The Buddhist Pantheon in Ceylon and Its Extensions. In *Anthropological Studies in Theravada Buddhism,* edited by Manning Nash. New Haven: Yale University Press.

1967   *Land Tenure in Village Ceylon.* Cambridge: Cambridge University Press.

1969   The Sanni Demons: Collective Representations of Disease in Ceylon. *Comparative Studies in Society and History* 11(2):174–216.

1970   The Idiom of Demonic Possession: A Case Study. *Social Science and Medicine* 4:97–111.

1975   Psychocultural Exegesis of a Case of Spirit Possession in Sri Lanka. *Contributions to Asian Studies* 8:41–89.

1978   The Firewalkers of Kataragama: The Rise of *Bhakti* Religiosity in Buddhist Sri Lanka. *Journal of Asian Studies* 37(3):457–76.

1981   *Medusa's Hair: An Essay on Personal Symbols and Religious Experience.* Chicago: University of Chicago Press.

1984   *The Cult of the Goddess Pattini.* Chicago: University of Chicago Press.

1990   *The Work of Culture: Symbolic Transformations in Psychoanalysis and Anthropology.* Chicago: University of Chicago Press.

Ortner, Sherry

1984   Theory in Anthropology since the Sixties. *Comparative Studies in Society and History* 26(1):126–66.

Perera, Jayantha

1985   *New Dimensions of Social Stratification in Rural Sri Lanka.* Colombo: Lake House Investments.

1992   Trends in Agrarian Change: Past and Present in Wewagama, a Village in the Mahaweli Development Project Area, Anuradhapura District. In *Agrarian Change in Sri Lanka,* edited by James Brow and Joe Weeramunda. New Delhi: Sage Publications.

Pieris, Ralph

1956   *Sinhalese Social Organization: The Kandyan Period.* Peradeniya: Ceylon University Press Board.

Popular Memory Group

1982   Popular Memory: Theory, Politics, Method. In *Making Histories: Studies in History-Writing and Politics,* edited by Richard Johnson et al. London: Hutchinson.

References Cited

Rahula, Walpola

1966   *History of Buddhism in Ceylon: The Anuradhapura Period.* 2d ed. Colombo: M. D. Gunasena.

Roberts, Michael, ed.

1979   *Collective Identities, Nationalisms, and Protest in Modern Sri Lanka.* Colombo: Marga Institute.

Robinson, Marguerite

1975   *Political Structure in a Changing Sinhalese Village.* Cambridge: Cambridge University Press.

Samaraweera, Vijaya

1973   Land Policy and Peasant Colonization, 1914–1948. In *University of Ceylon History of Ceylon,* vol. 3, edited by K. M. de Silva. Peradeniya: University of Ceylon.

1977   Land as "Patrimony": Nationalist Response to Immigrant Labour Demand for Land in Early 20th Century Sri Lanka. *Indian Economic and Social History Review* 14:341–62.

1978   Litigation, Sir Henry Maine's Writings and the Ceylon Village Communities Ordinance of 1871. In *Senarat Paranavitana Commemoration Volume,* edited by L. Indrapala and J. E. Van Lohuizen-De Leeuw. Leiden: Brill.

1981   Land, Labour, Capital and Sectional Interests in the National Politics of Sri Lanka. *Modern Asian Studies* 15:127–62.

Sarkar, N. K. and S. J. Tambiah

1957   *The Disintegrating Village: Report of a Socio-Economic Survey Conducted by the University of Ceylon.* Colombo: Ceylon University Press Board.

Scott, David

1992   Conversion and Demonism: Colonial Christian Discourse and Religion in Sri Lanka. *Comparative Studies in Society and History* 34(2):331–65.

1994   *Formations of Ritual: Colonial and Anthropological Discourses on the Sinhala Yaktovil.* Minneapolis: University of Minnesota Press.

Scott, James C.

1985   *Weapons of the Weak: Everyday Forms of Peasant Resistance.* New Haven: Yale University Press.

Seligmann, C. G., and B. Z. Seligmann

1911   *The Veddas.* Cambridge: Cambridge University Press.

Seneviratne, H. L.

1978   *Rituals of the Kandyan State.* Cambridge: Cambridge University Press.

Shanmugaratnam, N.

1980   Emerging Agrarian Trends and Some Reflections on the Agrarian Reforms in Sri Lanka. *Social Science Review* 2:56–111.

1983   Underdevelopment and Peasant Agriculture under British Colonialism. *Social Science Review* 3:61–85.

1985a   Colonial Agrarian Changes and Underdevelopment. In *Capital and Peasant Production: Studies in the Continuity and Discontinuity of Agrarian Structures in Sri Lanka,* edited by Charles Abeysekera. Colombo: Social Scientists' Association.

1985b   Some Aspects of the Evolution and Implementation of the Policy of Peasant Resettlement. In *Capital and Peasant Production: Studies in the Continuity and Discontinuity of Agrarian Structures in Sri Lanka,* edited by Charles Abeysekera. Colombo: Social Scientists' Association.

Shastri, Amita

1983a   Evolution of the Contemporary Political Formation of Sri Lanka. *South Asia Bulletin* 3(1):16–37.

1983b   The Political Economy of Intermediate Regimes: The Case of Sri Lanka, 1956–70. *South Asia Bulletin* 3(2):1–14.

Silva, Kalinga Tudor

1992   Capitalist Development, Rural Politics and Peasant Agriculture in Highland Sri Lanka: Structural Change in a Low Caste Village. In *Agrarian Change in Sri Lanka,* edited by James Brow and Joe Weeramunda. New Delhi: Sage Publications.

Social Scientists' Association, eds.

1985   *Ethnicity and Social Change in Sri Lanka.* Colombo: Social Scientists' Association.

Spencer, Jonathan

1990a   *A Sinhala Village in a Time of Trouble.* Delhi: Oxford University Press.

1990b   Writing Within: Anthropology, Nationalism, and Culture in Sri Lanka. *Current Anthropology* 31(3):283–91.

1990c   *Sri Lanka: History and the Roots of Conflict.* Edited by Jonathan Spencer. London: Routledge.

1992   Representations of the Rural: A View from Sabaragamuva. In *Agrarian Change in Sri Lanka,* edited by James Brow and Joe Weeramunda, pp. 357–87. New Delhi: Sage Publications.

Stein, Burton

1983   *Peasant, State and Society in Medieval South India.* Delhi: Oxford University Press.

References Cited

Stirrat, R. L.

    1977   Demonic Possession in Roman Catholic Sri Lanka. *Journal of Anthropological Research* 33:133–57.

    1984   The Riots and the Roman Catholic Church in Historical Perspective. In *Sri Lanka in Change and Crisis,* edited by James Manor. London: Croom Helm.

    1992   *Demons, Shrines and Holy Men: Catholicism in Contemporary Sri Lanka.* Cambridge: Cambridge University Press.

Tambiah, S. J.

    1958   The Structure of Kinship and Its Relationship to Land Possession and Residence in Pata Dumbara, Central Ceylon. *Journal of the Royal Anthropological Institute* 88(1):21–44.

    1965   Kinship Fact and Fiction in Relation to the Kandyan Sinhalese. *Journal of the Royal Anthropological Institute* 95(2):131–73.

    1976   *World Conqueror, World Renouncer.* Cambridge: Cambridge University Press.

    1977   The Galactic Polity: The Structure of Traditional Kingdoms in SE Asia. In *Anthropology and the Climate of Opinion,* edited by S. Freed. New York: New York Academy of Sciences.

    1986   *Sri Lanka: Ethnic Fratricide and the Dismantling of Democracy.* Chicago: University of Chicago Press.

    1992   *Buddhism Betrayed? Religion, Politics, and Violence in Sri Lanka.* Chicago: University of Chicago Press.

Tennekoon, Serena

    1988   Rituals of Development: The Accelerated Mahaväli Development Program of Sri Lanka. *American Ethnologist* 15:294–310.

Thompson, E. P.

    1963   *The Making of the English Working Class.* London: Gollancz.

    1978   *The Poverty of Theory and Other Essays.* New York: Monthly Review Press.

Tucker, Robert C., ed.

    1978   *The Marx-Engels Reader.* 2d ed. New York: W. W. Norton.

Turner, Victor

    1969   *The Ritual Process.* Chicago: Aldine.

Turton, Andrew

    1984   Limits of Ideological Domination and the Formation of Social Consciousness. In *History and Peasant Consciousness in South East Asia,* edited by Andrew Turton and Shigeharu Tanabe. Osaka: National Museum of Ethnology.

References Cited

Vitebsky, Piers

    1992   Shifting Cultivation Comes to Rest: Changing Values of Land and the Person in an Area of Monaragala District. In *Agrarian Change in Sri Lanka,* edited by James Brow and Joe Weeramunda. New Delhi: Sage Publications.

Weber, Max

    1956   *Staatssociologie.* Berlin: Duncker and Humblot.

    1958   *The Protestant Ethic and the Spirit of Capitalism.* Translated by Talcott Parsons. 1930. Reprint, New York: Charles Scribner's Sons.

    1978   *Economy and Society.* 2 vols. Berkeley: University of California Press.

Whitaker, Mark

    1990   A Compound of Many Histories: The Many Pasts of an East Coast Tamil Community. In *Sri Lanka: History and the Roots of Conflict,* edited by Jonathan Spencer. London: Routledge.

Williams, Raymond

    1977   *Marxism and Literature.* Oxford: Oxford University Press.

    1980   *Problems in Materialism and Culture.* London: Verso.

Willis, Paul

    1981   *Learning to Labor: How Working Class Kids Get Working Class Jobs.* New York: Columbia University Press.

Woost, Michael D.

    1990a   Rural Awakenings: Grassroots Development and the Cultivation of a National Past in Rural Sri Lanka. In *Sri Lanka: History and the Roots of Conflict,* edited by Jonathan Spencer. London: Routledge.

    1990b   *Constructing a Nation of Villages: Development and Community on the Singalese Frontier.* Ph.D. diss., University of Texas, Austin.

    1993   Nationalizing the Local Past in Sri Lanka: Histories of Nation and Development in a Sinhalese Village. *American Ethnologist* 20(3):502–21.

    1994   Developing a Nation of Villages: Rural Community as State Formation in Sri Lanka. *Critique of Anthropology* 14(1):77–95.

Wright, Patrick

    1985   *On Living in an Old Country: The National Past in Contemporary Britain.* London: Verso.

Yalman, Nur

    1960   The Flexibility of Caste Principles in a Kandyan Community. In *Aspects of Caste in South India, Ceylon and North-West Pakistan,* edited by E. R. Leach. Cambridge Papers in Social Anthropology, no. 2. Cambridge: Cambridge University Press.

Index

Page numbers for illustrations are in italics.

Index

Index

in Samadigama, 133, 152; reputation,
130–31; UNP official, 127
marriage: outside the caste, 115–21; among
Veddas, 10, 52, 54
Marx, Karl, 26
Mekichchawa, 64, 75, *90,* 110–11
Menikhamy, 160
Menikrala: conflict with Fernando family,
128–30, 152; and housing allocations,
96–100, 109; on new houses, 122; UNP
official, 112–13
Metcalfe, Charles: on village community,
81
Minneriya (god), 139
moneylending, 64–68
Moragahawela, 140, 157
Morakava, 103
MP (Member of Parliament): and conflict in
Samadigama, 124, 127, 129–30; control
of resources by, 92; in dream, 4; and
housing allocations, 96–101, 110; and la-
bor, 94. *See also* Herath, Yasapala
Mudalihamy: and conflict in Samadigama,
129, 134; on construction of houses, 92,
94; on housing allocations, 98; as
Seelawathie's priest, 165, 168–72; at Wijeratne's performance, 174
mul pavul (root families), 95–101, 108–9,
123, 156, 187
Muthubanda, 100–101, 109, 120

Naidurala: and allocation of houses, 95–
101, 187; assaulted by Jinadasa, 94–95;
and construction of houses, 92–95; president of the RDS, 91–92; president of the
UNP, 91–92, 97–98, 113–14, 127–29,
134
Nandasena, 101, 111
Nuvarakalaviya. *See* Anuradhapura District

Obeyesekere, Gananath: on kinship, 10; on
pantheon, 136; on Veddas, 12
ornaments, sacred. *See* gods

paddy cultivation: in Anuradhapura District, 35, 40; in Kukulewa, 47, 53–57, 68–
69; mentioned, 45, 46, 62
party politics, 73–77, 182, 187. *See also*
SLFP; UNP
past, the: authority of, 21–22, 190–92; as
site of struggle, 28

Pattini (god), 139–40, 162–63, 166, 168,
175
Perera, Albert, 126
Pinhamy, 163–65
Piyadasa, 111, 144–45
Podi Nona, 115–16
Podiya, 110
Polin Banda, 110
population, 37, 43, 55–56
populist legitimism, 85, 109
Potter caste, 13, 40
Premadasa: priest in Kukulewa, 159–64;
UNP official, 75–76, 112; at Wijeratne's
performance, 176
Premadasa, Ranasinghe: at opening of Sa-
madigama, 3–4, 102–7; petitions sent to,
108–10; and Village Awakening, 88, 105,
122
prēta (ghost), 142
priest *(kapurāla),* 4–8, 137, 147, 158–65,
173. *See also* Dingiribanda; Mudalihamy;
Premadasa; Ukkubanda
prime minister. *See* Premadasa, Ranasinghe
Pulleyar, 3, 7, 137–39, 155, 163
Punchibanda, 115–16, 143
Punchihamy, 125
Punchirala, 75–76

rājakāriya (king's duty), 40, 150
Rampathwila, 114
Ranbanda, 7, 101, 127
Ranmenike, 122
raṭe mahatmaya (district lord), 42–43, 61,
117
RDS (rural development society), 91–92,
109
Reriyakka (demon), 140, 146
rice cultivation. *See* paddy cultivation
rock inscription, 101, 104
root families. *See mul pavul*
Rosalyn, 115–16, 118–20, 143

Samadigama: conflicts in, 127–35, 188; demonic attacks in, 142–49, 188–89; *gambādi rājakāriya* in, 3–9, 17, 150–53;
housing in, 122–23; living conditions in,
124–27; location of, *90;* name of, 101;
opening ceremony, 101–7, 183–85, 188;
relations with Kukulewa, 4, 6–7, 123–24,
144–49, 188–89; Village Awakening in,
3, 14

Index

rule, 42, 61, 117; as regional lords, 37–39; and UNP, 64, 103–4

variga. *See* caste

Veddas: aboriginals, 12–13, 44, 47; descent from Kuveni and Vijaya, 12–13, 23, 47, 104, 180–81; and the gods, 137, 175, 181; in relation to Sinhalas, 13, 44–49, 80, 107, 180–81, 184–86, 188; mentioned, 31, 120, 173

vel vidānē (irrigation headman), 61–62

Vijaya, 12–13, 23, 47, 52, 104, 180–81

Village Awakening Program: allocation of houses, 95–101; construction of houses, 91–95; opening ceremony, 101–7; program for Kukulewa, 88–90; and Sinhala nationalism, 16, 23, 186–88

village community: and agriculture, 52–55; images of, 80–84, 107; in Kukulewa, 22–23, 50–51; and Sinhala nationalism, 82–87, 187–88, 190–91

violence, 94–95, 129, 131–34, 168, 174

wage labor: at construction site, 92–94; female, 57, 125–26; among kin, 11, 66–68, 70–71; outside Kukulewa, 124–26; spread of, 56–59, 70–71

Wannihamy: commercial activities, 62–66, 63, 68–71; on gods and demons, 142, 154, 157–58, 167–68; SLFP supporter, 74–76, 147; mentioned, 161, 182

Washerman caste, 13, 40

Weber, Max: on community, 18, 50; on devotion to labor, 71; on tradition, 21–22

Welewa, 119, 151–52

Wijeratne: and construction of houses, 92–95; and housing allocations, 95–101, 110–11, 156, 187, 192; leadership in Samadigama, 128–29, 132, 134; possessed, 4–9, 153–58, 166, 173–77, 188–92; UNP official, 91–92, 112–14, 127, 132; mentioned, 17, 152, 162

William, 111–13, 126

Williams, Raymond: on hegemony, 25–29, 86

Wimaladasa: and agriculture, 59–60, 65–71; on housing project, 97, 123; and party politics, 75–76, 123; at Wijeratne's performance, 176; mentioned, 134, 182

women: and conflict in Samadigama, 130–32; purity of, 5–6, 153–54; as wage laborers, 57, 125–26

Yalman, Nur: on kinship, 10

About the Author

James Brow is an associate professor of anthropology and Asian studies and chair of the Department of Anthropology at the University of Texas at Austin. Born and raised in the United Kingdom, he received his undergraduate education at Oxford University, where he studied modern history, and then moved to the United States, receiving his Ph.D. in anthropology from the University of Washington in 1974. He has taught at Swarthmore College, Washington University, and the University of Texas at Austin.

He has conducted ethnographic field research in Sri Lanka at various times since 1968, having been funded by the Smithsonian Institution, the National Science Foundation, the Wenner-Gren Foundation for Anthropological Research, the Joint Committee on South Asia of the American Council of Learned Societies and the Social Science Research Council, and the National Endowment for the Humanities.

His earlier study of Kukulewa, entitled *Vedda Villages of Anuradhapura: The Historical Anthropology of a Community in Sri Lanka,* was published by the University of Washington Press in 1978. He is also the senior editor (with Joe Weeramunda) of *Agrarian Change in Sri Lanka,* published by Sage Publications in 1992. His other writings on Sri Lanka have appeared in leading academic journals such as *American Ethnologist, Journal of Asian Studies, Anthropological Quarterly,* and *Ethnology.*

Brow's current research moves back in time from the present study, examining the historical provenance of those images of the village community that are centrally engaged in *Demons and Development.* He is particularly interested in the ways in which nationalist representations of the village community combine a fierce anticolonial rhetoric with substantial appropriation of the colonialist imagination.